Writing Stored Procedures for Microsoft® SQL Server™

Matthew Shepker

A Division of Macmillan USA
201 West 103rd St., Indianapolis, Indiana, 46290 USA

Writing Stored Procedures for Microsoft® SQL Server™

Copyright © 2000 by Sams Publishing

International Standard Book Number: 0-672-31886-5

Library of Congress Catalog Card Number: 99-067847

Printed in the United States of America

First Printing: June 2000

02   01   00   4   3   2   1

Trademarks

Warning and Disclaimer

ACQUISITIONS EDITOR
Sharon Cox

DEVELOPMENT EDITORS
Susan Shaw Dunn
Steve Rowe

MANAGING EDITOR
Charlotte Clapp

PROJECT EDITOR
Dawn Pearson

COPY EDITOR
Mike Henry

PROOFREADERS
Linda Seifert
Maryann Steinhart

TECHNICAL EDITOR
Ivan Oss

INTERIOR DESIGN
Anne Jones

COVER DESIGN
Anne Jones

Overview

Contents

About the Author

Matthew Shepker, MCSE and MCT, is currently working as a project manager in Overland Park, Kansas. He has been working with SQL Server for more than five years in various business applications, including online transaction processing, decision support systems, and other custom software. Matthew has written two books and co-authored five others. He lives in Gardner, Kansas, with his wife, Misty. When he's not working on writing books, he usually can be found working on the house, debugging his code, building and flying remote-control airplanes, or vegging out and petting his dog, Sam. He can be reached at mshepker@planetkc.com.

Contributing Author

James Sabbarton is a Microsoft Certified Systems Engineer and holds additional SQL Server qualifications. A consultant systems analyst and DBA, he is currently studying for his Microsoft Certified Solution Developer certification. He has worked within the IT industry in various locations throughout Europe for 18 years and has a broad spectrum of knowledge starting in the very early days when programming in Assembler. He has worked in many industries including retail, insurance, shipping, and finance. His recent roles have focused on Microsoft SQL Server development on the Windows NT platform. James lives in Brentwood, England, with his very tolerant wife, Lindsay; son, Harry; and Airedale, Copper.

Dedication

As always, to my wife, Misty, and our soon-to-be little one

Acknowledgments

Writing is always a group process, with only one person really getting the credit. A host of people behind the scenes helped create the book you are now holding in your hands. First of all, I want to thank Sharon Cox for allowing me to run with this book. It has been an interesting run of things with several bumps in the road, and I want to thank her for keeping on me to get this done. I want to think Steve Rowe and Susan Dunn for keeping me on track and giving me great feedback. Lastly, I want to thank Ivan Oss for keeping all the technical facts straight and accurate.

On a personal note, I would like to thank a lot of people putting up with me. Not just through the writing process, but in general. I have to thank my mother for all the advice she has given me through my life. Through all my dumb mistakes in life, she has always had some gem of wisdom that has helped me through it. I also have to thank my father for providing a great deal of insight into life. When I become a father, my children will be lucky if I can be half the father that you were to me and Becky. To my sister, Becky, and her soon-to-be husband, Norby, good luck. I love you, kid. Lastly, I have to thank my wife, Misty. She has always suffered in silence while I locked myself away to write. I love you, always.

Tell Us What You Think!

As the reader of this book, *you* are our most important critic and commentator. We value your opinion and want to know what we're doing right, what we could do better, what areas you'd like to see us publish in, and any other words of wisdom you're willing to pass our way.

As an associate publisher for Sams, I welcome your comments. You can fax, email, or write me directly to let me know what you did or didn't like about this book—as well as what we can do to make our books stronger.

Please note that I cannot help you with technical problems related to the topic of this book, and that due to the high volume of mail I receive, I might not be able to reply to every message.

When you write, please be sure to include this book's title and author as well as your name and phone or fax number. I will carefully review your comments and share them with the author and editors who worked on the book.

Fax: 317-581-4770

Email: adv_prog@mcp.com

Mail: Brad L. Jones, Associate Publisher
          Sams Publishing
          201 West 103rd Street
          Indianapolis, IN 46290 USA

Introduction

This book was written so that you can learn how to create stored procedures. I'm sure that you have created a few stored procedures already. The first stored procedures I created were simple queries that I encapsulated so that I didn't have to reload or retype them every time I wanted to run them. After a while, I learned how useful stored procedures can be. Hopefully, this book will assist you in moving down the path of creating useful and powerful stored procedures. You'll learn some techniques that will help you create stored procedures that will provide all the results your users expect while remaining friendly to the system.

Prerequisites

You must fulfill some prerequisites before you can effectively use the information presented in this book. First, you must have a solid understanding of the Transact-SQL (T-SQL) language. This book provides some review of the commands that make up T-SQL, but the review is not extremely in-depth and might cause you some frustration if you haven't previously seen how T-SQL works. The concepts you need to understand and be aware of are as follows:

- A solid understanding of Data Manipulation Language (DML). This includes SELECT, UPDATE, INSERT, and DELETE statements.
- Knowledge of Data Definition Language (DDL). This includes the syntax required to create tables, views, and indexes.
- Experience with Declared Referential Integrity (DRI). This includes the creation and maintenance of primary key/foreign key relationships.
- An understanding of mathematical, comparison, and logical operators.
- A solid grasp of programming fundamentals, including control-of-flow language.
- An understanding of application programming, including flowcharting and creating pseudocode.
- Knowledge and understanding of the creation and use of cursors.
- A basic understanding of XML and how it is used.
- Experience with the Query Analyzer.

System Requirements

Although you will be able to glean information from this book by just reading it, you will get much more out of this book if you actually write the code at the same time that you read about it. To do this, you must have access to a computer and to SQL Server. The following is exactly what you will need:

- Access to SQL Server 7.0 or SQL Server 2000. All the code presented in this book was written using SQL Server 2000 and was tested on SQL Server 7.0, so it should work on both platforms. The server you work on should be nonproduction so that any mistakes you make won't affect your users.
- Sufficient privileges on the SQL Server computer to allow you to create objects in the pubs database. All the code examples outlined in the book utilize the pubs database. The exception is Chapter 11, "Writing Utility Stored Procedures," in which you must be able to create objects in the master database.
- For Chapter 14, "SQL Server XML Support," you need access to Microsoft Internet Information Server (IIS).

CAUTION

In this book, you will be creating and dropping objects in the pubs and master databases. Be very careful while doing this; if you make a mistake, you can cause irreparable harm to your server—especially when you are dealing with the master database. For all examples presented in this book, use a nonproduction server with no vital information on it. This way, if you break something, it can easily be fixed.

How This Book Is Organized

This book is divided into four logical sections. For the most part, these sections progress from the easiest topics to grasp to the more difficult topics.

Part I: Introduction to Developing Stored Procedures

Part I is made up of four chapters:

- Chapter 1, "SQL Server and Stored Procedure Background," provides general background on SQL Server and stored procedures.
- Chapter 2, "Stored Procedure Camps," outlines the two basic camps that developers fall into when developing stored procedures and how you can find middle ground between those two camps.
- Chapter 3, "Processing Stored Procedures," goes through the creation and execution of stored procedures.
- Chapter 4, "Stored Procedures Rules," covers the rules outlined by Microsoft for the creation of stored procedures, as well as some suggestions that will make your stored procedure development much easier.

Part II: Simple Stored Procedures

Part II also consists of four chapters:

- Chapter 5, "Creating and Altering Stored Procedures," outlines the actual creation and alteration of stored procedure.
- Chapter 6, "Creating More Complex Stored Procedures," goes over the creation of more complex stored procedures.
- Chapter 7, "Creating Stored Procedures that Insert Data," covers the creation of stored procedures that insert data into tables.
- Chapter 8, "Creating Stored Procedures that Modify Data," covers the creation of stored procedures that modify data in tables.

Part III: Security and Advanced Procedure Development

Part III consists of five chapters:

- Chapter 9, "Providing Security for Stored Procedures," goes over the application of application and physical security for stored procedures.
- Chapter 10, "Programming Structures in SQL," covers the programming structures within the SQL language.
- Chapter 11, "Writing Utility Stored Procedures," introduces the idea of the creating stored procedures that enhance the functionality of SQL Server itself.
- Chapter 12, "Extended Stored Procedures," covers the creation of extended stored procedures.
- Chapter 13, "Creating Custom Functions," introduces the new feature of custom-defined functions.

Part IV: XML and Triggers

The three chapters in Part IV are as follows:

- Chapter 14, "SQL Server XML Support," covers the addition of XML support to SQL Server.
- Chapter 15, "Writing Triggers," covers the creation of triggers and introduces a new trigger type to SQL Server.
- Chapter 16, "Considerations When Using Stored Procedures and Triggers," goes over some of the considerations that you should keep in mind when you create stored procedures.

Conventions Used in This Book

The following typographic conventions are used in this book:

- Code lines, commands, statements, variables, and any text you type or see onscreen appear in a monospace typeface.

- Placeholders in syntax descriptions appear in an *italic monospace* typeface. Replace the placeholder with the actual filename, parameter, or whatever element it represents.

- *Italics* highlight technical terms when they're being defined.

- The ➡ icon is used before a line of code that's really a continuation of the preceding line. Sometimes a line of code is too long to fit as a single line on the page. If you see ➡ before a line of code, remember that it's part of the line immediately above it.

The book also contains notes and cautions to help you spot important or useful information more quickly. You'll also see tips, which provide shortcuts to help you work more efficiently.

Introduction to Developing Stored Procedures

IN THIS PART

SQL Server and Stored Procedure Background

IN THIS CHAPTER

Before you jump into creating stored procedures using SQL Server, you might want to be aware of some background information. This information won't necessarily change the way you write your stored procedures, but it might assist you in really knowing what you are talking about from a SQL Server perspective. I also cover some of the important new features in SQL Server 2000. With few exceptions, all the code presented in this book is backward-compatible to SQL Server 7.0, but to truly take advantage of some of the new features that I outline and show you how to use, you need to get a copy of SQL Server 2000.

In this chapter, I cover the following:

- History of databases
- History of SQL Server
- SQL Server in business today
- New features in SQL Server 2000
- Uses for stored procedures

The History of Databases

There probably is a true written account on how databases evolved throughout the last few years. I won't get too far into the specifics here. From a high level, databases have been around for quite some time, just not computerized. Originally, databases were known as ledgers and card catalogs. These were maintained by people and really took a lot of manpower to maintain. When computers came around, it was really a logical progression to move databases to that platform. As processing power and storage increased and overall cost decreased, databases became more prevalent in the business world. Many paper processes became computer-oriented and all the data that would have normally been stored on paper forms in filing cabinets began to be stored in computer databases. Today, almost every business has a database of some sort, whether it be a lower-end Microsoft Access database or a higher-end SQL Server or Oracle database.

SQL Server's History

SQL Server has actually been around for quite a while, in one form or another. SQL Server was originally introduced in 1988. The first version was a joint venture between Sybase and Microsoft, ran only on OS/2, and was a complete flop in the marketplace. In 1993, SQL Server 4.2 for Windows NT Advanced Server 3.1 was released. This version made some small advances in the marketplace, but still didn't have what it needed to make it an enterprise-class RDBMS. Microsoft and Sybase went their separate ways in 1994, and shortly afterward Microsoft released SQL Server 6.0. In 1996, SQL Server 6.5 was released. This version of SQL Server succeeded in the marketplace primarily because it had the speed, power, ease-of-use, and low cost that purchasers and IT staffers were looking for.

In addition to the features that administrators were looking for, part of SQL Server's success has to do with the direction that the marketplace took around the same time that SQL Server 6.5 was released. For the most part, the market was moving toward faster and cheaper Intel-based servers running Windows NT Server. This meant that, on abandoning other platforms, when there was a need for an RDBMS, SQL Server became the natural selection.

SQL Server 7.0, released in early 1999, moved SQL Server into the enterprise database arena. Although previous versions of SQL Server contained large amounts of the original Sybase code, SQL Server 7.0 is said to be 100% Microsoft code. It's even said that Microsoft developers threw a party when the final lines of original code were removed. If SQL Server 7.0 is not a complete rewrite, it is pretty close.

The latest version, SQL Server 2000, allows Microsoft to step a little further into the enterprise database arena. It has a large amount of new features that make it a stronger competitor of the largest, most widely accepted enterprise database—Oracle. SQL Server will probably never completely take over this particular database arena, but it will continue to make strides to do so.

SQL Server in Business Today

SQL Server has made huge inroads into the business market since its inception. The real advances have come since SQL Server 6.5. A huge number of applications in the marketplace have been written to utilize the advantages of SQL Server. A few categories of these systems are as follows:

- **Customer Relationship Management (CRM) Software**—A number of CRM packages on the market have been designed to take advantage of SQL Server in combination with other Microsoft products such as Exchange and Outlook. CRM products track customer information and all contact that has been made with the customers.

- **Data Collection Systems**—These applications are designed to capture real-time information and store it away for later processing and summarization. These systems usually require extremely high availability and reliability. To produce these types of results, SQL Server Enterprise Edition used with Windows NT Enterprise Edition in a clustered environment provides a platform with built-in redundancy and support for automatic failover.

- **Data Warehouses**—A data warehouse stores a large collection of data that can be analyzed for trends that are useful to the company that owns the data. For example, a simple data warehouse could show a company's inventory manager how a specific product has sold during a specific week over the past few years so that when the week in question rolls around, enough of that product is on hand to meet the projected need.

Data warehouses were all the rage a few years ago. Support for data warehouses dwindled because of the large investment it took to create them and their immense size. Smaller data warehouses, known as *data marts*, have lately begun to reemerge to provide this important information to companies that choose to implement them. SQL Server is a great choice for these types of applications because of built-in OLAP (Online Analytical Processing) support.

- **E-Commerce**—The surge in popularity of the Internet over the past few years has brought about a new way for companies to buy and sell products. Many companies have chosen SQL Server as the platform they base their e-commerce engines on because of its stability, high availability, and low cost.

Relational Database Management Systems

SQL Server 2000, the latest and greatest of the SQL Server platforms, is still a relational database management system (RDBMS). All RDBMSs share some qualities. These features are the basics of what make up any RDBMSs, and include the following:

- As its name implies, the purpose of an RDBMS is to manage relational databases. A *relational database* is a grouping of tables. The tables are broken down into rows, also known as *records*, and the records are broken down into columns, also known as *fields*. Without these, you would have nothing to manage.

- All RDBMSs use SQL, or a variation of it, to manipulate the data contained in any of the databases. SQL (correctly pronounced S-Q-L) was developed at IBM in the late 1970s.

- RDBMSs must maintain data integrity. In other words, every relational database needs to ensure that if data in multiple tables is updated, all the updates take place. For example, imagine a banking system that contains two tables: one for your savings account and one for your checking account. You call your bank and ask to transfer $100 from savings to checking. This process involves subtracting $100 from your savings account and adding $100 to your checking account. If the bank loses power after the $100 is deleted from the table, what happens? If there is no data integrity, you have just lost $100. With data integrity, when the server is powered back on, the RDBMS realizes that the subtraction completed but that the addition didn't, and it cancels the whole transaction.

- Most RDBMSs strive to maintain separation between the actual data and the business logic that ensures that the data in the database is maintained in a constant state. In most cases, you will want to try to limit the amount of business functionality that you maintain in the database server.

- Many RDBMSs store data in such a way that redundant data is eliminated through some of type of compression. That doesn't mean data is lost—rather, it means that less storage space is needed.

- All RDBMSs provide some sort of security for the databases they manage. This security is usually at least a two-level process. First, any user who wants to access the system must identify herself with a valid login and password. When she passes this level of authentication, most systems have rules, called *permissions*, that block a user from accessing data to which she shouldn't have access.

The Features of SQL Server 2000

SQL Server 2000 combines functionality that was available in previous versions of SQL Server and new functionality added only in this version. The older functionality is what made SQL Server popular to start with and the new functionality enables you to do things that were impossible in previous versions.

The Old Staple Functionality

The old staple functionality is what originally made SQL Server popular in the marketplace. Much of this popularity has to do with the ease of use and administration inherent in SQL Server as well as the ease of available application development and power. Some of the staple functionality is as follows:

- **Graphical Management Tools**—These tools, such as SQL Enterprise Manager, make it extremely easy to manage SQL Server. These tools provide information about the overall health of the server and data in a format that almost any user can understand. Anyone who has ever worked with any of SQL Server's competitors will quickly tell you that the tools that ship with SQL Server far outpace anything that ship with other databases.

- **Ease of Use**—SQL Server is a very easy-to-use database platform. When you take into account the graphical management tools and the familiar Windows environment, SQL Server is one of the easiest database platforms on the market to learn.

- **Centralized Management**—One great ability you have when working with SQL Server is remotely managing any server from a single centralized computer. As long as the centralized computer can access a server, it can manage how that server is operating.

- **Multiple Client Support**—SQL Server supports all types of client applications. The base product ships with a standard suite of applications, including SQL Enterprise Manager and SQL Query Analyzer, that you can use to manage the server and modify your data. SQL Server also supports the Open Database Connectivity (ODBC) standard. By using these tools, you can create custom applications that can connect to SQL Server or any other type of RDBMS for which a driver is available.

- **Development Platform Support**—When creating new applications that will access SQL Server, nearly any currently available development platform can be used. That means no matter what programming language you know, you can write applications tailored to SQL Server. One of the best development platforms available for SQL Server is a

Microsoft product known as Visual Studio. This suite contains several tools that enable you to quickly and easily create new SQL Server applications.

- **Enterprise-Class Database Server**—It's sad that SQL Server is sometimes looked at as one step away from being an enterprise-class database server. With its most recent releases, SQL Server has truly stepped into the world of enterprise-class database servers. SQL Server 2000 can support databases larger than several terabytes with more than 32 processors. SQL Server 2000 also includes support that will allow it to upgrade to 64-bit processor architecture when it becomes available.

- **Runs on Windows NT/2000 and Windows 95/98**—For most production purposes, SQL Server usually runs on Windows NT or Windows 2000. Unlike previous versions of SQL Server, this version also runs on both Windows 95 and Windows 98 computers. This might not sound like a big improvement, but for developers, this is one of the largest timesavers that you can imagine. Developers can create applications that communicate with a single database type. With previous versions of SQL Server, developers used SQL Server for the main data source and relied on a smaller and, frequently, less robust database, such as Microsoft Access, for the offline data source.

- **Supports Replication**—Replication ensures that the data your users need is where they need it when they need it. SQL Server has added a great deal of functionality into how replication currently works. Among other things, this version allows for merge replication, which enables users at any site to make changes to the data. The changes are sent to the master copy and then sent back out to any other subscribers.

- **Support for Distributed Transactions**—A distributed transaction occurs on several servers at the same time. If any server involved in a distributed transaction can't make the requested changes, the changes aren't made on any of the servers.

- **Data Warehousing**—SQL Server has made many advances in the way it handles large quantities of data. This makes SQL Server a good choice for managing data warehouses. Data warehouses are usually extremely large databases that contain data from transaction-oriented databases. These huge databases are used to identify trends that aren't apparent from a cursory examination of the data.

- **Built-in OLAP**—One of the largest advantages to SQL Server is that Online Analytical Processing (OLAP) services are built into the server. Many other servers on the market force you to purchase third-party applications to provide this functionality.

- **Lower TCO**—When you compare all the features of SQL Server to the features of its competitors, the overall total cost of ownership, or TCO, is much lower for SQL Server than for any other database server on the market. Hardware, software, client licenses, ongoing management costs, and development costs are all less expensive than any other database management system on the market.

New Functionality

SQL Server 2000 is a new advance in SQL Server technology. Although on the surface SQL Server 2000 still looks a lot like SQL Server 7.0, a number of new advances set SQL Server 2000 apart from all the others. The majority of the enhancements that you are interested in as a developer have to do with the underlying SQL Server engine. Here are some of the most exciting new features:

- **XML Support**—There's currently a large push in the marketplace for applications to support XML (Extensible Markup Language). With the release of SQL Server 2000, Microsoft has effectively made SQL Server an XML-enabled database server. SQL Server's XML support enables you to access a database server directly though a URL in a Web browser, perform a SELECT statement that returns an XML string, and support XML-based interaction between SQL Server and a client application.

- **Cascading Referential Integrity (RI)**—SQL Server 2000 now supports functionality that's described as cascading RI. *Cascading RI* enables you to define relationships between tables that are maintained when the tables are updated or deleted. In past versions of SQL Server, when a user performed an update against a column in a table that was referenced in another table using standard RI, the update was cancelled and an error was returned to the user. With the addition of cascading RI, the user can make the update and the referenced columns are also updated, ensuring that no orphaned records are produced.

- **Indexed Views**—One recent event was the Million Dollar Challenge issued to Microsoft by the chairman of Oracle Corporation. This challenge basically said that if anyone could prove that SQL Server wasn't 100 times slower than Oracle when running a particular query, that person would win $1 million. Oracle utilized its ability to create indexes on views to come up with query times that were difficult to beat using SQL Server alone. Microsoft was able to beat it by using SQL Server's built-in OLAP services, but couldn't produce the same results using SQL Server alone. SQL Server 2000 provides the ability for a developer to create an index on a view that spans multiple tables. This allows SQL Server to know exactly where the information it's looking for resides in both tables, and can return the information much more quickly.

- **Trigger Modifications**—Microsoft has greatly expanded the way triggers operate in SQL Server 2000. With all previous versions of SQL Server, a trigger could be created that fired in response to a data modification. These triggers could be created only on tables and fired only after all table constraints, such as unique constraints, are checked. SQL Server 2000 enables you to create a new type of trigger, called an INSTEAD OF trigger, that fires before any table constraints are checked. These triggers can also be created on views, enabling you to perform multitable inserts into a view.

- **New Data Types**—SQL Server 2000 adds several extremely useful data types for you to use. These data types include `table`, which enables you to return several rows from a user-defined function; `sql_variant`, which allows you to have columns and variables that contain any data type except for `text`, `ntext`, `image`, `timestamp`, or `sql_variant`; and `bigint`, which enables you to store an 8-bit integer between the range of -2^{63} to $2^{63} - 1$ or $-9,223,372,036,854,775,808$ to $9,223,372,036,854,775,807$.

- **Function Enhancements**—SQL Server 2000 introduces the ability to create custom user functions. These functions can be used much like any other SQL Server function.

- **Index Modifications**—Microsoft has added a great deal of new functionality to indexes in SQL Server 2000. With this version of SQL Server, you can create indexes on computed columns, specify the order in which index values are sorted, and create indexes on `bigint`, `sql_variant`, and bit columns. Also, indexed columns no longer have a maximum length of 900 bytes.

- **New Backup Functionality**—Aside from increasing the overall performance of the backups performed using SQL Server, SQL Server 2000 also adds new functionality to the backup and restore processes. This new functionality includes the capability to recover from certain problems, such as unqualified update and delete statements, without taking the entire database offline. SQL Server 2000 also provides the capability for the recovery process to process through the transaction log to a specific named transaction.

- **Collation Changes**—Microsoft has added new functionality to the way SQL Server collates, or sorts, data. SQL Server no longer requires you to choose a collation during the install process. It picks up this information from the collation settings on the Windows NT Server on which it's being installed. You also can set different collations on SQL Server instances, databases, columns, variables, and constants in the database.

- **Extended Properties**—SQL Server 2000 enables developers to add extended properties to objects created in the database. These properties can be anything that the developer wants and are normally used to store information that's specific to an application or site. Properties can be up 7,500 bytes long.

- **Session Context**—Like Web sessions, SQL Server now enables you to create session contexts for users who are logged in to the SQL Server. Developers can use this session information to assign special application-level information to specific users. A user-session context can hold up to 128 bytes of data.

- **Security Enhancements**—Several new security enhancements have been added to SQL Server 2000, including the Kerberos security protocol, delegation, and new encryption schemes.

- **SQL Server Instancing**—One feature missing from previous versions of SQL Server was the ability to run multiple instances, or copies, of SQL Server on the same computer. SQL Server 2000 enables you to have as many instances of SQL Server running on the same machine as your hardware can handle.

- **Federated Database Server** —SQL Server 2000 allows you to create views that encompass tables residing on more than one server. This way, you can build out a group of database servers, thus creating an almost cluster level of performance.

- **Performance Enhancements**—SQL Server 2000 has greatly improved database engine performance. This performance increase can be seen in faster queues and data modifications.

Uses for Stored Procedures

You might already have a good idea of what can be done with stored procedures. However, probably much more can be done with stored procedures than you've ever thought of. Truthfully, probably quite a bit more can be done than I have ever thought of. The great thing about stored procedures is that, as a developer, you can create stored procedures that do whatever you need them to do. The following is a list of some of what you can do with stored procedures and reasons for using them. Most of these items are covered in this book; over time, you will discover others.

- **Encapsulation of Queries**—One of the first uses I discovered for stored procedures was to encapsulate queries so that I didn't have to worry about where they were saved, and I could execute them from anywhere on the network. The first queries I wrote were simple SELECT statements that returned extremely simple information. At that time, the only query tool available to the users of the system I was working with was ISQL/w, the precursor to Query Analyzer, so I also used stored procedures to roll out the queries to the users. All the users had to do was log in to the system and execute the stored procedure and they would get all the results they needed.

- **Parameterized Queries**—After I figured out how basic stored procedure worked and mastered the SELECT statement, the next thing that I did was start to work on parameterized queries. These stored procedures accepted one or two parameters and returned a subset of the information in the tables in which the user was interested. This enabled the users to return only those results that were important to them.

- **Encapsulation of Data Modification Statements**—Another great use of stored procedures is to encapsulate data modification statements. When you type data modification statements into a query window and execute them, there is a possibility that you will mistype something and cause severe problems in the database. If you encapsulate the data modification statements into a stored procedure that has been adequately tested, you are able to better control the statement and limit the amount of damage that can be done in the statement.

- **Maintainability of Application Logic**—One very widespread use of stored procedures is to use them as a container for application logic. This way, you can maintain all your company's business rules and logic in a single location, which makes them extremely easy to maintain. If a business rule changes, all you have to do is change the code in the stored procedure, and all users would have the new code.

- **Standardization**—If you roll all the data access, data modification, and business logic statements into stored procedures, you are virtually guaranteed that all access to your database will be standardized. That means if a user accesses a particular table, you know exactly what he is doing and how he is doing it.

- **Ease of Troubleshooting**—This point closely follows the previous point. If you standardize all your database access through a common set of stored procedures, troubleshooting is much easier. This ease is because you have only one place to look to find the problems and, when the problem is fixed, one place to roll the changes to.

- **Security**—One of the best, but least implemented, uses for stored procedures is as a security measure. If you create a stored procedure that accesses a table, you can revoke access to that table; the only way your users can access that table is through the stored procedure you've created. This is an extremely powerful method for locking down the server and keeping users from accessing information they aren't supposed to.

- **Automation of Administration Tasks**—The most fun and most interesting types of stored procedures to write (for me at least) are procedures that assist in the automation of the SQL Server. Like system stored procedures, the core set of procedures installed with SQL Server, these procedures are used to perform low-level system functions and to return information about the server and the objects on the server. I call these procedures *utility stored procedures*. Later in this book, I present some of the most useful utility stored procedures that I have written for you to use and learn from.

Conclusion

SQL Server, and specifically SQL Server 2000, is an extremely powerful application that can be used in almost any business context that relies on collecting and managing large quantities of data. In this chapter, I outlined some of the new features of SQL Server that you will most likely use when you are developing stored procedures and applications that reside on SQL Server. After you had a chance to see what SQL Server itself can do, I covered some of the things that you can do with stored procedures. The rest of the book actually shows you how to create stored procedures and what you can do with them.

Stored Procedure Camps

IN THIS CHAPTER

When working with SQL Server stored procedures, you will discover that most developers are in one of two camps concerning what types of functionality should be provided in stored procedures. You will usually find that the developers in both camps are willing to battle it out to determine the direction in which the development will move on a specific application. Some developers are determined to put as much business logic as possible into stored procedures that they write. Other developers want to put as little functionality as necessary into the stored procedures. Both approaches offer certain advantages and, of course, both have disadvantages. In this chapter, you will get a chance to see the advantages and disadvantages of both camps as well as look at some ways to find some middle ground.

In this chapter, we will cover the following:

- Definition of business logic
- Why the differences have come about
- The All Business Logic Camp
- The No Business Logic Camp
- Finding Middle Ground

What Is Business Logic?

Before I get too far into the discussion of the pros and cons of putting business logic into stored procedures, you really need to know what business logic is. *Business logic*, sometimes called *business rules*, is the code in your application that forces your users to follow the processes that makes your business work. These rules can be process flows or data formatting. The business logic will provide the definition of how and what type of data is stored in the tables of your database. This might not seem important at first glance, but if you don't follow these rules, it can really break your business.

A simple example of business logic is the formatting of a phone number. It is pretty common to want all the phone numbers stored in your database to look the same. Not only does this make the phone numbers more readable, but it also forces your users to create consistency. If you don't have consistency, you could end up with phone numbers that look like the following examples:

- 9995551212
- 999-555-1212
- (999) 555-1212
- 999 555 1212

Granted, this type of inconsistency is not a big deal in most instances. As long as your users are collecting all the data you need, this first rule is just formatting.

Business logic is more than formatting, however. There are cases when not following these rules can cost your company customers or even incur extremely large fines. The following examples are true accounts of two large businesses. One of these businesses lost an extremely large customer because a business rule was not followed. The other business was fined hundreds of thousands of dollars when a rule was not followed.

In the first case, the company (which I will call ABC Computer Hardware) was in the business of supplying parts—most notably hard disk drives—to major computer manufacturers. ABC had an agreement with one computer manufacturer to supply hard drives at a 15% discount. When the manufacturer needed more hard drives, it would call up and order them, and the person taking the order would look up the discount on a sheet of paper and manually put the discount in the order. Everything was fine for a few months, until the manufacturer called to request more hard drives and instead of the 15% reduction, it received only a 1.5% reduction. This mistake was enough to cause the manufacturer to find another hard drive supplier. If hard and fast business rules were defined and adhered to, ABC Computer Hardware would not have lost one of its largest customers.

In the second case, one of the largest computer manufacturers in the United States was fined hundreds of thousands of dollars for shipping computers to the wrong address. The United States has export laws that define which countries can receive high-tech equipment. For the most part, American companies can ship computers only to countries in North America. The particular company in question shipped several systems to a country that was not supposed to receive this type of equipment. The United States government found out about this and issued an extremely large fine. In this case, if the correct business logic had been in place in the manufacturer's order-taking system, it would have saved the company a great deal of money.

Why Differences Have Come About

When looking at the history of SQL Server and development in general, it is easy to see why the differences around the creation of stored procedures have come about. During the infancy of computing, when all processing occurred on a centralized mainframe, all data and business logic were stored in the same place. It was very easy to make changes to the application and business logic because they were all in one place.

As decentralized computing became more prevalent, more of the processing of business logic was moved to the smaller and less expensive PCs, and the more expensive central servers were utilized to store and serve up data. Administrators and developers soon learned that, in this scenario, it was very difficult to make changes to business and application logic because changes had to be rolled out to several places. This could be very time-consuming and, hence, very expensive.

Today, it is interesting to note that with the recent explosion of the Internet and network computers, computing is moving back into the arena of centralized computing. On the World Wide Web, almost all processing (with the exception of some simple data validation) is performed on central computers. With network computers, all processing is performed at a central location. The only functions performed by the hardware sitting on the user's desk are to display information to the user and to gather input in the form of keystrokes and mouse movements, which is then sent back to the server for processing.

The All Business Logic Camp

The first major camp came about when administrators and developers found out that maintaining all the business logic surrounding an application in the client could be very difficult and time-consuming. This is known as having a *fat client*. Any change in a fat client results in having to recompile the entire client. Recompiling does not, in and of itself, require much work. The problem is that in order for all users to take advantage of the new client, it must be installed on their computers. For large companies with hundreds or even thousands of PCs, this could pose major logistical problems. This process could be very time-consuming and extremely cost prohibitive. To solve this problem, many developers began to place all the business and application logic in stored procedures that reside in the database layer. This enabled developers to make changes whenever they needed to and, as long as the modifications to the stored procedures did not return any unexpected data, the client would continue to work as it had in the past. Take, for example, the code in Listing 2.1. This piece of code is a subroutine out of a fat Visual Basic 6.0 application. This application pulls the title ID and title from the titles table in the pubs database.

LISTING 2.1   A Fat Visual Basic Routine

```
Private Sub Command1_Click()
Dim adcConnection As New ADODB.Connection
Dim adrRecordset As ADODB.Recordset
Dim strSQL As String

    adcConnection.ConnectionString = "driver={SQL Server};" & _
        "server=tophat;uid=sa;pwd=;database=pubs"
    adcConnection.ConnectionTimeout = 30
    adcConnection.Open

    strSQL = "SELECT title_id, title FROM titles"

    Set adrRecordset = adcConnection.Execute(strSQL)
    MSFlexGrid1.Clear
    MSFlexGrid1.AddItem adrRecordset.Fields(0).Name + Chr(9) + _
        adrRecordset.Fields(1).Name
```

```
Do While Not adrRecordset.EOF
    MSFlexGrid1.AddItem adrRecordset.Fields(0) + Chr(9) +
    ➥adrRecordset.Fields(1)
    adrRecordset.MoveNext
Loop
MSFlexGrid1.FixedRows = 1
Set adrRecordset = Nothing
adcConnection.Close
Set adcConnection = Nothing
```

End Sub

Now imagine that the person who originally requested this application changes his or her mind and now wants the code to return the author's name and the name of the book. To make this change, the developer would have to edit the code, as seen in Listing 2.2, and then roll it out to every user who needs it.

LISTING 2.2   Changing a Fat Application

```
Private Sub Command1_Click()
Dim adcConnection As New ADODB.Connection
Dim adrRecordset As ADODB.Recordset
Dim strSQL As String

    adcConnection.ConnectionString = "driver={SQL Server};" & _
        "server=tophat;uid=sa;pwd=;database=pubs"
    adcConnection.ConnectionTimeout = 30
    adcConnection.Open

    strSQL = "SELECT SUBSTRING((RTRIM(a.au_lname) + ', ' + " & _
            "RTRIM(a.au_fname)), 1, 25) AS Name, t.title AS Title " & _
            "FROM authors a INNER JOIN titleauthor ta " & _
            "ON a.au_id = ta.au_id INNER JOIN titles t " & _
            "ON t.title_id = ta.title_id " & _
            "ORDER BY au_lname ASC, au_fname ASC"

    Set adrRecordset = adcConnection.Execute(strSQL)
    MSFlexGrid1.Clear
    MSFlexGrid1.AddItem adrRecordset.Fields(0).Name + Chr(9) + _
        adrRecordset.Fields(1).Name
    Do While Not adrRecordset.EOF
        MSFlexGrid1.AddItem adrRecordset.Fields(0) + Chr(9) +
        ➥adrRecordset.Fields(1)
        adrRecordset.MoveNext
    Loop
```

continues

LISTING 2.2   Continued

```
MSFlexGrid1.FixedRows = 1
Set adrRecordset = Nothing
adcConnection.Close
Set adcConnection = Nothing

End Sub
```

As you can see, not much code was changed, but the resulting work required to roll out the new program is where the difficulty lies. To enable users to request changes and developers to make changes easily, people began to make the client a *thinner* client, placing more of the application logic into the database. This allows more generic code to be used in the client and the actual work to be placed in the stored procedure that is being called. Going back to the examples shown in Listings 2.1 and 2.2, the client can be written to call a single stored procedure and then, if needed, the stored procedure can be rewritten. The code in Listing 2.3 shows the stored procedure required to create the resultset created in Listing 2.1.

LISTING 2.3   Thin Client Stored Procedure

```
USE pubs
GO
CREATE PROC usp_report1
AS
SELECT title_id, title FROM titles
GO
```

The client code is written so that it calls the stored procedure created in Listing 2.3, as shown in Listing 2.4.

LISTING 2.4   Thin Client Visual Basic Routine

```
Private Sub Command1_Click()
Dim adcConnection As New ADODB.Connection
Dim adrRecordset As ADODB.Recordset
Dim strSQL As String

    adcConnection.ConnectionString = "driver={SQL Server};" & _
        "server=tophat;uid=sa;pwd=;database=pubs"
    adcConnection.ConnectionTimeout = 30
    adcConnection.Open

    strSQL = "usp_report1"
```

```
Set adrRecordset = adcConnection.Execute(strSQL)
MSFlexGrid1.Clear
MSFlexGrid1.AddItem adrRecordset.Fields(0).Name + Chr(9) + _
    adrRecordset.Fields(1).Name
Do While Not adrRecordset.EOF
    MSFlexGrid1.AddItem adrRecordset.Fields(0) + Chr(9) +
    ➥adrRecordset.Fields(1)
    adrRecordset.MoveNext
Loop
MSFlexGrid1.FixedRows = 1
Set adrRecordset = Nothing
adcConnection.Close
Set adcConnection = Nothing

End Sub
```

When this code is executed, the results (as seen in Figure 2.1) look the same as those generated from Listing 2.1. The only difference is that the code that generates the results is contained in a stored procedure.

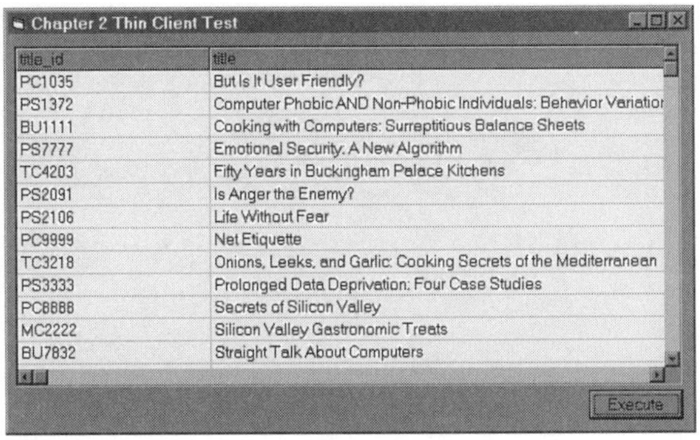

FIGURE 2.1
The results from the execution of the code in Listing 2.4 give no clue that a stored procedure was used.

To change this application so that it executes like the one in Listing 2.2, the only thing that must happen is to change the stored procedure so that it returns the desired resultset, as shown in Listing 2.5.

LISTING 2.5   Stored Procedure Change

```
ALTER PROC usp_report1
AS
SELECT SUBSTRING((RTRIM(a.au_lname) + ', ' +
       RTRIM(a.au_fname)), 1, 25) AS Name, t.title AS Title
FROM   authors a INNER JOIN titleauthor ta
       ON a.au_id = ta.au_id INNER JOIN titles t
       ON t.title_id = ta.title_id
ORDER BY au_lname ASC, au_fname ASC
```

Now, without changing the client at all, all users will get the new results, as shown in
Figure 2.2.

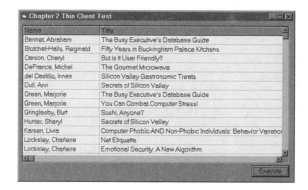

FIGURE 2.2
The results from the code in Listing 2.5 show how easy it is to change a stored procedure.

Another reason for using this method to write your applications is to enforce business rules.
For example, imagine that the owner of a regional shipping company asks you to write an
application that enables him to track his customers. Currently, his company serves companies
only in the Kansas and Missouri area. He wants you to limit the state entries that can be placed
into the database to ensure that no one mistakenly picks up a client in another state. If you create this application as a fat client and you ever have to make any changes, you must recode
and recompile. On the other hand, if you create this application as a thinner client with the
logic that limits the states contained in stored procedures, it will be much easier to make the
required changes.

Now that you have seen how this approach works, you must be made aware of the pros and
cons of creating your code in this manner.

Advantages of Business Logic in the Database

As you have seen, the biggest advantage to writing applications by using this approach is that it is extremely easy to make most minor changes (and even some major changes) to the way your application works. It is also possible to make major changes to the back-end processing of your application without modifying the client code.

Another advantage to maintaining your business and application logic in stored procedures at the server is that you can create applications with extremely small memory footprints. This is because all logic is contained at the server level, so there is very little code other than formatting at the client level. These applications can then run more efficiently on computers with less memory.

Disadvantages of Business Logic in the Database

Just as there are some major advantages to this approach, there are some major disadvantages as well. One of the biggest disadvantages is the lack of ability to grow the application to enterprise levels. Often, the business logic contained in an application is quite complex. If all this logic resides in the database, you will run into locking and blocking issues as well as general slow response times. This is because SQL Server is designed as a database server, not an application server.

Other issues of using this approach come if you ever have to migrate your application from SQL Server to another RDBMS, such as Oracle. SQL Server functions and datatypes do not necessarily have an exact correspondence in Oracle. Take, for example, the code in Listings 2.6 and 2.7.

LISTING 2.6   SQL Server Stored Procedure

```
CREATE PROCEDURE uspAddCustomer
@vchName        VARCHAR(32),
@vchStreet      VARCHAR(64),
@vchCity        VARCHAR(32),
@chrState       CHAR(2),
@vchZip         VARCHAR(10),
@numTaxRate     NUMERIC(2, 1) OUTPUT
AS

IF (UPPER(@chrState) IN ('CA', 'WA', 'NV'))
BEGIN
    SELECT @numTaxRate = 2.5
END ELSE
IF (UPPER(@chrState) IN ('NJ', 'FL', 'OR'))
```

continues

LISTING 2.6   Continued

```
BEGIN
    SELECT @numTaxRate = 3.5
END ELSE
BEGIN
    SELECT @numTaxRate = 2.5
END

IF EXISTS (SELECT * FROM Customers WHERE CustomerName = @vchName)
BEGIN
    RAISERROR ('Customer Name Not Unique', 11, 1)
    RETURN 1
END

INSERT INTO Customers VALUES (@vchName, @vchStreet, @vchCity,
                             @chrState, @vchZip, @numTaxRate)

IF (@@ROWCOUNT = 0)
BEGIN
    RAISERROR('An unknown error occured during the insert', 11, 1)
    RETURN 1
END

RETURN 0
```

Listing 2.6 creates a stored procedure that inserts an order record into a table called `Customers`. It also returns the tax rate for the state where the customer lives. There is only allowed one customer in the `Customers` table that has the same name, so if there is more than one, an error will be returned to the user. The code in Listing 2.7 does the same thing on an Oracle server.

LISTING 2.7   Oracle Stored Procedure

```
create or replace procedure add_cust
(name    in varchar2,
 street in varchar2,
 city    in varchar2,
 state   in char,
 zip     in varchar2) is
    tax_rate number(2,1);
begin
    dbms_output.enable;
    if (upper(state) in ('CA', 'WA', 'NV')) then
        tax_rate := 2.5;
    elsif (upper(state) in ('NJ', 'FL', 'OR')) then
        tax_rate := 3.5;
```

```
    else
        tax_rate := 2.0;
    end if;

    insert into "Customer" values
    (custid_seq.nextval, name, street, city, upper(state), zip, tax_rate);

exception
    when dup_val_on_index then
        dbms_output.put_line('Customer name is not unique');
    when value_error then
        dbms_output.put_line('Add failed. Value inconsistent with definition');
    when others then
        declare
            error_code number        := sqlcode;
            error_msg  varchar2(300) := sqlerrm;
        begin
            dbms_output.put_line('Error adding customer: ' || error_msg);
            dbms_output.put_line('Error code: ' || to_char(error_code));
        end;
end;
```

As you can see, it is not possible for you simply to transfer the code from SQL Server to Oracle. While the code looks similar, you must rewrite all the code in order to make it work.

Another problem you might encounter if you put all your logic in the database is that you are somewhat limited by what you can do using the Transact-SQL language. Unlike other languages, such as Visual Basic or C++, Transact-SQL is not very powerful.

Also, you must remember that every time you place logic into the database, you are taking processor cycles away from the true use of the database server: serving data. As an example, one client I consulted for asked me to investigate some performance issues they were having. When the client started using this system, the system ran very well. When the client scaled the system to more users, they began to see major performance problems. After some investigation, I determined that most of the client's problems centered on one stored procedure. After more investigation, I determined that the stored procedure, which was being executed approximately once a second by about 75 clients, was performing a simple conversion from kilograms to pounds. After I removed this functionality from the database and placed it back into the client, the performance issues were pretty much eliminated.

The last major issue that people deal with when putting all the business logic into the database is that of code versioning. When you write an application in Visual Basic or C++, you have the ability to add a version number so that you can tell the difference between versions if you make changes. This way, you can easily check which version is installed on each user's computer and revert to a previous version if you need to do so. The major problem with using SQL Server to support your application and business logic is that no versioning is built into the stored procedures. The only way to track the versions is to maintain the scripts used to create the stored procedures. Because there is no internal versioning, there is no easy way to see which version of a stored procedure is running on a particular server.

The No Business Logic Camp

At the other end of the stored procedure spectrum lies the camp that wants no part of application or business logic in the database. This camp wants the database to do nothing but store data. At the farthest end of this spectrum, you will find developers who go as far as to require that the application take care of all referential integrity. Most developers do not go this far, but they are out there.

After many developers and administrators were burned by putting all the logic into the database, many of them moved toward putting all the logic into the client. This made for an extremely fat client and an extremely thin database layer. All the database does in this scenario is store data. No advantage is taken of the more powerful features of the database. This poses some definite problems when rolling out changes to the client, but many administrators feel that the trade-off is worth it. Because you have already seen how the code for this type of scenario works in Listing 2.1 and Listing 2.2, you should be aware of the advantages and disadvantages associated with it.

Advantages of the No Business Logic Camp

The major advantage of not putting any business or application logic into the database is the advance in speed that you gain. When application logic is placed in stored procedures and triggers in the database, it is possible to run into performance issues. The performance issues arise because while the procedure or trigger is running, all locks held by the process are held until the process is complete. If a stored procedure takes half a second to run, you might not have a problem if the database does not have many users or the procedure is not called frequently. On a heavily utilized database where that procedure is frequently accessed, this execution time could cause definite problems.

Disadvantages of the No Business Logic Camp

Clearly, one of the biggest disadvantages to having no business logic in the database is that you have to place the logic someplace else. The easiest solution is to put the logic into the application later. The problem with this solution is that it makes your users dependent on you to ensure that they are running the latest version of the client software. This falls back into the logistical problems that I discussed earlier in the chapter. If even one person is not running the correct version of the front end, it could cause major problems.

Another disadvantage to removing the business logic from the database is that making logic changes is more difficult and time-consuming. For the most part, database administrators are able to look at a stored procedure or trigger and make the required changes if a business rule needs modification. On the other hand, if all the logic is stored in the application, making changes will require a programmer.

Finding Middle Ground

You will find that most developers and managers reside in one of the two groups that I have outlined here. This can result in almost religious arguments during the design phase of an application. The good thing is that technologies are available that allow both sides to get their way.

One example of such technology is a Web-enabled application. A Web application can solve both of the major issues that are brought up on both sides. First of all, distribution of the application is not a big issue. If changes to the application must be made, they are rolled out to the Web server. Assuming that the users already have Web browsers installed on their computers, they don't have to worry about installing anything new. The changes will be reflected the next time that the users access the Web site. This type of approach solves the "no logic in the database" issue as well. It is possible to store all the logic at the Web server. This removes the logic from the database and allows for a single point of change if any of the logic must be modified at a later date.

Another recent technology that can help find middle ground is network computing. In network computing, a powerful server sits on the network and provides all the processing required for the clients. The client computers are simple machines that contain as little as a network card, a video display, a mouse, and a keyboard. When these computers are turned on, they connect to the remote server through the network. The server provides data processing, data collection, video services, and keystroke and mouse movement capturing. In this case, the application resides only on the server, so it eliminates the need to roll out a new client to every computer in the event that business logic changes. All the administrator would have to do is change the application on the server.

The last technology that can establish middle ground is a middle-tier framework, such as Microsoft Transaction Server, or MTS. Technologies such as MTS enable developers to create applications that connect to other computers to acquire vital pieces of code to make them work. These pieces of code, called *components*, can contain business and application logic. Components are interesting because of the way they are accessed by the application. Components are accessed through interfaces. These interfaces are known to the application. As long as the interfaces look the same to the application, you can change the logic contained in the component. This eliminates the need to redistribute the application if you must change the business logic.

Conclusion

When you are designing an application, it is important to realize that there are several schools of thought on how and where the business logic of the application should be stored. Some people feel that the logic should reside in the database layer. This keeps the application from doing anything but displaying the data that is returned from the database. Other people feel that the logic should reside in the application layer. This allows the database to do the only things it is designed to do: store and serve data. When designing an application, you must be aware of both these camps and also be aware of the different ways available to you to mitigate the issues. This includes Web-enabling your applications, using network computing, or using middle-tier application servers such as Microsoft Transaction Server. It is also important to remember that you do not have to be rooted in one camp or another. Depending on the needs of your users and the functionality required by the application, you may have certain portions of the application in which the business logic resides in the database and others where the logic is in the application itself.

Processing Stored Procedures

IN THIS CHAPTER

When working with SQL Server stored procedures, you need to be aware of several aspects of how stored procedures work. These aspects include how stored procedures are created, how they are stored, and how they are processed. In this chapter, you will learn about the following:

- How SQL Server creates stored procedures
- How SQL Server processes stored procedures
- SQL Server execution plans

How SQL Server Creates Stored Procedures

Unfortunately, despite the title of this section, SQL Server doesn't create stored procedures for you. You have to plan out how the stored procedure will work, write the code, and then debug the code. Nevertheless, when you finally have your code written and execute the CREATE PROCEDURE statement, SQL Server has to go through a couple of steps before the code is actually created as a stored procedure.

Prior to SQL Server 7.0, when you executed the CREATE PROCEDURE statement, SQL Server would parse the statement, resolve the names of all objects referenced in the procedure, and partially compile the stored procedure. The precompiled statement was stored until the procedure was executed. This saved compilation time when the procedure was executed, thus speeding up the server's response time.

With SQL Server 7.0 and beyond, Microsoft changed the way this worked. Now, when CREATE PROCEDURE is executed, SQL Server first parses the statement to ensure that all statements are syntactically correct. If the server encounters any sort of syntax error, the creation of the procedure is cancelled and an error is returned to the user. If there are no syntax errors, SQL Server stores the text of the stored procedure in the syscomments table in the database that the user who created the stored procedure was using at the time CREATE PROCEDURE was executed. Nothing else happens until the stored procedure is actually executed. After the stored procedure is run for the first time, SQL Server prepares the code contained in the procedure to be executed.

How SQL Server Processes Stored Procedures

When you first execute a stored procedure, the SQL Server query processor reads the code of the stored procedure from the syscomments table and begins the deferred name resolution process.

Deferred Name Resolution

Deferred name resolution is the process of checking the names of all objects that a stored procedure uses to make sure that they exist. Tables, stored procedures, or other objects referenced by the stored procedure don't have to exist when the procedure is first created. SQL Server doesn't resolve the names of the objects until the stored procedure is actually executed. The resolution process occurs whenever a stored procedure needs to be compiled, such as when the server is first restarted or after the query plan is aged out of memory. During the resolution process, not only does SQL Server check the objects that are referenced in the stored procedure, but it also performs other validation, such as the following:

- Ensuring that the column data types in any referenced tables are compatible with any variables that reference those columns

- Checking that any variables and columns passed into SQL Server functions are compatible with the expected inputs for the functions

- Making sure that any data being passed out of the stored procedure is compatible with any variables that it's being passed into

If any object being referenced by the stored procedure is renamed or deleted, an error will be returned to the user when the stored procedure is executed. If an object referenced in the stored procedure is deleted and a different one is created with the same name, the stored procedure uses the new object, assuming that all the data types in the new object are compatible. The stored procedure doesn't have to be recompiled for this to occur.

This activity is extremely different from the way prior versions of SQL Server worked. In previous versions of SQL Server, you had to recompile the stored procedure if you made any changes to the underlying objects. This could lead to some very difficult-to-troubleshoot problems. For example, if you renamed an object referenced by a stored procedure and then created a new object with the old name, the stored procedure would continue to use the old object, even though the name had changed. This was because SQL Server used to precompile the stored procedure and resolve the names of any objects referenced in the stored procedure to their object IDs. When the old object was renamed, SQL Server didn't—and still doesn't—change the object ID. Because the stored procedure had been precompiled and all the names had already been resolved, everything continued to execute exactly as it had.

If any errors are encountered during the name resolution process, an error is returned and execution halts. If the name resolution process is successful, the stored procedure is analyzed to create an execution plan.

Creation of an Execution Plan

After all the object names referenced in the stored procedure are successfully resolved, the SQL Server query optimizer analyzes all the stored procedure code and creates an execution plan. An *execution plan* is basically a roadmap that shows that fastest method for SQL Server to access the data that the stored procedure is attempting to access. When SQL Server is

3

PROCESSING STORED PROCEDURES

creating the execution plan, the query optimizer takes several variables into account. Some of these variables include the following:

- The quantity of data in the tables that are referenced.
- The types of indexes that have been created on the tables referenced in the query.
- The indexed columns. It's extremely important that you analyze how the data in your tables is accessed. When a certain column or group of columns is used to identify the rows that need to be retrieved from the table, you should ensure that there's an index on those columns. It's also important that you know the order in which the columns will be referenced in the queries. You must make sure that the columns in the index are in the same order as the columns that are most frequently listed in queries. If the columns are listed differently in the query than they are listed in the index, the index won't be used.
- The data distribution in the indexes.

> **NOTE**
>
> To determine the distribution, SQL Server uses distribution statistics that are kept on the indexes. It's possible for these distribution statistics to become old and obsolete. To keep this from occurring, run UPDATE STATISTICS on any table that experiences large changes in the indexed values or if you perform a large insert or delete from the table.

- The types of comparison operators and the values being compared to in the WHERE clause.
- The presence and types of joins being used in the query.
- The existence of the UNION, GROUP BY, or ORDER BY keyword.

After all these factors are analyzed and SQL Server determines the fastest way to access the data, the stored procedure is compiled into an execution plan. The execution plan is cached into memory and used to run the stored procedure. SQL Server will reuse this execution plan whenever the stored procedure is executed until the SQL Server is stopped or needs memory and swaps out that execution plan.

Execution Plans

With the release of SQL Server 7.0, Microsoft changed the way execution plans were used and maintained in memory. With SQL Server 6.5 and earlier, the chances of an execution plan being reused were pretty slim. This caused some extra overhead because SQL Server would have to reevaluate the stored procedure every time it was executed. With SQL Server 7.0 and beyond, execution plans have a much higher chance of being reused.

As with previous versions of SQL Server, after the memory for system data structures is allocated from the overall amount of memory, the remaining memory is divided into two portions:

- A percentage of the memory is allocated for use as procedure cache, which is used for storing execution plans.
- The other portion of available memory is used for data buffers.

The overall pool of available memory as well as the amount of memory for the procedure cache and data buffers fluctuates depending on the current load on the system. This load includes other applications and services running on the machine, the number of user connections to the machine, and the number of open files and network connections to the machine.

CAUTION

Be very careful about running other applications directly on the SQL Server. The more applications run on the server, the less memory available to SQL Server. Also be very cautious about what screen savers you run on your SQL Server. I know that the OpenGL screen savers look cool, but don't run them on your SQL Server—or any other production server for that matter. I have seen the 3D Pipes screen saver drop available memory by 60 percent and peg processor utilization.

3

PROCESSING STORED PROCEDURES

Execution Plan Makeup

As mentioned previously, with the release of SQL Server 7.0, there is a much greater chance that the query optimizer will reuse an execution plan. Microsoft increased the chances that execution plans will be reused by changing the makeup of the plans. There are two main components to a SQL Server execution plan: the query plan and the execution context.

The majority of a SQL Server execution plan is made up of an object known as a *query plan,* a read-only reusable structure that any user on the system can use. The query plan is essentially a roadmap that is used to get to the data in the tables quickly. The query plan doesn't contain any information about a user's query parameters, only how to get to the data. SQL Server will maintain a maximum of only two query plans in memory at any point in time: one handles all serial executions, the other handles all parallel executions.

The second part of an execution plan contains all the parameters unique to a specific user's execution. This structure is known as the *execution context.* Although there is no set number of execution context structures, SQL Server will reuse any that have become inactive.

This separation allows SQL Server to reuse query plans for queries that have the same query plan with different parameters in the WHERE clause.

Putting it all together, SQL Server reuses available execution plans when a user executes a SQL query or stored procedure. The parameters or search criteria that the user passes in are stored in the execution context. The execution context is specific to the individual user. A visual representation of the correspondence between the query plan and the execution context is shown in Figure 3.1.

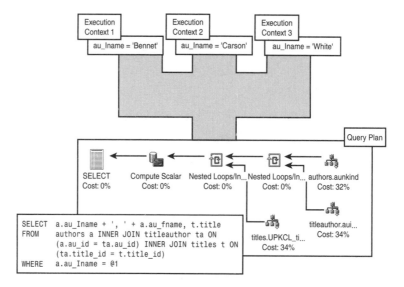

FIGURE 3.1

This is a visual representation of a query plan and execution context.

How SQL Server Chooses Query Plans

When a stored procedure—or any other SQL statement—is sent to the SQL Server, the query engine checks through the procedure cache to see whether an execution plan has been created for that stored procedure or SQL statement. If a plan has been stored in the procedure cache, SQL Server loads and uses that plan, thus saving the time and overhead required to re-create a new query plan. If the query engine doesn't find an execution plan, it must create one and store it in the procedure cache for future use.

When SQL Server searches the procedure cache to see whether an execution plan exists, it uses an extremely efficient method that almost always uses fewer system resources than compiling a new procedure. One major caveat to the search method SQL Server uses is that it requires that all object names be fully qualified for it to work. Look at the following code:

```
SELECT    *
FROM      pubs.dbo.authors
GO
SELECT    *
FROM      authors
GO
```

The first SELECT statement in this listing will be matched to an existing execution plan, if one exists. The second SELECT statement will be recompiled, even if there's an existing plan. The reason is that if the names aren't fully qualified, the database doesn't truly know the exact object that you are looking for. Remember that it is possible to have more than one table with the same name in the database as long as each table has a separate owner. If you don't specify an owner for the object in your query, even if there are no tables with the same name in the database, SQL Server must still act as though there are. Therefore, to effectively reuse execution plans, you should always ensure that the objects referenced in the SQL statements you create are fully qualified.

Aging and Deallocating Execution Plans

After an execution is created, it's placed in the procedure cache. Execution plans aren't removed from the procedure cache until SQL Server needs space to add new execution plans. When an execution plan is created, a cost factor and an age number are associated with the query plan and the user execution context. The cost factor is based on a combination of the server overhead and the amount of time that was required to create the execution plan. The age number is incremented by the cost factor every time the execution is pulled from the procedure cache and reused by another user. Every time the lazy writer process scans the procedure cache, it decrements the age field on every execution context in the procedure cache.

3

PROCESSING
STORED
PROCEDURES

The Lazy Writer

The *lazy writer* is a system process that flushes out dirty and aged buffers and makes them available for system or user processes. A *dirty buffer* contains changes that haven't yet been written back to the hard drive. The lazy writer performs the function of writing these changes to disk. This process helps eliminate the need to run frequent checkpoints for the purpose of creating buffers.

Take, for example, an execution plan that has a compilation cost factor of 12. Each time this query plan is used, it increments the age number by this value. After the execution plan is referenced three times, it has an age of 36. On each scan by the lazy writer, the age is decremented by one. After 36 scans, the age number for the query plan is 0 unless another user has referenced the plan.

The lazy writer can deallocate the query plan when the following three conditions have been met:

- SQL Server needs memory to store an object and all available memory earmarked for procedure cache is already in use.
- The age field for a particular object has been decremented to 0.
- No user is referencing the object.

Because the age value is incremented every time an execution plan is used, frequently used plans are never removed from the procedure cache. Other, less frequently used query plans usually have their age values decremented to 0 rather quickly and, hence, are eligible for deallocation much sooner.

Execution Plan Recompilation

When certain database changes occur, they can have a major impact on existing execution plans. This impact can be anything from the execution plan becoming inefficient to it becoming invalid. SQL Server tracks and detects any changes that will cause an execution plan to become invalid. When any change occurs that will negatively impact an execution plan, SQL Server marks that plan as being invalid and automatically sets the age field associated with that plan to 0. This will cause the execution plan to be removed from the procedure cache and a new plan to be generated on the next execution of the statement. The actions that can cause an execution plan to become invalid are as follows:

- Any changes to the structure of a table or view that's referenced by a query such as ALTER TABLE or ALTER VIEW.
- New distribution statistics being generated that are extremely different from the current statistics. These statistics can be generated automatically or explicitly through the use of the UPDATE STATISTICS command.
- Dropping or modifying an index that's referenced in the execution plan.
- An explicit call to the sp_recompile stored procedure that references a table used in the execution plan.
- A large change in the quantity of keys being referenced in the execution plan. Such changes are caused by INSERT and DELETE statements being run against referenced tables.
- For trigger execution plans, if the number of rows in the inserted or deleted tables changes drastically.

Viewing and Interpreting Execution Plans

When you are developing stored procedures and other SQL Server queries, it's a good idea for you to be able to see what the execution plan will look like. This enables you to create well-written stored procedures without the need to perform a great deal of redevelopment after the procedure goes into production. The execution plan also shows where you can speed up query execution. For example, it will show tables that don't have statistics created on them. There are two ways to view the execution plan. You can view the estimated execution plan or the actual execution plan.

All execution plans are viewed in SQL Query Analyzer, using a feature called the graphical showplan. To view an estimated query plan, click the Display Estimated Execution Plan button on the Query Analyzer toolbar. This scans all the code in the stored procedure or query and returns the query plan. This plan enables you to see how the entire script runs. If there are conditional operators in the script or stored procedure, all options are shown. Figure 3.2 shows an example of an estimated query plan.

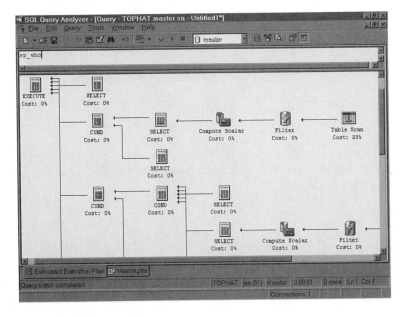

3

PROCESSING
STORED
PROCEDURES

FIGURE 3.2
SQL Query Analyzer displays an estimated query plan for the sp_who *system stored procedure.*

To view the actual execution plan, select the Show Execution Plan option from the drop-down list next to the execute button and then execute the stored procedure. It adds a tab at the bottom of the query window that contains the actual query plan used to execute the stored procedure or query. Figure 3.3 shows the true query plan for the same query estimated in Figure 3.2. Notice how these plans are extremely different.

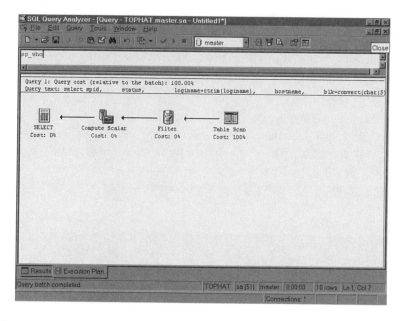

FIGURE 3.3

The true query plan for the sp_who *system stored procedure looks very different from the estimated plan.*

As you can see from Figures 3.2 and 3.3, quite a few icons are used to explain the different physical operators that SQL Server uses during the execution of a query. Table 3.1 outlines each icon and what it means.

NOTE

Notice that several of these descriptions refer to an arguments section. To view this arguments section, hover your mouse cursor over the icon in question in the graphical showplan.

TABLE 3.1   Graphical Showplan Icons

Icon	Operator	Description
	Assert	Verifies a condition. For example, it verifies referential integrity, checks constraints, or checks that a subquery returns a single row. Each row is evaluated against the value in the argument.

Icon	Operator	Description
	Bookmark Lookup	Uses a bookmark such as a row ID or clustered index key to look up a corresponding row in a table or clustered index. The argument contains the bookmark used to find the row in the table or clustered index.
	Clustered Index Delete	Deletes rows from the clustered index specified in the arguments section.
	Clustered Index Insert	Inserts the value specified in the argument into a clustered index.
	Clustered Index Scan	Scans the clustered index that's specified in the argument. Only those rows that satisfy the search criteria are returned.
	Clustered Index Seek	Uses an index seek to retrieve rows from a clustered index. The argument will contain the name of the index and a value used to specify rows to retrieve.
	Clustered Index Update	Updates rows in a clustered index.
	Collapse	Speeds up update processing.
	Compute Scalar	Evaluates an expression to produce a scalar value that can either be returned to the user or used within the query.
	Concatenation	Scans multiple inputs, combines them, and returns each row scanned.
	Constant Scan	Introduces a constant row into a query. It returns either zero or one row that contains no column. This operator is usually present with the Compute Scalar operator.
	Deleted Scan	Scans the deleted table when a trigger is executed.

continues

TABLE 3.1   Continued

Icon	Operator	Description
	Filter	Scans the input and returns only those rows that satisfy the filter expression, which is contained in the argument.
	Hash Match	Builds a hash table by creating a hash table for each row it received. The passed-in argument is a list of columns that are used to create the hash.
	Hash Match Root	Coordinates the operation of the Hash Match Root operators. The Hash Match Root and Hash Match Team operators share the same hash function and partitioning strategy.
	Hash Match Team	Is a part of a team of hash operators that share a common hash function and partitioning strategy.
	Index Delete	Deletes input rows from a clustered index. The arguments section contains the nonclustered index and a specification of the rows to be deleted.
	Index Insert	Inputs a specified value into a nonclustered index that's specified in the arguments section. The arguments section also contains the value being inserted.
	Index Scan	Retrieves all rows from the index listed in the arguments section. The arguments section can also contain an operator specifying that only certain rows be returned.
	Index Seek	Uses the ability to seek in an index to retrieve rows from a nonclustered index.
	Index Spool	Scans the input rows, places the data into a hidden spool file, and then builds an index on those rows.
	Index Update	Updates rows in a nonclustered index as specified in the arguments section.
	Inserted Scan	Scans the inserted table that's created by a trigger.
	Log Row Scan	Scans the transaction log.

Icon	*Operator*	*Description*
	Merge Join	Performs inner joins, left outer joins, left semi joins, left anti semi joins, right outer joins, right semi joins, right anti semi joins, and unions.
	Nested Loops	Performs inner joins, left outer joins, left semi joins, and left anti semi joins.
	Parallelism	Performs distribute streams, gather streams, and repartition streams.
	Parameter Table Scan	Scans an internal table that acts as a parameter in a query. This table is most commonly used in stored procedures that perform INSERT queries.
	Remote Delete	Deletes rows from a remote object.
	Remote Insert	Inserts rows into a remote object.
	Remote Query	Queries a remote object. The actual query is sent to the remote server in the arguments section.
	Remote Scan	Scans a remote object.
	Remote Update	Updates a remote object.
	Row Count Spool	Checks all input rows and counts the number of rows present and the number of rows with no data in them.
	Sequence	Executes each input in sequence and updates many different objects.
	Sort	Sorts all incoming rows.
	Stream Aggregate	Groups a set of columns and calculates one or more aggregate expressions returned by the query.
	Table Delete	Deletes rows from a table. The name of the table and a specification of which rows to delete are stored in the arguments section.

continues

3

PROCESSING
STORED
PROCEDURES

TABLE 3.1 Continued

Icon	Operator	Description
	Table Insert	Adds new rows to the table specified in the arguments section.
	Table Scan	Retrieves all rows from the table specified in the arguments section.
	Table Spool	Scans the input and places a copy of each row into a spool table.
	Table Update	Updates rows in a table that are specified in the arguments section.
	Top	Retrieves a specified number or percentage of rows in a table.
	Dynamic	Specifies that all changes to the underlying tables can be seen in the cursor.
	Fetch Query	Retrieves rows from a cursor.
	Keyset	Specifies that it can see updates made by other users, but not inserts.
	Population Query	Populates the cursor's work table when the cursor is first opened.
	Refresh Query	Fetches current data into the cursor fetch buffer.
	Snapshot	Specifies that any changes made to the underlying data can't be seen by the cursor.

Most of the icons that you have seen here will be seen only in special circumstances. Most frequently, you will see a group of only five to ten of them. To get an idea of how to interpret a query plan, type in the following query and execute it with the Show Execution Plan option turned on:

```
SELECT    a.au_fname + ' '+ a.au_lname AS 'Author Name', t.title
FROM      authors a INNER JOIN titleauthor ta
          ON (a.au_id = ta.au_id) INNER JOIN titles t
          ON (ta.title_id = t.title_id)
```

To view what an icon means and what its impact on the query is, hover your cursor over that particular icon to display information about that operation (see Figure 3.4).

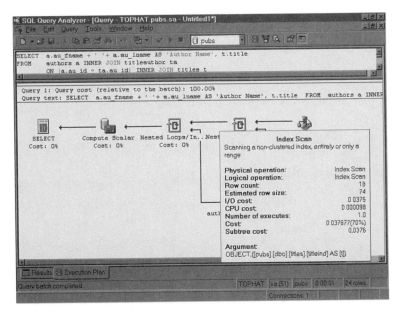

FIGURE 3.4
Hover your cursor over an icon in the query plan to determine that operation's impact on the query.

Conclusion

In this chapter, you have seen how SQL Server processes stored procedures. First, SQL Server parses all the code that's passed. When the procedure is first executed, SQL Server compiles the code into an execution plan. The execution plan is made up of a *query plan*, which is the actual way to get to the data, and the *execution context*, which is the specifics for that particular execution. Lastly, you saw how the graphical showplan works and how to interpret the data returned.

Stored Procedures Rules

IN THIS CHAPTER

When using any sort of programming language, there are rules. Many of these rules are *inferred rules*, meaning that they are not defined by anyone other than your peers. For example, Hungarian notation in Visual Basic code is not a requirement. It just makes for good, easily interpreted code. Other rules, such as how and what types of procedure can be created where, are required. In this chapter, you will go over different rules regarding the creation of SQL Server stored procedures. Like any other programming language, SQL Server requires some of these rules and others are suggestions about how you should handle the creation of stored procedures. This chapter will cover the following:

- Programming stored procedure rules
- Variable naming conventions
- Object naming conventions
- Special stored procedure naming conventions

Programming Stored Procedure Rules

When you are developing an application that relies on SQL Server stored procedures, you must take into account a number of rules. Those rules govern the following:

- How the stored procedure is created
- How objects inside the stored procedure are referenced
- How to protect your stored procedure source code from being read
- How ODBC interacts with stored procedures

Basic Rules

Several rules must be dealt with when creating stored procedures. These rules define the way in which the stored procedure itself is created and how the stored procedure can interact with other objects in the database. The following is a list of the major things you must keep in mind when creating stored procedures:

- The CREATE PROCEDURE statement must be the first statement in a SQL Server batch. If the procedure is not the first statement, SQL Server returns an error to the user and fails to create the procedure.
- Stored procedures can execute any SQL statement available to the creator, except for the following statements: CREATE DEFAULT, CREATE TRIGGER, CREATE PROCEDURE, CREATE VIEW, and CREATE RULE.
- Any database object, except for those SQL statements listed earlier, can be created and used within a stored procedure.
- Stored procedures can create and reference temporary tables.

- If you create a local, or private, temporary table inside a stored procedure, that table is in the database only for the use of the stored procedure that created it. When the stored procedure has completed its execution, the temporary table is dropped from the database.

- If you create a stored procedure that executes a second stored procedure, all objects created in the first stored procedure are available to the second stored procedure. This includes both private and public temporary tables.

- If you execute a remote stored procedure that modifies data on a remote server, those changes cannot be rolled back. This is because remote stored procedures do not take place as a part of the local transaction.

- SQL Server stored procedures can take a maximum of 1,024 parameters. This includes both input and output parameters.

- SQL Server places no logical limit on the number of internal variables that can be defined in a stored procedure. The amount of available memory determines how many variables can be used.

- Parameters passed into the stored procedures are NULL by default. This can pose problems when SQL Server is adding or modifying data in tables that do not allow NULL values. If the stored procedure attempts an UPDATE or INSERT into a table that does not allow a NULL, SQL Server returns an error. To keep this from occurring, place logic in the stored procedure to check for the NULL and replace it with a valid value or put a default value on the table.

- SQL Server stored procedures are limited to a maximum of 128MB, depending on the amount of memory in the server. If you need to create a stored procedure that is larger than 128MB, you should create two separate stored procedures that are called by a third.

Referencing Objects in Stored Procedures

When you create a stored procedure, object names that are referenced inside the stored procedure are assumed to be owned by the creator of the stored procedure. If the creator of the stored procedure does not use the fully qualified names of the objects referenced in the stored procedure, access to that stored procedure is restricted to the user who created it. When statements such as ALTER TABLE, CREATE TABLE, DROP TABLE, TRUNCATE TABLE, CREATE INDEX, DROP INDEX, UPDATE STATISTICS, and DBCC are used, you must qualify the names of the objects if other users will use the procedure. This is because SQL Server does not resolve the names of the tables until the procedure is actually run. To alleviate problems with this, you should ensure that all the objects in your database are owned by the same person. For those of you who have worked in other databases, such as Oracle, this may seem like an extremely unwise thing to do from a security standpoint. Let me assure you that you can keep adequate security with SQL Server even with all objects having the same owner.

Source Code Protection

After the stored procedures that make up your SQL Server application have been installed, there are times that you will want to protect your code from being viewed by the users and administrators of your system. Of course, if the users or administrators actually have to run a script to install the procedures, this step is a moot point.

When a stored procedure is created, SQL Server stores the actual code for the stored procedure in the syscomments system table in the database in which the stored procedure resides. In earlier versions of SQL Server, people simply deleted the information contained in that table to keep other people from seeing the code. This worked for that purpose, but it did not allow your users to upgrade to the next version of SQL Server when it was released. Now, the best option you have to keep your users from viewing the code that was used to create the procedure is to encrypt the information using the WITH ENCRYPTION option. After the syscomments table has been encrypted, it cannot be decrypted and cannot be viewed by anyone. Take a look at the example in Listing 4.1.

LISTING 4.1 Encrypting Stored Procedures

```
CREATE PROCEDURE uspTestProcedure
AS
SELECT    *
FROM    authors
GO

sp_helptext uspTestProcedure
GO

ALTER PROCEDURE uspTestProcedure
WITH ENCRYPTION
AS
SELECT    *
FROM    authors
GO

sp_helptext uspTestProcedure
GO
```

When you look run the sp_helptext system stored procedure against the unencrypted stored procedure, it returns the code exactly as you typed it in. When the stored procedure is then encrypted, sp_helptext returns a message saying that the source has been encrypted with no other information.

ODBC Options

When an ODBC application first connects to SQL Server, it will set several options that might affect the way your stored procedures operate. Those options are as follows:

- SET QUOTED_IDENTIFIER ON
- SET TEXTSIZE 2147483647
- SET ANSI_DEFAULTS ON
- SET CURSOR_CLOSE_ON_COMMIT OFF
- SET IMPLICIT_TRANSACTIONS OFF

Because non-ODBC applications do not set these options, you should test every stored procedure that will interact with ODBC applications. Test with these options both on and off to ensure that the application will work exactly the way you expect. If a particular stored procedure needs one of these options set differently than the way it is set by ODBC, you must issue the SET command at the beginning of the stored procedure. That SET statement will be in effect only until the execution of the stored procedure has completed. After the procedure has completed its execution, the server reverts to the original settings.

Deferred Name Resolution and Query Plan Creation

When you create a stored procedure, the code in the procedure is parsed to ensure that no syntax errors exist. If a syntax error is encountered at this point, SQL Server stops the creation of the procedure and returns an error to the user. If the syntax of the command is correct, the text of the procedure is stored in the syscomments system table in the database in which the procedure is being created.

The first time the stored procedure is executed, the SQL Server query processor reads the data from the syscomments table and checks whether all the objects referenced in the stored procedure are contained in the database. This process is known as *deferred name resolution*.

If any errors are encountered during deferred name resolution, SQL Server returns an error and halts the execution of the stored procedure. Because of the deferred name resolution process, any objects referenced in a SQL Server stored procedure do not need to be in the database when the stored procedure is created. The objects must be there only when the stored procedure is first run. This type of resolution is used because it enables the user to drop and recreate tables (and other objects in the database) without having to recompile every stored procedure that references that object.

In previous versions of SQL Server, you could rename a table that was referenced in a stored procedure and create a new table with the same name. When you executed the stored procedure, it executed against the old table. This is because, in previous versions of SQL Server, all the objects would be resolved to their object IDs at the time they were created. The object ID of the object is not changed when you change the object's name, so the stored procedure does not recognize the new object. Deferred resolution solves this problem. By executing the code in Listing 4.2, you can see an example of deferred name resolution.

LISTING 4.2   Deferred Name Resolution

```
CREATE PROCEDURE usp_4_1_1
@vchAuthorLastNamePattern    VARCHAR(16) = '%'
AS

SET NOCOUNT ON

SELECT @vchAuthorLastNamePattern = @vchAuthorLastNamePattern + '%'

EXEC usp_4_1_2

IF (SELECT COUNT(*) FROM ##TempAuthors WHERE AuthorName LIKE
    ➥@vchAuthorLastNamePattern) = 0
BEGIN
    RAISERROR ('No names found matching this pattern.', 0, 1)
    RETURN 101
END ELSE
BEGIN
    SELECT     *
    FROM    TempAuthors
    WHERE    AuthorName LIKE @vchAuthorLastNamePattern
END
DROP TABLE TempAuthors
GO


CREATE PROCEDURE usp_4_1_2
AS

SET NOCOUNT ON

SELECT    au_lname + ', ' + au_fname AS AuthorName, phone AS PhoneNumber
INTO    TempAuthors
FROM    authors
GO
```

As you can tell from the code in this listing, two objects that do not exist are referenced in the first stored procedure. These objects are the second stored procedure and the table

`TempAuthors`. In previous versions of SQL Server, the creation of this stored procedure would have failed. Because of the deferred resolution process, this stored procedure can be created and, when it is executed, it will work as expected.

During the deferred resolution process, SQL Server also performs some other validation activities. These activities include checking variable and column data types, ensuring the parameters that are passed in are of the proper data type, and making sure the nullability of any referenced column is maintained.

If the stored procedure has made it past the resolution stage, the query optimizer analyzer examines all the SQL statements in the stored procedure and creates an execution plan. The execution plan is the fastest method to execute the stored procedure. The execution plan is based on information such as the following:

- The overall quantity of data in the tables that are referenced by the stored procedure
- The types and presence of any indexes on the tables
- The distribution of the data in the columns that are indexed
- The comparison operators and values being compared in the `WHERE` clause
- Whether there are `UNION`, `GROUP BY`, or `ORDER BY` clauses in the SQL statements

After all these factors have been taken into account, SQL Server compiles the stored procedure into an execution plan and stores it in memory. This optimized execution plan is used to execute the stored procedure. The plan stays in memory until SQL Server is restarted or until the server must make room for a different execution plan. An execution plan is reused when the stored procedure is reexecuted, assuming that the plan is still in memory and is still valid. For more information on query plans, refer to Chapter 3, "Processing Stored Procedures."

Using Naming Conventions

As a developer, I am sure that you have found that for almost everything, someone somewhere has established naming conventions for how things are described. When dealing with SQL Server, no one has decided what the naming standards for objects in the database are. Naming conventions allow you to write code that is self documenting and, hence, easier to read.

Microsoft Discrepancies in Naming Convention

Looking at some of Microsoft's code, you will find that even Microsoft does not use a standard naming convention. Take a look at the code snippets in Listings 4.3 and 4.4 from the `sp_help` and `sp_rename` system stored procedures, respectively.

4

STORED PROCEDURES RULES

LISTING 4.3   Old sp_help

```
create proc sp_help
@objname nvarchar(776) = NULL          -- object name we're after
as
-- PRELIMINARY
set nocount on
declare     @dbname     sysname
-- OBTAIN DISPLAY STRINGS FROM spt_values UP FRONT --
declare @no varchar(35)
declare @yes varchar(35),
declare @none varchar(35)
```

LISTING 4.4   Old sp_rename

```
CREATE PROCEDURE sp_rename
@objname     nvarchar(776),          -- up to 3-part "old" name
@newname     sysname,                -- one-part new name
@objtype     varchar(13) = null      -- identifying the name
as
Set nocount      on
Set ansi_padding on
Declare      @objtypeIN         varchar(13),
    @ExecRC          integer,
    @CurrentDb          sysname,
    @CountNumNodes      integer,
    @UnqualOldName      sysname,
    @QualName1          sysname,
    @QualName2          sysname,
    @QualName3          sysname,
    @OwnAndObjName      nvarchar(517),    -- "[owner].[object]"
    @objid          integer,
    @xtype          char(2),
    @indid          smallint,
    @colid          smallint,
    @cnstid          integer,
    @parent_obj      integer,
    @xusertype          smallint,
    @ownerid          smallint,
    @objid_tmp          integer,
    @xtype_tmp          char(2),
    @retcode        int,
    @replinfo        int,
    @replbits          int
```

In the `sp_help` code shown in Listing 4.3, both the `@objname` and `@objid` variables start with the prefix `obj`, but have different data types. In the `sp_rename` code shown in Listing 4.4, `@objname`, `@newname`, and `@objtype` are all declared as `varchar`, yet they have different prefixes. Lastly, notice that some of the variables—specifically `@Int1` and `@Int2`—indicate the data type.

It is more efficient to name these variables so that their names reflect the type of data they hold, as shown in Listing 4.5 and Listing 4.6.

LISTING 4.5   New sp_help

```
create proc sp_help
@ncvobjname nvarchar(776) = NULL     -- object name we're after
as
set nocount on
declare @dbname      sysname
declare @vchNo         varchar(35)
declare @vchYes      varchar(35)
declare @vchNone       varchar(35)
```

LISTING 4.6   New sp_rename

```
CREATE PROCEDURE sp_rename
@nvcObjName      nvarchar(776),        -- up to 3-part "old" name
@NewName      sysname     ,         -- one-part new name
@vchObjType      varchar(13) = null    -- identifying the name
AS
SET NOCOUNT ON
SET ANSI_PADDING ON
Declare      @vchObjTypeIN        varchar(13)
Declare      @intExecRC         integer
Declare      @CurrentDb         sysname
Declare      @intCountNumNodes     integer
Declare      @UnqualOldName        sysname
Declare      @QualName1        sysname
Declare      @QualName2        sysname
Declare      @QualName3        sysname
Declare      @nvcOwnAndObjName     nvarchar(517)     -- "[owner].[object]"
Declare      @intObjID        integer
Declare      @chrXType        char(2)
Declare      @insIndID        smallint
Declare      @insColID        smallint
Declare      @intCnstID        integer
Declare      @intParentObj        integer
```

4

continues

LISTING 4.6 Continued

```
Declare    @insXUserType      smallint
Declare    @insOwnerID        smallint
Declare    @intObjIDTmp        integer
Declare    @chrXType_Tmp       char(2)
Declare    @intRetCode        int
Declare    @intReplInfo        int
Declare    @intReplBits        int
```

As you can see from this new code, it is much easier to tell what data is being stored in the variables. So far, there has been very little activity from Microsoft to establish naming conventions for use when you are developing with SQL Server. Falling back on other programming languages, we can develop some conventions of our own.

Microsoft Identifier Rules

In this section, I attempt to establish naming conventions for both data types and objects. The largest issue I must tackle is that of standards for variable names. To do this, I must establish a case standard and a set of prefixes. Title case has always been a popular standard for variables, and I carry on that standard here. As for the prefixes, I cover those in a moment. First, you need to be aware of the following restrictions that apply for naming variables and objects in SQL Server:

- Identifier names cannot exceed 128 characters. Although this seems like a lot, it can occasionally be restricting, particularly when you are accurately trying to describe the role an object plays in the database. More than likely, for most everyday development needs, you will never exceed this limit.

- Names can begin only with a letter or one of the following characters: _ (underscore), # (pound or hash), or @ (at symbol). The @ and # symbols have special meanings. The @ symbol represents a local variable to SQL Server, so you cannot use it when naming a database object. The # symbol represents a temporary object. A local variable cannot use an initial # in its name.

- Identifiers can contain alphanumeric characters or any of the following symbols: # (pound or hash), $ (dollar), or _ (underscore). You have no restrictions on placement within the name, as long as the initial character follows the rule previously mentioned.

- You cannot use a SQL Server reserved word as an identifier.

- Spaces and other characters are not allowed in identifier names. Also, you cannot use a keyword, such as table, as an object name.

Suggested Naming Conventions

When determining naming conventions for use in SQL Server development, you must still adhere to the rules for identifiers as described by Microsoft. The conventions listed here describe conventions that are in accordance with those rules.

The naming convention I suggest is as follows: Local variables should use a lowercase, three-letter prefix with all remaining words in title case. You should avoid using any symbols—such as the # (pound or hash), the $ (dollar), or the _ (underscore)—in any of your variable names. This convention is not set in stone, and, if you need to, you can change these to suit your needs. I use these in most of my code because it makes the code much more readable.

Table 4.1 lists some suggestions for naming conventions for data types and some examples.

TABLE 4.1   Data Type Naming Conventions

Data Type	Prefix	Example
int	int	@intObjectId
smallint	ins	@insCounter
tinyint	iny	@inyQuantity
float	flt	@fltValue
real	rel	@relInterest
numeric	num	@numMass
decimal	dec	@decVolume
money	mny	@mnyTotal
smallmoney	mns	@mnsSalary
bit	bit	@bitTerminated
datetime	dtm	@dtmBirth
smalldatetime	dts	@dtsBeginAccount

4

STORED
PROCEDURES
RULES

continues

TABLE 4.1 Continued

Data Type	Prefix	Example
char	chr	@chrLastName
varchar	vch	@vchAddress1
nvarchar	nvc	@nvcFirstName
binary	bny	@bnyFlags
varbinary	bnv	@bnvData
text	txt	@txtMemo
ntext	ntx	@ntxNotes
image	img	@imgPicture
cursor	cur	@curTableNames
uniqueidentifier	uid	@uidIdentifier

Although ntext, text, and image are valid data types, most likely they will not be declared as local variables. Keep in mind that local variables must begin with a single @ (at) symbol.

Objects commonly use a lowercase, two-letter prefix with all remaining words in title case. Tables and columns normally do not use a prefix, although the title case rule still applies. Table 4.2 lists the object naming conventions..

TABLE 4.2 Object Naming Conventions

Object	Prefix	Example
Table	None	SalesReps
Column	None	AuthorId
View	vw	vwContractAuthors
Rules	rl	rlZipCheck
Defaults	df	dfStandardQuantity
User-defined data types	dt	dtAddressLine
Index (clustered)	ic	icAuthorFullName
Index (nonclustered)	in	inClientStateCity
Primary key (clustered)	pc	pcCustomerId
Primary key (nonclustered)	pn	pnStateLookupId
Foreign key	fk	fkRepCompanyId
Trigger	tr	trStoreDelete
Cursor	cr	crTables

Notice that there is one glaring omission from Table 4.2. That omission is the naming standard for stored procedures. Most people automatically assume that you should use the sp_ prefix for all stored procedures. This is incorrect, and I will discuss the reasons for this later in the chapter. Some people suggest using the pr prefix for all stored procedures. You have probably noticed that so far, I have used usp to prefix all user stored procedures.

Again, everything I have covered dealing with naming conventions is *suggested*. No one has declared any definite naming conventions for use with SQL Server. As long as you remain consistent throughout your coding, you are okay.

Special Stored Procedure Naming Conventions

You must be aware of a couple of important things when working with SQL Server stored procedures. When you look at the system stored procedures included with SQL Server, you will see that they all begin with the prefix sp_. When I started programming with SQL Server, I assumed that all stored procedures should begin with sp_. I created hundreds of procedures using that prefix, until I ran across a small note in a SQL Server manual that said sp_ is the prefix for system stored procedures. Even then, that did not mean much to me. Finally, I read up on the sp_ prefix to find out what made that prefix so special.

If the first three letters of the stored procedure are sp_, SQL Server first searches the master database for the procedure. If the procedure is not found, SQL Server searches the master database assuming that the owner name is dbo. Finally, after it has exhausted those locations, SQL Server looks in the local database assuming that the owner name is the currently logged-in user. This enables you to create stored procedures that can be accessed in the master database when you are using any database on the server.

Although this might not sound like a big deal, SQL Server processes stored procedures with the sp_ prefix in a special way. Not only does SQL Server handle this prefix in a special way, so do external tools that you might use. One of those tools is ER*win*, a frequently used data modeling tool. One of the most powerful features of this tool is the capability to reverse engineer any database to which you have access. ER*win*, like other tools, looks at stored procedures with the sp_ prefix as system stored procedures and ignores them completely. This can make life pretty difficult when working with these tools.

What does all this mean to you? It means you should avoid using the sp_ prefix for stored procedures for normal application stored procedures. If you are creating systemwide utility stored procedures, it is acceptable to use this prefix. Otherwise, leave it alone.

4

STORED PROCEDURES RULES

Conclusion

In this chapter, you got a look into some of the rules you must follow when you create stored procedures. First, you saw how stored procedures are created and added to the server. Next, you saw how stored procedures are pulled from the server, compiled and executed. Lastly, you tackled the rules for identifiers and some suggested conventions for naming variables and other objects in your databases. Some of these rules are enforced by SQL Server. Other rules, such as the naming conventions, are not. These rules simply make your life easier during development of the procedures.

Simple Stored Procedures

IN THIS PART

Creating and Altering Stored Procedures

IN THIS CHAPTER

Now that you have learned how SQL Server stored procedures work, it is time to start creating stored procedures. Almost any query you write can be turned into a stored procedure. This approach enables you to run any query by executing a single command. This helps to insulate the application and the application developers by hiding the complexities of the SQL queries. Creating the actual stored procedure is relatively easy, after the query has been written and debugged. In this chapter, you will look at the basics of creating and altering stored procedures.

In this chapter, I will cover the following:

- Creating stored procedures
- SELECT statements
- Using the CREATE PROCEDURE command
- Using cursors in stored procedures
- Altering stored procedures

Creating Stored Procedures

The actual creation of a stored procedure is quite easy. The work that happens before you actually create the procedure is difficult. Before you create the procedure, you must first create and debug the query that is executed inside the procedure. The first part of this might be to create pseudocode that outlines the functionality contained in the stored procedure you are creating. This pseudocode will act as a roadmap during creation of the query.

The query can be as complex or as simple as you need. In this chapter, the stored procedures you will create are simple SELECT statements. Users who are experienced with the SELECT statement, logical operators, comparison operators, and Boolean expressions will want to skip forward to the section "Using Cursors." The following section is a basic review of the SELECT statement.

SELECT Statements

As a review, the syntax of the SELECT statement is as follows:

```
SELECT <select_list>
FROM <table_source>
WHERE <search_condition>
```

Where the following are the options:

Option	Description
`<select_list>`	This is either a list of the individual columns you want to select out of a table or an asterisk (*), which symbolizes that you want to select all data from the table.
`<table_source>`	This is a list of all the tables from which you are selecting. If you add more than one table here, you must also create a link (called a *join*) between the two tables to ensure that you receive the expected results. There is more information on joins in the next chapter.
`<search_condition>`	The search condition is used to limit the number of rows returned from a SELECT statement. Many options can be used in this section. Most of those options are covered in the next chapter.

You can use many options within this basic framework of the SELECT statement. I discuss some of these options in this chapter and the rest of them in the next chapter. When you SELECT data from a table, you must always provide something in the `<select_list>` and `<table_source>` options. The simplest SELECT statement you can use is one that SELECTs all rows and all columns from a table. An example of this type of SELECT statement can be seen in Listing 5.1.

LISTING 5.1   Simple SELECT Statement

```
SELECT *
FROM authors
```

The results from this SELECT statement are shown in Figure 5.1. This statement results in a lot of data being returned. In very large tables, this can be more information than you want to sort through.

Limiting the Number of Columns

To limit the number of columns returned, you need to list the names of the columns that you want to see. Listing 5.2 outlines a query that would return all the authors' first names, last names, and phone numbers from the authors table.

5

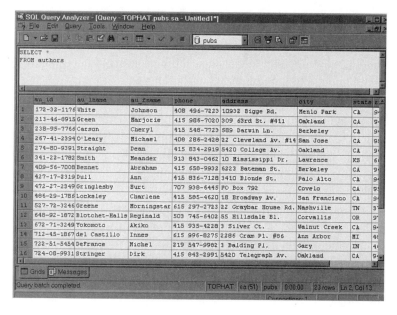

FIGURE 5.1

A simple SELECT statement can produce a lot of data.

LISTING 5.2   Limiting the Number of Columns Returned

```
SELECT au_fname, au_lname, phone
FROM authors
```

As you can see, we have replaced the asterisk (*) in the select list with a list of column names separated by commas. The rest of the SELECT statement is the same as before. The result set from this query is shown in Figure 5.2.

There is one issue that you must be able to handle when creating a SELECT statement. As I mentioned previously, in order to limit the number of columns returned to the user, you must list the names of the columns that you want to see. The problem comes when you are dealing with a database you are not familiar with. If you don't know the name of the columns, there are two ways in which you can easily get the names of the columns without returning all of the rows from the database. The first is to use the sp_help system stored procedure. The sp_help system stored procedure will return all the data about a particular table when you pass the table name into the stored procedure. You will not normally use the sp_help stored procedure in any of the stored procedures that you write. Rather, you will use it to research the underlying table structure before you write the query. An example of the use of the sp_help system stored procedure is shown in Listing 5.3.

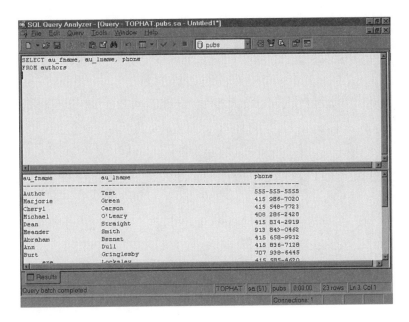

FIGURE 5.2
The result set from Listing 5.2 contains the three specific columns we asked for.

LISTING 5.3   The sp_help System Stored Procedure

```
sp_help authors
```

The results from the execution of this stored procedure are shown in Figure 5.3. Quite a bit of information about the table is included in these results, including information about the columns, indexes, constraints, and any other tables that reference the table.

If you don't want to sort through all that information, it is possible to get only the names of the columns by executing a query that selects all columns with a false WHERE clause, as shown in Listing 5.4.

LISTING 5.4   Getting the Table Structure Without the sp_help Stored Procedure

```
SELECT *
FROM authors
WHERE 1=0
```

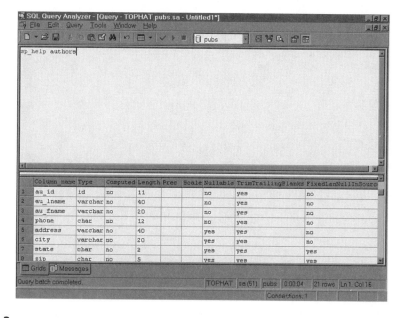

FIGURE 5.3

The sp_help *stored procedure provides a lot of information about a table.*

This query tells SQL Server to return all the columns and rows where one equals zero. Because one can never equal zero, SQL Server will return the column names from the table with no data, as seen in Figure 5.4.

As you have seen, it is relatively easy to limit the number of columns returned from a SELECT statement. It is also possible to limit the number of rows returned from a SELECT statement.

Limiting the Number of Rows

So far, we have discussed the information you need to create a SELECT statement that selects all or a subset of the columns in a table. Frequently, though, you will also want to limit the number of rows that you return. This provides even more control for finding specific records in the table in which you are interested. In order to do this, all you need to do is use the WHERE keyword.

Comparison Operators

Normally when you are selecting a subset of rows out of a table, you compare a value in a row to a known value. This is done through the use of comparison operators. A list of the comparison operators is in Table 5.1.

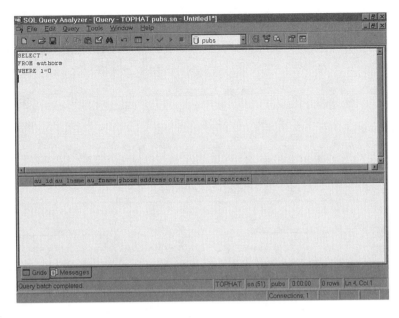

FIGURE 5.4

A false WHERE *clause in a* SELECT *statement produces the column names of a table.*

TABLE 5.1   SQL Server Comparison Operators

Operator	Definition
=	*Equal to*. This operator returns true for values that are exactly alike. For example, 1 = 1 is true.
<>	*Not equal to*. This operator returns true for values that are not exactly alike. For example, 1 <> 3 is true.
!=	*Not equal to*. This operator returns true for values that are not exactly alike. This operator is the same as the <> operator. For example, 1 != 3 is true.
>	*Greater than*. This operator returns true for values that are greater than the specified value. For example, 3 > 1 is true.
>=	*Greater than or equal to*. This operator returns true for values that are greater than or exactly the same as the specified value. For example, 3 >= 1 is true and 3 >= 3 is true as well.
!>	*Not greater than*. This operator returns true for values that are less than the specified value. For example, 1 !> 3 is true. This operator is not commonly used and is the same as the < operator.

continues

TABLE 5.1 Continued

Operator	Definition
<	*Less than.* This operator returns true for values that are less than the specified values. For example, 1 < 3 is true.
<=	*Less than or equal to.* This operator returns true for values that are less than or exactly the same as the specified value. For example, 1 <= 3 is true and 1 <= 1 is true as well.
!<	*Not less than.* This operator returns true for values that are greater than the specified value. For example, 3 !< 1 is true. This operator is not commonly used and is the same as the > operator.

As you can see, there are quite a few comparison operators that you can use. In the table, all the examples used numeric values. You can use all the numeric operators with string values as well. When using the greater than and less than symbols with string values, you might run into some interesting results. If you use the standard case-insensitive sort order with SQL Server, a < b and A < b. If you use a case-sensitive sort order, a < b but A > b. You must plan for this type of functionality when you design your application.

By effectively using comparison operators, you can limit the number of rows returned by SQL Server to the user. Let's look at a couple of these comparison operators in action. Listing 5.5 shows you how to implement the WHERE keyword in combination with the SELECT statement that we used earlier to return only those authors who live in California.

LISTING 5.5 An Example of Comparison Operators

```
SELECT au_lname, au_fname, phone
FROM authors
WHERE state = 'CA'
```

What I have done in this statement is to put a WHERE clause after the FROM clause of the SELECT statement. In the WHERE clause, I specify that I want only those rows in which the state column in the table is exactly like CA, or the abbreviation of California. You can see that I do not have to return the column referenced in the WHERE clause to the user, it just has to be in the table. The result set from this query is shown in Figure 5.5.

It is possible for you to specify more than one criteria in the WHERE clause through the use of Boolean operators that join the criteria together. You are essentially telling SQL Server to perform the SELECT based on multiple WHERE statements. Table 5.2 outlines the Boolean operators you can use to join together criteria in a WHERE clause.

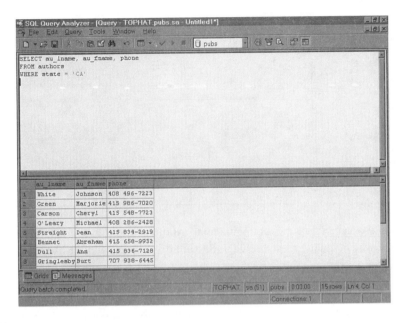

FIGURE 5.5

The result set from Listing 5.5 includes only authors from California.

TABLE 5.2   Boolean Operators

Operator	Description
AND	The AND Boolean operator is used to combine two criteria and evaluates as true only if both of the specified criteria are true. For example, 1 < 6 AND 5 = 5 would be evaluated as true because both of the criteria evaluate as true.
OR	The OR Boolean operator is used to combine two criteria and evaluates as true if either of the specified criteria is true. For example, 1 > 6 OR 5 = 5 would still evaluate as true, even though 1 > 6 is a false statement.
NOT	The NOT Boolean operator is used in conjunction with either of the other two operators listed here. It negates the value of the criteria that is listed in conjunction with it. For example, 5 = 5 AND NOT 1 > 6 would be evaluated as true because 1 is not greater than 6.

These operators can be used to string together as many comparison criteria as you want. Taking the previous query, assume you want to get a listing of all authors who live in California and have a contract status of 1, but who do not live in the city of Oakland. There are a couple of ways to do this. The queries shown in Listing 5.6 show two different ways to perform this query. How you write it is up to you.

5

CREATING AND
ALTERING STORED
PROCEDURES

LISTING 5.6   Using Logical Operators

```
SELECT au_lname, au_fname, phone
FROM authors
WHERE state = 'CA' AND
      contract = 1 AND
      city <> 'Oakland'

SELECT au_lname, au_fname, phone
FROM authors
WHERE state = 'CA' AND
      contract <> 0 AND NOT
      city = 'Oakland'
```

As you can see, you can do quite a bit with comparison operators, especially when you know the values for which you are querying. SQL Server also provides you the ability to query data that falls between a certain range of values.

Using Ranges

Ranges provide you the ability to use the BETWEEN keyword to search for a group of unknown values that fall between two known values. To perform these searches, you must know the value at which you want SQL Server to start including and the top value that you want included. The minimum and maximum values are separated by the word AND. Listing 5.7 uses the BETWEEN keyword to find any book names in the titles table where the price is between $15.00 and $20.00.

LISTING 5.7   Using Ranges

```
SELECT title
FROM titles
WHERE price BETWEEN 15.00 AND 20.00
```

The query in Listing 5.7 tells SQL Server to go into the table and find every book where the price is between $15.00 and $20.00, and to return the titles of those that do. Figure 5.6 shows the results of this query. We can also use the BETWEEN keyword in conjunction with the NOT keyword to return all rows that fall outside a certain range.

Another option is to look into the tables for information that falls in a certain list.

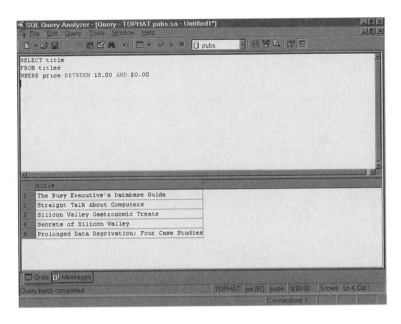

FIGURE 5.6
The titles in this result set are priced between $15 and $20.

Using Lists

SQL Server also enables you to search for values that fall within a specified list of values by using the IN keyword. To perform a search like this, you need to know the values that are required. For instance, refer to the phone list example. Let's say that the vice president now asks you to create a phone list of all authors who reside in both California and Oregon. You could do this using two comparison operators separated with the AND keyword, but using the IN keyword in this case will save you a little typing. When you start to get larger lists, the IN keyword can save you a great deal of typing. Listing 5.8 shows how the IN keyword works.

LISTING 5.8 Using the IN Keyword

```
SELECT au_lname, au_fname, phone
FROM authors
WHERE state IN ('CA', 'OR')
```

This query uses the IN keyword, followed by a list of values that we want to search for, separated by commas and enclosed by parentheses. The results from this query are shown in Figure 5.7. You can also use the NOT keyword in conjunction with the IN keyword to retrieve all rows that do not match the values in the list.

5

CREATING AND
ALTERING STORED
PROCEDURES

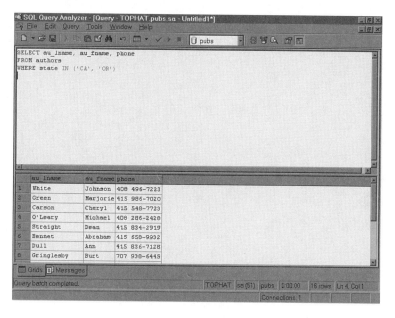

FIGURE 5.7

Using the IN *keyword can save you some typing.*

All the operations we have looked at so far for limiting the number of rows returned will work with any SQL Server data type. There is one last method we can use to limit the number of rows that works only with string type data.

Using the LIKE Keyword

The LIKE keyword is used in conjunction with string data. LIKE enables you to search string columns for a certain pattern. This option enables you to use wildcard searches to find the data you are looking for. When searching with the LIKE keyword, any specific characters you search for must match exactly, but wildcard characters can be anything. Table 5.3 lists the wildcard characters you can use in conjunction with the LIKE keyword.

TABLE 5.3   Wildcard Characters

Character	Description	Example
%	Matches any string of characters from 0 to any length	WHERE au_lname LIKE 'M%' retrieves out of the table rows where the author's last name starts with the character M.

Character	Description	Example
_	Matches any single character	`WHERE au_fname LIKE '_ean'` retrieves out of the table all rows where the author's first name begins with any letter followed by the three letters *ean*. For example, Dean, Sean, and Jean.
[ ]	Matches a specified range of characters or a set of characters	`WHERE phone LIKE '[0-9]19%'` retrieves all rows where the author's phone number starts with 019, 119, 219, and so on.
[^]	Matches any characters that fall outside a specified range or set of characters	`WHERE au_fname LIKE '[^ABER]%'` retrieves all rows where the author's first name does not start with the characters A, B, E, or R.

Now that you have reviewed the SELECT statement, there is another way to use SELECT in conjunction with cursors to return information to the user.

Using Cursors

Another way to return information to the user is to use cursors. A *cursor* is an object you can create in the database that is used to store multiple rows of data. This object can be looped through on a row-by-row basis, and operations can be performed against each row. In basic terms, cursors are similar to arrays in any other programming language.

Creating Cursors in SQL Server

There are five steps to working with cursors in SQL Server:

Cursor Step	Explanation
DECLARE the cursor	This process tells SQL Server that you are going to create a specific type of cursor. During the declaration, you specify a name for the cursor and SELECT statement, which will make up the rows through which the cursor loops.
OPEN the cursor	During the open, the object is actually created and filled.

continues

Cursor Step	Explanation
Perform FETCH statements	A fetch actually returns rows from the cursor so that they can be used by the application.
CLOSE the cursor	Clears out the cursor.
DEALLOCATE the cursor	Removes all references to the cursor from memory.

Using the DECLARE Statement

The most complicated part of creating the cursor is the DECLARE statement. This is because all the declaration about the exact data that you want to return is defined in this section through a SELECT statement. The syntax for this is as follows:

```
DECLARE cursor_name CURSOR
[LOCAL | GLOBAL]
[FORWARD_ONLY | SCROLL]
[STATIC | KEYSET | DYNAMIC | FAST_FORWARD]
[READ_ONLY | SCROLL_LOCKS | OPTIMISTIC]
[TYPE_WARNING]
FOR select_statement
[FOR UPDATE [OF column_name [,...n]]]
```

The following are the options for the DECLARE statement:

Option	Description
DECLARE	The DECLARE keyword tells SQL Server that you are going to create an object. In this case, you will create a cursor.
cursor_name	This is a placeholder indicating the name that will be used to reference the cursor that you create.
CURSOR	This keyword tells SQL Server that you are going to create a CURSOR object.
LOCAL	The LOCAL keyword defines the scope of the cursor. LOCAL means that only the calling batch, stored procedure, or trigger can utilize the cursor. The cursor is implicitly deallocated when the batch, stored procedure, or trigger completes processing.
GLOBAL	The GLOBAL keyword is also used to define the scope of the cursor. When a cursor is declared as GLOBAL, the cursor has a life of the connection. When the user who created the cursor logs off, the cursor is implicitly deallocated.
FORWARD_ONLY	FORWARD_ONLY declares a cursor that can only be scrolled from the first row to the last row. With a FORWARD_ONLY cursor, FETCH NEXT is the only way you can get data from the cursor.

SCROLL	The SCROLL keyword indicates that you can move in any direction through the data in the cursor.
STATIC	The STATIC keyword is used to indicate that SQL Server should make a copy of the data and place it into tempdb. If data in the base table is modified, the changes will not be reflected in the cursor.
KEYSET	A KEYSET cursor is one in which the order of the rows within the cursor is fixed when the cursor is first opened. A set of identifying keys is copied into a table in tempdb called keyset. Any changes made to the nonidentifying keys are displayed when the cursor is scrolled through. Inserts to the table are not shown in the cursor. If a row in the cursor is deleted, SQL Server returns an @@FETCH_STATUS of -2 when the user attempts to fetch that row.
DYNAMIC	A DYNAMIC cursor is one in which any changes made to the base data are available during the fetch. The data, number of rows, and order of the rows can change from fetch to fetch.
FAST_FORWARD	The FAST_FORWARD option specifies a FORWARD_ONLY, READ_ONLY cursor with certain performance enhancements turned on. If FAST_FORWARD is specified, you cannot also specify SCROLL, FOR_UPDATE, or FORWARD_ONLY.
READ_ONLY	The READ_ONLY option is used to specify a cursor through which no data can be changed. The type of cursor cannot be referenced in a WHERE CURRENT OF statement.
SCROLL_LOCKS	The SCROLL_LOCKS option causes SQL Server to lock each row as it is read into the cursor. This is done to ensure that locks and updates made through the cursor will succeed.
OPTIMISTIC	The OPTIMISTIC keyword specifies that SQL Server will not lock each row as it reads it. In this scenario, if a row that is being updated or deleted has changed since the cursor was opened, the modification will fail.
TYPE_WARNING	The TYPE_WARNING option is used to instruct SQL Server to return an error to the client if the specified cursor type is implicitly changed from one type to another.
FOR	This keyword is used to tell SQL Server that you are about to begin the SELECT statement that will make up the cursor.
select_statement	This is a placeholder indicating where the SELECT statement begins.
FOR UPDATE	This optional keyword defines a cursor as updatable. This allows you to update columns that are a part of the cursor. If you don't specify any columns with OF column_name, all columns in the cursor can be updated.

5

CREATING AND
ALTERING STORED
PROCEDURES

| OF `column_name` | This option lists the columns that can be updated in the cursor. If you list columns in this section, only those columns can be updated. |
| `,...n` | The *n* is used as a placeholder to show that you can specify multiple columns. |

After the cursor has been declared, the next step is to OPEN it. The syntax for opening the cursor is extremely simple. The following outlines the OPEN syntax:

```
OPEN cursor_name
```

`cursor_name` is the name of the cursor you previously declared. After the cursor has been declared and opened, you must use the FETCH statement to loop through the cursor to return rows. The FETCH statement has several options that enable you to move through the cursor. The following is the syntax for the FETCH statement:

```
FETCH
[[NEXT | PRIOR | FIRST | LAST | ABSOLUTE {n | @n} | RELATIVE {n | @n}] FROM]
cursor_name
[INTO @variable1,...n]
```

The following are the options for the FETCH statement:

Directive	Description
NEXT	Retrieves the next row in the cursor. This option is good for any type of cursor.
PRIOR	Retrieves the previous row in the cursor. This option is only good for KEYSET, STATIC, and SCROLL cursors.
FIRST	Retrieves the first row in the cursor. This option is only good for KEYSET, STATIC, and SCROLL cursors.
LAST	Retrieves the last row in the cursor. This option is only good for KEYSET, STATIC, and SCROLL cursors.
ABSOLUTE	Using a literal int, smallint, tinyint, or a variable of one of these data types, retrieves the *n*th physical row in the cursor. For negative values of *n* or @*n*, the cursor counts backward from the last row of the cursor. This option is only good for KEYSET, STATIC, and SCROLL cursors.
RELATIVE	Using a literal int, smallint, tinyint, or a variable of one of these data types, retrieves the *n*th relative row from the current row position of the cursor. For negative values of *n* or @*n*, the cursor counts backward from the current row of the cursor. This option is only good for KEYSET, STATIC, and SCROLL cursors.
FROM	This keyword tells SQL Server the cursor from which you are going to retrieve data.

cursor_name	This is the name of the cursor from which you are going to retrieve data.
INTO	This optional keyword tells SQL Server that you are going to return into the listed variables. If you are returning data into variables, you must provide one variable for each column contained in the cursor.
@variable1, ...n	This is a placeholder showing you where the variable will be listed.

While you are fetching data from the cursor, you must monitor the @@FETCH_STATUS system variable. This variable will contain information about the last fetch that was made from the current connection. If the @@FETCH_STATUS variable is -1, you have reached the end of the cursor and it is time to exit the loop. After you have fetched the data you need out of the cursor, the last two steps are to CLOSE and DEALLOCATE the cursor. This clears the cursor of any rows contained in it and then removes any references to the cursor from memory. The code in Listing 5.9 outlines the full cycle of cursor creation.

LISTING 5.9   Simple Cursor Creation

```
DECLARE @vchAuthorLName     VARCHAR(32)
DECLARE @vchAuthorFName     VARCHAR(32)
DECLARE @vchPhone           VARCHAR(11)
DECLARE @vchSQLStatement    VARCHAR(64)

DECLARE curAuthorInformation CURSOR FOR
    SELECT  au_fname, au_lname, phone
    FROM    authors

OPEN curAuthorInformation
FETCH NEXT FROM curAuthorInformation INTO @vchAuthorLName,
        @vchAuthorFName, @vchPhone

WHILE (@@FETCH_STATUS <> -1)
BEGIN
    SELECT @vchSQLStatement = @vchAuthorLName + ', ' + @vchAuthorFName +
            ':    ' + @vchPhone
    PRINT @vchSQLStatement
    FETCH NEXT FROM curAuthorInformation INTO @vchAuthorLName,
                @vchAuthorFName, @vchPhone
END

CLOSE curAuthorInformation
DEALLOCATE curAuthorInformation
```

5

CREATING AND ALTERING STORED PROCEDURES

In this code, you first declare the variable that will be used during the execution of the stored procedure. After the variables have been declared, the cursor itself is declared. When the cursor is created, it is opened and the first row is retrieved from the cursor. After the first row is retrieved, the @@FETCH_STATUS variable is checked in a WHILE loop. The WHILE loop checks the @@FETCH_STATUS variable after each execution. When this variable becomes -1, the loop exits and the cursor is closed and deallocated.

Now that you have seen how to use the SELECT statement and cursors to return data to the user, you can create procedures using them.

CREATE PROCEDURE

After you have planned, written, and debugged the code that will be executed inside the stored procedure, you can create the procedure. The CREATE PROCEDURE statement is required to create a stored procedure, as outlined in the following syntax:

```
CREATE PROCEDURE <procedure_name>
{<@parameter> <data type>} [VARYING] [= default] [OUTPUT]][,...n]
[WITH {RECOMPILE | ENCRYPTION | RECOMPILE, ENCRYPTION}]
AS
<sql_statements>
```

Table 5.4 lists the options for the CREATE PROCEDURE statement.

TABLE 5.4   Stored Procedure Options

Option	Description
<procedure_name>	This is the name of the stored procedure you are creating.
<@parameter>	If you want to pass parameters into a stored procedure, you must define them in the declaration of the stored procedure. This declaration includes the name of the parameter, the data type of the parameter, and a few other special options depending on their use.
<data type>	If you specify a parameter, you must specify the data type of that parameter. This can be any valid data type, including text and image.
[VARYING]	This option is specified when you are returning a cursor as a parameter.
[= default]	This option is used to specify a default value for a particular parameter. If the procedure is executed without specifying a value for the parameter,

Option	Description
	this value is used instead. This can be a NULL or any other valid value for that data type. For string data, this can include wildcards if the parameter is used in conjunction with the LIKE parameter.
[OUTPUT]	This optional keyword specifies that the parameter is a return parameter. The value of this parameter can then be returned to the executing procedure when execution has completed. Text and image data types cannot be used as OUTPUT parameters.
[,...n]	This symbol indicates that you can specify multiple parameters with a stored procedure. SQL Server allows up to 1,024 parameters for use in a single stored procedure.
WITH RECOMPILE	This option forces SQL Server to recompile the stored procedure every time it is executed. You should use this when you are using temporary values and objects.
WITH ENCRYPTION	This option forces SQL Server to encrypt the text of the stored procedure that is stored in the syscomments table. This enables you to create and redistribute a database without worrying about users figuring out the source code of your stored procedures.
WITH RECOMPILE, ENCRYPTION	This option forces SQL Server to recompile and encrypt the stored procedure.
AS	This indicates that the definition of the stored procedure is about to begin.
<sql_statements>	This is a placeholder for the different statements that will make up the stored procedure.

Admittedly, this looks like a lot of choices. You can use a number of options, but most of them (particularly the RECOMPILE and the ENCRYPTION options) are only used in certain circumstances. I will go over these options later in the chapter. First, you must see how a basic stored procedure is created. As I mentioned earlier, the first and most important part of creating a stored procedure is the planning phase. You must first create the script that will be executed in the stored procedure. For this example, the first stored procedure is pretty simple. The stored procedure shown in Listing 5.10 selects all the rows and all the columns from the authors table in the pubs database.

5

LISTING 5.10   A Simple Stored Procedure

```
CREATE PROCEDURE proc_c5_1
AS
SELECT * FROM authors
```

The stored procedure in Listing 5.10 is an extremely simple one and produces extremely simple results when executed. The results of this stored procedure are shown in Figure 5.8. These results are the same as if you executed the SELECT statement contained inside the procedure.

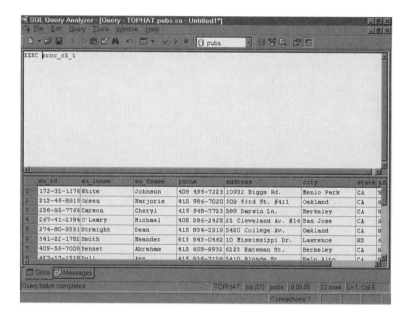

FIGURE 5.8

The results from the execution of the stored procedure created in Listing 5.10 are very simple.

Notice that the stored procedure was executed in the figure using the EXEC command. A stored procedure does not always have to be executed in this manner. If a stored procedure is the first thing executed in a batch, the EXEC statement is not required. However, if the stored procedure is executed later in a batch or multiple stored procedures are executed in a batch, you must use the EXEC command. The syntax of the EXEC command is as follows:

```
EXEC[UTE]
[@return_status =] <procedure_name>
[[@parameter =] value [OUTPUT] | [DEFAULT]] [,...n]
[WITH RECOMPILE]
```

The parameters for this syntax are shown in Table 5.5.

TABLE 5.5   EXECUTE Statement Options

Option	Description
@return_status	This is an optional variable you can use to track the execution status of the stored procedure. This variable must be declared before it is used.
<procedure_name>	This is the name of the stored procedure you are executing.
[@parameter =]	If the stored procedure you are executing accepts parameters, this structure can be used to specify the parameter into which you are passing a value.
value	This is the value that you are passing into the stored procedure.
[DEFAULT]	This option specifies that you want to use the default value for a particular parameter.
[OUTPUT]	This optional keyword specifies that the parameter is a return parameter. The value of this parameter can then be returned from the executing procedure when execution has completed.
[,...n]	This symbol indicates that you can specify multiple parameters with a stored procedure. SQL Server allows up to 1,024 parameters for use in a single stored procedure.
[WITH RECOMPILE]	This option forces SQL Server to recompile the stored procedure every time it is executed. You should use this when you are using temporary values and objects.

The EXECUTE command is not limited to executing a single stored procedure. When you are running multiple stored procedures in the same batch, you must use the EXECUTE command. Look at the code in Listing 5.11. The code in this listing shows you the types of problems that can arise when you run two stored procedures in the same batch without using the EXECUTE statement. The second portion of this listing is the same two stored procedures that are run with the EXECUTE statement.

LISTING 5.11   Multiple Stored Procedures in the Same Batch

```
sp_who active
sp_who 1
GO

EXECUTE sp_who active
EXECUTE sp_who 1
GO
```

5

CREATING AND
ALTERING STORED
PROCEDURES

In this example, the code in the first batch fails to run and returns an error. The code in the second batch runs correctly. Another use of the EXECUTE command is to create strings at runtime that can be executed. This is useful when you are running several commands based on values in a table. The following code snippet is a portion of a stored procedure that updates the statistics on all the indexes on all the user tables in the database. The full code for this stored procedure can be found in Chapter 11, "Writing Utility Stored Procedures."

```
DECLARE tnames_cursor CURSOR FOR SELECT name FROM sysobjects
    WHERE type = 'U'
OPEN tnames_cursor
FETCH NEXT FROM tnames_cursor INTO @table_name
WHILE (@@fetch_status <> -1)
BEGIN
    EXEC ("UPDATE STATISTICS " + @table_name )
    FETCH NEXT FROM tnames_cursor INTO @table_name
END
```

This stored procedure loops through a list of all the user tables in the database and executes the UPDATE STATISTICS command on each table. Now that you have seen how to create and execute simple stored procedures, you should be aware of how stored procedures are changed.

The Changing of the Code—Altering Stored Procedures

Anyone who has ever programmed can tell you that there are times when the original code you rolled out to your users does not provide the correct functionality. Sometimes this is because of a minor problem with the code; other times, it is because the code is completely wrong. It used to be very difficult and somewhat complicated to modify stored procedures. SQL Server 2000 provides an easy way to modify stored procedures without losing any important information.

The Old Way

If you worked with any of the 6.x versions of SQL Server, you know that modifying stored procedures could be very difficult. This is because none of those versions provided a real way to perform this functionality. Instead, the only way to modify stored procedures was to drop the stored procedure and run a script to re-create the procedure. Although this works, several flaws are inherent in this approach.

Usually the first problem you will notice deals with the permissions assigned to the original stored procedure. Although the actual drop and re-creation of the stored procedure takes very little time, often milliseconds, your users will begin to complain that they cannot execute the procedure. That is because when the original stored procedure is dropped, all permissions associated with that procedure are dropped as well. If you do not remember to reassign the permissions to the procedures, your users will not be able to execute the stored procedure.

A second problem you will notice when you modify a stored procedure the old way is not as problematic for your users. Instead, you as the developer will notice the problem. As with the permissions associated with a stored procedure, the dependencies associated with that stored procedure are also dropped. A *dependency* is an object in the database that relies on another object in the database. For example, a stored procedure that returns data out of a particular table is known to depend on that table. When you create a stored procedure, the object IDs of any objects referenced in that stored procedure are stored in the sysdepends table in the database in which the procedure is created. The inverse of this is true as well: If you create a stored procedure or trigger that references the original procedure, that information is also stored in the sysdepends table. Later on, this information is very useful when determining what objects in the database can be dropped without affecting anything else.

The problem comes if you drop and re-create a stored procedure that is referenced by any other stored procedure. All dependency information regarding that procedure is deleted from the sysdepends table. Even though the original object is still in the database and the old stored procedure was re-created, there is no record in the database regarding the dependency. The only way to get that dependency information back is to drop and re-create all the dependent objects, which is a big hassle. It is such a big hassle that most developers do not bother to re-create the dependency information and learn not to rely on it.

Viewing Dependency Information

There are two ways that you can view dependency information available to you. One is to use the sp_depends system stored procedure. The other way to view this information is using SQL Enterprise Manager. The syntax of the sp_depends stored procedure is as follows:

```
sp_depends <object_name>
```

<object_name> is the name of the object on which you are trying to get information. The results of this stored procedure will give you all the objects that depend on and are dependent upon the object specified.

The other way to view the dependency information is to use SQL Enterprise Manager. To do this, open the stored procedures folder, right-click the stored procedure for which you want to view the dependencies, and select All Tasks -> View Dependencies. This opens the Dependencies dialog box shown in Figure 5.9.

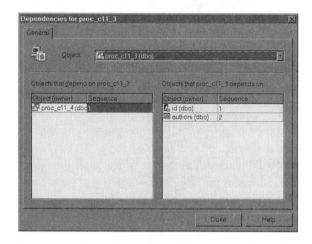

FIGURE 5.9
The Dependencies dialog box shows you which objects depend on and which objects are dependent upon the selected stored procedure.

The Old Problems

Just so that you know what we used to be up against, type in the script in Listing 5.12. Run it in two sections as outlined in the code.

LISTING 5.12 The Old Problems

```
/** First Section **/
CREATE PROCEDURE proc_c11_1
AS
    SELECT au_lname, au_fname, phone
    FROM    authors
GO
CREATE PROCEDURE proc_c11_2
AS
    EXEC proc_c11_1
GO
GRANT EXECUTE ON proc_c11_1 TO public
GO
sp_helprotect proc_c11_1
GO
```

```
sp_depends proc_c11_2
GO
/** Stop Here **/

/** Second Section **/
DROP PROCEDURE proc_c11_1
GO
CREATE PROCEDURE proc_c11_1
AS
    SELECT au_lname, au_fname, phone, state
    FROM  authors
GO
sp_helprotect proc_c11_1
GO
sp_depends proc_c11_2
GO
```

As you can see from the results in the first section, all the permissions and dependencies show up correctly. In the second section, after the proc_c11_1 procedure was dropped and re-created, all the permissions and dependency information are gone. This could be problematic to say the least, and has been the cause of many DBAs being called at odd hours of the night. That was the situation until SQL Server 7.0 was released with the ALTER PROCEDURE command.

The New Way—ALTER PROCEDURE

With the release of SQL Server 7.0, Microsoft provided developers and DBAs with a new and very useful way to modify stored procedures. Instead of first dropping and then re-creating the stored procedure, all you have to do is use the ALTER PROCEDURE command. This command alleviates all the issues discussed earlier.

The ALTER PROCEDURE command actually modifies a stored procedure that was previously created using the CREATE PROCEDURE command without losing the permissions or information about objects that are dependent on the procedure. Any other procedures on which the procedure being re-created depends will also be re-created. The syntax of the ALTER PROCEDURE command is as follows:

```
ALTER PROCEDURE <procedure_name>
{<@parameter> <data type>} [VARYING] [= default] [OUTPUT]][,...n]
[WITH {RECOMPILE | ENCRYPTION | RECOMPILE, ENCRYPTION}]
AS
<sql_statements>
```

5

CREATING AND
ALTERING STORED
PROCEDURES

The following are the options for the ALTER PROCEDURE command:

Option	Description
<procedure_name>	The name of the stored procedure that you are going to alter.
<@parameter>	If you want to pass parameters into a stored procedure, you must define them in the declaration of the stored procedure. This declaration includes the name of the parameter, the data type of the parameter, and a few other special options depending on their use.
<data type>	If you specify a parameter, you must specify the data type of that parameter. This can be any valid data type, including text and image.
[VARYING]	This option is specified when you are returning a cursor as a parameter.
[= default]	This option specifies a default value for a particular parameter. If the procedure is executed without specifying a value for the parameter, this value is used instead. This can be a NULL or any other valid value for that data type. For string data, this value can include wildcards if the parameter is used in conjunction with the LIKE parameter.
[OUTPUT]	This optional keyword specifies that the parameter is a return parameter. The value of this parameter can then be returned to the executing procedure when execution has completed. Text or image data types cannot be used as OUTPUT parameters.
[,...n]	This symbol indicates that you can specify multiple parameters with a stored procedure. SQL Server allows up to 1,024 parameters for use in a single stored procedure.
WITH RECOMPILE	This option forces SQL Server to recompile the stored procedure every time it is executed. You should use this when you are using temporary values and objects.
WITH ENCRYPTION	This option forces SQL Server to encrypt the text of the stored procedure that is stored in the syscomments table. This enables you to create and redistribute a database without worrying about users figuring out the source code of your stored procedures.
WITH RECOMPILE, ENCRYPTION	This option forces SQL Server to recompile and encrypt the stored procedure.

AS	This indicates that the definition of the stored procedure is about to begin.
<sql_statements>	This is a placeholder for the different statements that will make up the stored procedure.

Type in the code in Listing 5.13 to see exactly how the ALTER PROCEDURE command works. Run it in two sections, as you did in Listing 5.12.

LISTING 5.13   ALTER PROCEDURE in Action

```
/** First Section **/
CREATE PROCEDURE proc_c11_3
AS
   SELECT au_lname, au_fname, phone
   FROM   authors
GO
CREATE PROCEDURE proc_c11_4
AS
   EXEC proc_c11_3
GO
GRANT EXECUTE ON proc_c11_3 TO public
GO
sp_helprotect proc_c11_3
GO
sp_depends proc_c11_4
GO
/** Stop Here **/

/** Second Section **/
ALTER PROCEDURE proc_c11_3
AS
   SELECT au_lname, au_fname, phone, state
   FROM   authors
GO
sp_helprotect proc_c11_3
GO
sp_depends proc_c11_4
GO
```

Notice that unlike the results in Listing 5.12, after proc_c11_3 is rebuilt using the ALTER PROCEDURE command, SQL Server has still maintained the permissions and dependency information.

Alteration Considerations

When you alter stored procedures, there a couple of things you must take into consideration. These considerations are extremely important and if they are not taken into account, your application might stop functioning completely.

The major issue that you must consider is the question of parameters that are present in previous versions of the stored procedure. If dependent stored procedures or triggers expect to be able to pass data into the altered stored procedure, and you have modified the data types or the number or order of the parameters in the stored procedure, the dependent stored procedures or triggers will fail.

Another important issue is that you must ensure that any output parameters are handled within the dependent stored procedures. If you modify how these parameters are passed or received, you might get unexpected results during the execution.

An example of this type of unexpected result can be seen by executing the query in Listing 5.14. Make sure to run the first section up until the /** Stop Here **/ comment before running the second section.

LISTING 5.14   Problems with ALTER PROCEDURE

```
/** First Section **/
CREATE PROCEDURE proc_c11_5
    @intTestValue     INT
AS
    PRINT @intTestValue + @intTestValue
GO


CREATE PROCEDURE proc_c11_6
AS
    EXEC proc_c11_5 5
GO


EXEC proc_c11_6
GO
/** Stop Here **/

/** Second Section **/
ALTER PROCEDURE proc_c11_5
    @chrTestValue     CHAR(1)
AS
    PRINT @chrTestValue + @chrTestValue
GO

EXEC proc_c11_6
GO
```

In the first section, a procedure is created that accepts numeric values and adds them together. The second procedure is a wrapper of the first procedure. When it executes, it returns a value of 10. In the second section, the first stored procedure is modified to accept a character value instead of a numeric value. When this procedure is executed after the change has been made, it returns a value of 55. Although both these results are technically correct, they are completely different. If your applications are expecting one result and getting another one, this can cause some very difficult-to-trace problems.

Conclusion

In this chapter, you have seen the basics of creating stored procedures. It is imperative that you realize how important it is to plan out exactly how the stored procedure will work before you actually create the procedure. This will keep you from having to re-create the procedure over and over again. First, you saw an overview of the SELECT statement. Then you saw how you can use cursors to return data to the users. Then came the important stuff: the actual creation of some procedures. These procedures were relatively simple, but don't worry, there are some more complicated ones in the future. The last thing you saw in this chapter was a discussion of how to modify stored procedures that are already created.

Creating More Complex Stored Procedures

IN THIS CHAPTER

Now that you have seen how to create some simple stored procedures using the SELECT statement, there are things that you should know to assist you in creating more powerful stored procedures. These include returning information and error messages that are useful to the user.

In this chapter, I will cover the following points:

- Creating more complex stored procedures
- Passing values as parameters into stored procedures
- Exiting stored procedures using the RETURN keyword
- Returning data using OUTPUT variables
- Using RAISERROR to return errors to the user

Complex Stored Procedure Creation

In Chapter 5, "Creating and Altering Stored Procedures," I discussed the creation of simple stored procedures that return very simple data by using the SELECT statement. These procedures were pretty simple, but the framework is now there to create more complex stored procedures that can accept parameters, pass values into variables, and contain error-trapping routines that return errors to the user. These stored procedures can be extremely complicated and they enable developers to create powerful applications that reside in the database layer.

Passing Parameters into Stored Procedures

With any development language, it is always important to be able to pass data into functions so that it can be processed or acted upon in some way. SQL Server is no different. As I discussed in Chapter 1, "SQL Server and Stored Procedure Background," stored procedures can be considered application functions and you will need to pass data into them as well. First, take a look at the stored procedure created in Listing 6.1.

LISTING 6.1 Stored Procedure Without Parameters

```
CREATE PROCEDURE usp_c6_1
AS
SELECT au_lname + ', ' + au_fname, phone
FROM authors
GO
EXEC usp_c6_1
```

This stored procedure returns all the names and phone numbers of all entries in the authors table. Although there are some uses for this stored procedure, it is likely more useful to be able to look up a single author's phone number. You could perform this retrieval in a couple ways.

One method is to create separate stored procedures for each author's name, as shown in Listing 6.2.

LISTING 6.2   One Way to Perform Lookups

```
CREATE PROCEDURE usp_6_2_bennet
AS
SELECT au_lname + ', ' + au_fname, phone
FROM authors
WHERE au_lname = 'Bennet'
GO


CREATE PROCEDURE usp_6_2_blotchethalls
AS
SELECT au_lname + ', ' + au_fname, phone
FROM authors
WHERE au_lname = 'Blotchet-Halls'
GO


CREATE PROCEDURE usp_6_2_yokomoto
AS
SELECT au_lname + ', ' + au_fname, phone
FROM authors
WHERE au_lname = 'Yokomoto'
GO
```

Although this approach would work, there are several problems with it. First of all, it is extremely inefficient to have to create a new stored procedure every time a new author is hired. This requires a developer or some other power user who has knowledge of SQL Server to create the procedure. This approach will also clutter the database with many extra procedures. Another issue with this approach is that it does not take into account multiple authors with the same last name. In this case, if multiple authors with the same last name are contained in the database, the code will return all those authors to the user. The last problem with this approach is that you always have to know the exact spelling of the author's name. If you don't know the exact spelling, you will not be able to access that author's information.

A better approach is to pass the author's name into a stored procedure. This enables you to create one stored procedure that returns the information you require. The code to create this type of stored procedure is shown in Listing 6.3.

LISTING 6.3   Using Parameters

```
CREATE PROCEDURE usp_6_3
@vchAuthorLName         VARCHAR(40)
AS
SELECT au_lname + ', ' + au_fname, phone
FROM authors
WHERE au_lname = @vchAuthorLName
GO
EXEC usp_6_3 'Bennet'
EXEC usp_6_3 'Blotchet-Halls'
EXEC usp_6_3 'Yokomoto'
```

From the source code of this stored procedure, you can see that all you have to do to create a stored procedure that accepts a parameter is declare the stored procedure after the CREATE statement and before the code for the stored procedure. The syntax for the declaration is as follows:

```
<@parameter> <data type> [,...n]
```

Option	Description
`<@parameter>`	If you want to pass parameters into a stored procedure, you must define them in the declaration of the stored procedure. This declaration includes the name of the parameter, the data type of the parameter, and a few other special options depending on their use.
`<data type>`	If you specify a parameter, you must specify the data type of that parameter. This can be any valid data type, including text and image.
`[,...n]`	This symbol indicates that you can specify multiple parameters with a stored procedure. SQL Server allows up to 1,024 parameters for use in a single stored procedure.

The results of the execution of this stored procedure show that it returns the same information as the stored procedures you created and executed earlier, while keeping you from cluttering your database with many redundant procedures.

There are a couple of issues with this stored procedure. First, if you do not pass in the parameter that the stored procedure is expecting, as shown in Listing 6.4, the stored procedure will fail. This is because the stored procedure requires that the user pass something in. It does not matter if the parameter that is passed in does not exist in the database, something must be there.

LISTING 6.4   Problems with Parameters

```
EXEC usp_6_3
--- Results start here ---
Server: Msg 201, Level 16, State 1, Procedure usp_6_3, Line 0
Procedure 'usp_6_3' expects parameter '@vchAuthorLName', which was not
supplied.
```

To solve this problem, you can add a default to the parameter. If the user does not pass any value into the stored procedure, SQL Server uses the default instead. This default value is usually very generic; it allows the stored procedure to run, but not much more than that. In this case, you could either use an author's last name, the value NULL, or a wildcard character. Which of these options you use depends on the needs of your application. If your application always expects your stored procedure to return a value, you would probably use an author's last name. If your application can handle the stored procedure not returning any value, you could use the value NULL as the default. Lastly, if your application can handle many results being returned from the stored procedure, you could use the wildcard character. Note that when you use the wildcard character, you also must use the LIKE keyword instead of the equal sign (=). Each of these options is shown in Listing 6.5.

LISTING 6.5   Using Default Parameters

```
CREATE PROCEDURE usp_6_5_1
@vchAuthorLName        VARCHAR(40) = 'Bennet'
AS
SELECT au_lname + ', ' + au_fname, phone
FROM authors
WHERE au_lname = @vchAuthorLName
GO
EXEC usp_6_5_1
GO


CREATE PROCEDURE usp_6_5_2
@vchAuthorLName        VARCHAR(40) = NULL
AS
SELECT au_lname + ', ' + au_fname, phone
FROM authors
WHERE au_lname = @vchAuthorLName
GO
EXEC usp_6_5_2
GO


CREATE PROCEDURE usp_6_5_3
@vchAuthorLName        VARCHAR(40) = '%'
AS
```

continues

LISTING 6.5 Continued

```
SELECT au_lname + ', ' + au_fname, phone
FROM authors
WHERE au_lname LIKE @vchAuthorLName
GO
EXEC usp_6_5_3
GO
```

When you type in and execute this code, you can see the major differences in the results. You must take into account how the application will process the results when choosing which method to use.

Returning Information to the User

So far, you have primarily seen how to return results from SELECT statements to the user. With more complex stored procedures, you will find that you need to return error codes and text, contents of variables, and internal errors and exit codes that your procedure has generated during its execution. There are several different ways to return this information, with the simplest way being to return a numeric value you can use in your application.

The RETURN Statement

The RETURN statement is used to stop unconditionally the execution of a stored procedure. No commands that follow the RETURN statement are processed after the RETURN statement is executed. When you use the RETURN statement in a stored procedure, you have the option of specifying an integer value that is returned to the application, batch, or stored procedure that executed the stored procedure. If you do not specify a value for the RETURN statement, SQL Server automatically returns a value of 0. Almost all Microsoft's system stored procedures follow the convention of returning a value after the execution of the stored procedure. You must decide whether this or one of the other approaches works best for your applications. One note: When using the RETURN statement, returning a value of 0 indicates that the stored procedure completed execution correctly and without encountering any problems. Returning a value other than 0 indicates that a problem occurred in the processing.

Take the code in Listing 6.6 as an example. This code creates a stored procedure that searches the titles table in the pubs database for a particular title pattern. In other words, it looks for all titles that match the word or phrase that the user supplies. In this procedure, we are going to take for granted that the calling application cannot handle more than a single row of results. You must be very specific about which book you are looking for, or the application will fail.

LISTING 6.6   Using the RETURN Statement

```
CREATE PROCEDURE usp_6_6
@vchTitlePattern     VARCHAR(80) = '%'
AS

SELECT @vchTitlePattern = '%' + @vchTitlePattern + '%'

IF (SELECT COUNT(*) FROM titles WHERE title LIKE @vchTitlePattern) < 1
BEGIN
    RETURN 1
END

IF (SELECT COUNT(*) FROM titles WHERE title LIKE @vchTitlePattern) > 1
BEGIN
    RETURN 2
END

SELECT     title, price
FROM       titles
WHERE      title LIKE @vchTitlePattern

RETURN 0
GO

DECLARE @intReturnValue     INT

EXEC @intReturnValue = usp_6_6 'the'

IF (@intReturnValue = 1)
BEGIN
    PRINT 'There are no corresponding titles.'
END

IF (@intReturnValue = 2)
BEGIN
    PRINT 'There are multiple titles that match this criteria.
    ➥Please narrow your search.'
END

GO

DECLARE @intReturnValue     INT

EXEC @intReturnValue = usp_6_6 'blah'
```

continues

LISTING 6.6 Continued

```
IF (@intReturnValue = 1)
BEGIN
    PRINT 'There are no corresponding titles.'
END

IF (@intReturnValue = 2)
BEGIN
    PRINT 'There are multiple titles that match this criteria.
    ➥Please narrow your search.'
END
GO

DECLARE @intReturnValue    INT

EXEC @intReturnValue = usp_6_6 'Database'

IF (@intReturnValue = 1)
BEGIN
    PRINT 'There are no corresponding titles.'
END

IF (@intReturnValue = 2)
BEGIN
    PRINT 'There are multiple titles that match this criteria.
    ➥Please narrow your search.'
END
```

Note that when calling a stored procedure that returns a value from within a SQL script, you must call the procedure in a specific way in order to trap the return value. This is done by declaring a variable and setting the variable equal to the stored procedure when it is executed, as shown in the following code snippet:

```
DECLARE @intReturnValue    INT
EXEC @intReturnValue = <stored procedure name>
```

Another option you have for returning information to the user is to use the PRINT command.

The PRINT Command

The PRINT function enables you to display custom messages to the user. These messages can have up to 8,000 characters and include variables. The variables can be local or global, but if they are not CHAR or VARCHAR data types, they must be changed by using either the CONVERT or CASR function.

Listing 6.7 shows the creation of a stored procedure that uses the PRINT function to return a message to the user. Notice that the CONVERT function is used to change the integer data type to character data types.

LISTING 6.7   Using the PRINT Statement to Return Data

```
CREATE PROCEDURE usp_6_7
@intMinQty          INT
AS
DECLARE     @intNumOrders      INT
DECLARE     @chrOutputText     CHAR(60)

SELECT      @intNumOrders = COUNT(*) FROM sales WHERE qty > @intMinQty

SELECT      @chrOutputText = 'There are ' + CONVERT(VARCHAR, @intNumOrders) +
    ' orders that contain more than ' + CONVERT(VARCHAR, @intMinQty) +
    ' units.'

PRINT @chrOutputText
GO

EXEC usp_6_7 15
GO

EXEC usp_6_7 12
GO

EXEC usp_6_7 8
GO
```

For two reasons, when returning information from stored procedures, you should use a PRINT statement rather than a SELECT statement. First, SELECT statements should be reserved for data processing or output. Second, the SELECT statement uses a different type of formatting, with a line over the returned data, which makes it difficult to read a large list of returned data. The PRINT statement is useful for communicating the status or outcome of a procedure to the user, but it should not be used to send critical messages. A better solution for returning error messages is the RAISERROR function.

The RAISERROR Function

The RAISERROR function offers many more options when returning errors to the user than the PRINT function does. The RAISERROR function returns a string outlining the information that must be returned to the user and then sets a flag on SQL Server that tells the client that an error has occurred. This error can then be trapped and dealt with by the client as a server error.

With RAISERROR, the text of the error message can be either retrieved from the sysmessages table in the master database or it can be generated dynamically with user-defined state and severity. The syntax of the RAISERROR function is as follows:

```
RAISERROR ({msg_id | msg_str}{, severity, state}
   [, arguments [,...n]] )
   [WITH LOG | NOWAIT | SETERROR]
```

The following are the options:

Option	Description
msg_id	The *msg_id* is the ID of a user-defined error message that has been stored in the sysmessages table. User-defined error messages should have error numbers larger than 50,000. Ad-hoc error messages are always returned with an error number of 50,000. The maximum value for the *msg_id* is 2,147,483,647.
msg_str	The *msg_str* is an ad-hoc message that is formatted similarly to the PRINTF function in C. The format of the *msg_str* is outlined later in this section.
severity	The *severity* is the user-defined severity level for the message being returned. Levels 0–18 can be returned by any user. Levels 19–25 can be used only by members of the sysadmin server role and must use the WITH LOG option. Severity levels of 19–25 are considered fatal errors. If one of these errors is encountered, the error is logged into the SQL Server error log and the Windows NT Application log, and then the client connection is terminated.
state	The *state* option is an arbitrary integer value from 1 to 127 that returns information about the invocation state of the error. The state information is not displayed when using Query Analyzer unless the severity is higher than 11.
arguments	The arguments option is used to substitute for the variables defined in the *msg_str* or the message that corresponds to the *msg_id*. The upper limit to the number of substitution arguments is 20.
WITH LOG	The WITH LOG option forces the error to be written to the SQL Server error log and the Windows NT Application log. Errors logged to the SQL Server error log are limited to 440 bytes.
WITH NOWAIT	The WITH NOWAIT option forces SQL Server to send the error message back to the client immediately. If this option is not specified, SQL Server might wait to send the error back to the client until the batch completes or until the server buffer gets full.

WITH SETERROR	The WITH SETERROR option forces SQL Server to set the @@ERROR values to the value of the msg_id or 50000, regardless of the severity level. Normally, for severities of 1–10, SQL Server sets the @@ERROR value to 0.

The format for the message string is as follows:

```
% [[flag] [width] [precision]] [{h | 1}]] type
```

The following are the options:

Option	Description
flag	The flag option enables you to specify spacing and justification in the user-defined error message. These options are
	- Left justified.
	+ For signed types, preface the output with a plus or minus.
	# For hexadecimal data, preface the output with 0x.
	0 Pad the output with zeros until the maximum width has been reached.
	blank Preface the output with a space if the value is signed and positive.
width	The width option defines the minimum width for the particular parameter.
precision	The precision is the maximum number of characters printed for the output field or the maximum number of digits printed for integer values.
{h | 1}type	Defines the type of the data that is accepted for a particular option. The accepted types are
	d or i Signed integer
	o Unsigned octal
	p Pointer
	s String
	u Unsigned integer
	x or X Unsigned hexadecimal

There is quite a bit to the RAISERROR function. To break it down, the easiest way to use RAISERROR is to provide it with a *msg_str*, a *severity*, and a *state*, as shown in Listing 6.8.

LISTING 6.8   The RAISERROR Function

```
RAISERROR ('This is a test', 1, 1)
```

This simple statement returns a message number, level, and state on one line and the message text on the next line. Using some of the other options available to you, you can create much more complex error messages, as shown in Listing 6.9.

LISTING 6.9   Using RAISERROR with Replacement Parameters

```
DECLARE     @intErrorNumber    INT
DECLARE     @vchUserName    VARCHAR(16)
DECLARE     @dtmDateTime    VARCHAR(32)

SELECT     @intErrorNumber = 50000
SELECT     @vchUserName = SUSER_NAME()
SELECT     @dtmDateTime = CONVERT(VARCHAR(32), GETDATE())

RAISERROR ('Error # %i was raised by %s at %s', 11, 1, @intErrorNumber,
➥@vchUserName, @dtmDateTime)
```

These examples show the usage of the RAISERROR function in a SQL script. When you use the RAISERROR function inside a stored procedure, you must also use the RETURN function to exit the stored procedure when the error has been encountered. The procedure created in Listing 6.10 revisits the procedure that was created in Listing 6.6. In this case, instead of placing the error checking outside the procedure, the error checking is placed inside the procedure, thus making the stored procedure and the error checking self-contained.

LISTING 6.10   Using the RAISERROR Function in a Stored Procedure

```
CREATE PROCEDURE usp_6_9
@vchTitlePattern    VARCHAR(80) = '%'
AS
DECLARE     @intTitleCount    INT

IF @vchTitlePattern = '%'
BEGIN
    RAISERROR ('ERROR:  Expected a title pattern. Useage:
    ➥usp_6_9 <search expression>', 11, 1)
    RETURN 99
END
```

Creating More Complex Stored Procedures

CHAPTER 6

105

6

CREATING MORE
COMPLEX STORED
PROCEDURES

```
SELECT @vchTitlePattern = '%' + @vchTitlePattern + '%'
SELECT @intTitleCount = COUNT(*) FROM titles WHERE title LIKE @vchTitlePattern

IF @intTitleCount = 0
BEGIN
    RAISERROR ('There are no titles that match that search criteria.', 10, 1)
    RETURN 1
END

IF @intTitleCount > 1
BEGIN
    RAISERROR ('There are %i titles that match that description.
    ➥Please refine the search criteria.', 10, 1, @intTitleCount)
    RETURN 2
END

SELECT      title, price
FROM        titles
WHERE       title LIKE @vchTitlePattern

RETURN 0
```

There are times in which you will need to pass data out of an executing stored procedure into a
variable for use in other portions of your application. This is done through the use of OUTPUT
parameters.

OUTPUT Parameters

As you learned earlier, stored procedures communicate with outside applications by using
parameters. Data is passed into the stored procedure for processing through parameters. Data
can also be passed out of the procedure by using output parameters. When you create a stored
procedure, you can tell the procedure that a particular parameter is going to be used to pass
data back to the application. Then, when the stored procedure is executed, you must use the
OUTPUT keyword again to specify that the stored procedure will be passing data out and you
want to capture it. As a review, the syntax important for the creation of a stored procedure that
returns data from a parameter is as follows:

```
CREATE PROCEDURE <procedure_name>
{<@parameter> <data type>} [VARYING] [= default] [OUTPUT]][,...n]
AS
<sql_statements>
```

The following are the options:

Option	Description
<procedure_name>	This is the name of the stored procedure you are going to create.
<@parameter>	If you want to pass parameters into a stored procedure, you must define them in the declaration of the stored procedure. This declaration includes the name of the parameter, the data type of the parameter, and a few other special options depending on their use.
<data type>	If you specify a parameter, then you must specify the data type of that parameter. This can be any valid data type, including text and image.
[VARYING]	This option is specified when you are returning a cursor as a parameter.
[= *default*]	This option is used to specify a default value for a particular parameter. If the procedure is executed without specifying a value for the parameter, this value will be used instead. This can be NULL or any other valid value for that data type. For string data, this value can include wildcards if the parameter is used in conjunction with the LIKE parameter.
[OUTPUT]	This optional keyword is used to specify that the parameter is a return parameter. The value of this parameter can then be returned to the executing procedure when execution has completed. Text and image data types cannot be used as OUTPUT parameters.
[,...*n*]	This symbol indicates that you can specify multiple parameters with a stored procedure. SQL Server allows up to 1,024 parameters for use in a single stored procedure.

It is important to remember that you must use the OUTPUT parameter in both the declaration of the stored procedure and the execution of the stored procedure. An example of this is shown in Listing 6.11.

LISTING 6.11   Returning Data Through OUTPUT Parameters

```
CREATE PROCEDURE usp_6_11
@vchTitle    varchar(80),
@intYTDSales    int OUTPUT
AS
```

Creating More Complex Stored Procedures

CHAPTER 6

107

6

CREATING MORE
COMPLEX STORED
PROCEDURES

```
SELECT      @intYTDSales = ytd_sales
FROM        titles
WHERE       title = @vchTitle

RETURN 0
GO

DECLARE @intTitleYTDSales int

EXECUTE usp_6_11 "The Busy Executive's Database Guide",
@intYTDSales = @intTitleYTDSales OUTPUT

PRINT 'Sales for "The Busy Executive''s Database Guide": $' +
convert(varchar(6), @intTitleYTDSales) + '.00'
GO
```

Classing Input Variables as OUTPUT Variables

Input variables can also be classed as OUTPUT variables, enabling you to pass data into a stored procedure, perform some sort of operations on it, and then pass it back to the calling stored procedure. This is known as passing the data *by-reference*. An example of this is shown in Listing 6.12.

LISTING 6.12   Passing Data By-Reference

```
CREATE PROCEDURE usp_6_12
@intValue INT OUTPUT
AS
SELECT @intValue = @intValue * @intValue
RETURN 0
GO

DECLARE @intResult INT
SET @intResult = 5
PRINT 'Value of @intResult before execution: ' + CAST(@intResult AS VARCHAR(6))
EXEC usp_6_12 @intResult OUTPUT
PRINT 'Value of @intResult after execution: ' + CAST(@intResult AS VARCHAR(6))
GO
```

Returning Data and Status Messages with OUTPUT

Another use of the OUTPUT keyword is to return data and status messages from a stored procedure. This enables you to return very pertinent information about the execution of the stored procedure to the application or user that called the stored procedure. Consider the code in Listing 6.13. This stored procedure enables a user to search the authors table in the pubs database for an author's author ID, first and last name, phone number, and ZIP code. If the user does not pass in the correct criteria, the stored procedure returns an error to the user through the two output variables, @vchStatus and @vchStatusMessage. Following the creation of the stored procedure, it is executed by several queries. These queries try out all the different criteria that the stored procedure checks.

Listing 6.13   Returning Errors Through Output Parameters

```
CREATE PROC usp_6_13
@vchAuthorID          VARCHAR(11) = '%',
@vchAuthorLastName    VARCHAR(40) = '%',
@vchZipCode           VARCHAR(5) = '%',
@vchStatus            VARCHAR(16) = '%' OUTPUT,
@vchStatusMessage     VARCHAR(128) = '%' OUTPUT
AS
SET NOCOUNT ON
IF ((@vchAuthorID = '%') AND (@vchAuthorLastName = '%')
➥AND (@vchZipCode = '%'))
BEGIN
    SELECT @vchStatus = 'ERROR'
    SELECT @vchStatusMessage = 'You must supply at least one search criteria.'
    RETURN 100
END

IF ((@vchAuthorID != '%') AND (@vchAuthorID NOT LIKE '___-__-____'))
BEGIN
    SELECT @vchStatus = 'ERROR'
    SELECT @vchStatusMessage = 'The AuthorID must be in the form ###-##-####.'
    RETURN 101
END

IF ((@vchAuthorID != '%') AND (SELECT COUNT(*) FROM authors
➥WHERE au_id = @vchAuthorID) = 0)
BEGIN
    SELECT @vchStatus = 'ERROR'
    SELECT @vchStatusMessage = 'There are no authors with an author id of '
    ➥+ @vchAuthorID + '.'
    RETURN 102
END

IF ((@vchAuthorLastName != '%') AND (SELECT COUNT(*) FROM authors
➥WHERE au_lname = @vchAuthorLastName) = 0)
BEGIN
    SELECT @vchStatus = 'ERROR'
    SELECT @vchStatusMessage = 'There are no authors with the last name ' +
    ➥@vchAuthorLastName + '.'
```

```
    RETURN 103
END

IF ((@vchZipCode != '%') AND (@vchZipCode NOT LIKE
➥'[0-9][0-9][0-9][0-9][0-9]'))
BEGIN
    SELECT @vchStatus = 'ERROR'
    SELECT @vchStatusMessage = 'The zip code must be in the form #####.'
    RETURN 104
END

IF ((@vchZipCode != '%') AND (SELECT COUNT(*) FROM authors
➥WHERE zip = @vchZipCode) = 0)
BEGIN
    SELECT @vchStatus = 'ERROR'
    SELECT @vchStatusMessage = 'There are no authors that live in the zip
    ➥code ' + @vchZipCode + '.'
    RETURN 105
END

IF (SELECT COUNT(*) FROM authors WHERE au_id LIKE @vchAuthorID AND
➥au_lname LIKE @vchAuthorLastName AND zip LIKE @vchZipCode) = 0
BEGIN
    SELECT @vchStatus = 'ERROR'
    SELECT @vchStatusMessage = 'There are no authors that match the given
    ➥search criteria.' + CHAR(10) +
                    'AuthorID: ' + @vchAuthorID + CHAR(10) +
                    'AuthorLastName: ' + @vchAuthorLastName + CHAR(10) +
                    'ZipCode: ' + @vchZipCode
    RETURN 106
END ELSE
BEGIN
    SELECT au_id, au_lname + ', ' + au_fname, phone, zip
    FROM authors
    WHERE au_id LIKE @vchAuthorID AND au_lname LIKE @vchAuthorLastName
    ➥AND zip LIKE @vchZipCode
    SELECT @vchStatus = 'OK'
    SELECT @vchStatusMessage = 'SUCCESS'
    RETURN 0
END
GO

DECLARE @vchStatus          VARCHAR(16)
DECLARE @vchStatusMessage    VARCHAR(128)

EXEC usp_6_13 @vchStatus = @vchStatus OUTPUT, @vchStatusMessage =
                @vchStatusMessage OUTPUT
```

continues

LISTING 6.13   Continued

```
PRINT @vchStatus
PRINT @vchStatusMessage

EXEC usp_6_13 @vchAuthorID = '123121234', @vchStatus = @vchStatus OUTPUT,
              @vchStatusMessage = @vchStatusMessage OUTPUT
PRINT @vchStatus
PRINT @vchStatusMessage

EXEC usp_6_13 @vchAuthorID = '123-12-1234', @vchStatus =
              @vchStatus OUTPUT, @vchStatusMessage = @vchStatusMessage OUTPUT
PRINT @vchStatus
PRINT @vchStatusMessage

EXEC usp_6_13 @vchAuthorLastName = 'Jones', @vchStatus =
              @vchStatus OUTPUT, @vchStatusMessage = @vchStatusMessage OUTPUT
PRINT @vchStatus
PRINT @vchStatusMessage

EXEC usp_6_13 @vchZipCode = '5123B', @vchStatus = @vchStatus OUTPUT,
              @vchStatusMessage = @vchStatusMessage OUTPUT
PRINT @vchStatus
PRINT @vchStatusMessage

EXEC usp_6_13 @vchZipCode = '12345', @vchStatus = @vchStatus OUTPUT,
              @vchStatusMessage = @vchStatusMessage OUTPUT
PRINT @vchStatus
PRINT @vchStatusMessage

EXEC usp_6_13 @vchAuthorLastName = 'Smith', @vchZipCode = '94025', @vchStatus =
              @vchStatus OUTPUT, @vchStatusMessage = @vchStatusMessage OUTPUT
PRINT @vchStatus
PRINT @vchStatusMessage

EXEC usp_6_13 @vchAuthorLastName = 'White', @vchZipCode = '94025', @vchStatus =
              @vchStatus OUTPUT, @vchStatusMessage = @vchStatusMessage OUTPUT
PRINT @vchStatus
PRINT @vchStatusMessage
```

When returning error and status messages from stored procedures by using OUTPUT parameters, you must set your application to check the return values to ensure that everything worked. If you don't, there might be results returned that you never knew about.

Passing an Open Cursor

Another use for OUTPUT parameters is to use them to pass an open cursor back to the calling stored procedure or trigger. This enables you to pass back a recordset that can be scrolled through, enabling you to perform operations on multiple rows. There are some things that you must be aware of before you use CURSOR OUTPUT parameters.

- Stored procedures can use only the CURSOR data type for OUTPUT parameters. If you use the CURSOR data type, you must also use the VARYING and OUTPUT parameters. Likewise, if you specify the VARYING keyword, you must use the CURSOR datatype and it must be an OUTPUT parameter.

- When using forward-only cursors, only the rows past the current position are passed back to the calling procedure. For example, if a cursor is opened containing 500 rows, and 100 rows are fetched from it before it is passed back to the calling procedure, the calling procedure will get a forward-only cursor that has only rows 101 through 500. The 101st row will be considered the first row in the new cursor.

- If a forward-only cursor is positioned before the first row when it is passed back to the calling procedure, only the rows in the original cursor are passed back.

- If a forward-only cursor is positioned at the last row in the cursor when it is passed back to the calling procedure, a NULL value is passed back.

- If a scrollable cursor is being used, all the rows in the cursor are returned to the calling procedure, no matter how many rows have been fetched. The current position in the cursor is maintained when it is passed back.

- If a cursor is closed before it is passed back to the calling procedure, a NULL value will be passed back.

The two stored procedures in Listing 6.14 show how to pass a cursor from one stored procedure to another. This procedure enables you to determine the quantity of any book that was ordered by all book stores.

LISTING 6.14   Cursor and Stored Procedures

```
CREATE PROC usp_6_14_1
@vchTitleID    VARCHAR(6) = '%',
@curOrders     CURSOR VARYING OUTPUT
AS
SET @curOrders = CURSOR FORWARD_ONLY STATIC FOR
    SELECT    title_id, stor_id, qty, ord_date
    FROM      sales
    WHERE     title_id LIKE @vchTitleID
    ORDER BY ord_date
```

continues

LISTING 6.14   Continued

```
OPEN @curOrders
GO

CREATE PROC usp_6_14_2
@vchTitlePattern    VARCHAR(80) = '%'
AS
DECLARE @vchTitleID      VARCHAR(6)
DECLARE @intRecordCount      INT
DECLARE @curTitleOrder      CURSOR
DECLARE @vchTitleIDOut      VARCHAR(6)
DECLARE @intStoreIDOut      INT
DECLARE @intQTYOut      INT
DECLARE @dtmDate      DATETIME
DECLARE @vchTitleOut      VARCHAR(80)
DECLARE @vchStoreOut      VARCHAR(40)
DECLARE @mnyTotalOut      MONEY
DECLARE @vchRetMessage      VARCHAR(255)

SET NOCOUNT ON

IF (@vchTitlePattern != '%')
BEGIN
    SELECT @vchTitlePattern = '%' + @vchTitlePattern + '%'

    SELECT  @intRecordCount = COUNT(*)
    FROM    titles
    WHERE    title LIKE @vchTitlePattern

    SELECT  @vchTitleID = title_id
    FROM    titles
    WHERE    title LIKE @vchTitlePattern

    IF @intRecordCount = 0
    BEGIN
        RAISERROR ('There are no matching records.', 0, 1)
        RETURN 101
    END
    IF @intRecordCount > 1
    BEGIN
        RAISERROR('There are multiple records that match that keyword.', 0, 1)
        RETURN 102
    END
    EXEC usp_6_14_1 @vchTitleID, @curTitleOrder OUTPUT
END ELSE
```

```
BEGIN
    EXEC usp_6_14_1 @curOrders = @curTitleOrder OUTPUT
END
FETCH NEXT FROM @curTitleOrder INTO @vchTitleIDOut, @intStoreIDOut,
                @intQTYOut, @dtmDate
WHILE (@@FETCH_STATUS = 0)
BEGIN
    SELECT @vchTitleOut = title, @mnyTotalOut = price
    FROM titles
    WHERE title_id = @vchTitleIDOut
    SELECT @vchStoreOut = stor_name FROM stores WHERE stor_id = @intStoreIDOut
    SELECT @vchRetMessage = @vchStoreOut + ' purchased ' +
            CONVERT(VARCHAR(2), @intQTYOut) + ' copies of ' + @vchTitleOut +
            ' on ' + CONVERT(VARCHAR(16), @dtmDate, 101) +
            ' for a total of $' + CONVERT(VARCHAR(10),
            (@intQTYOut * @mnyTotalOut))
    PRINT @vchRetMessage
    FETCH NEXT FROM @curTitleOrder INTO @vchTitleIDOut, @intStoreIDOut,
                    @intQTYOut, @dtmDate
END
CLOSE @curTitleOrder
DEALLOCATE @curTitleOrder
GO

EXEC usp_6_14_2
EXEC usp_6_14_2 'microwave'
EXEC usp_6_14_2 'database'
GO
```

Conclusion

In this chapter, I discussed some of the more powerful features of SQL Server stored procedures. First, you saw how to pass parameters into stored procedures, enabling you to create powerful and extensible procedures. Next, I looked at several ways to return data to the users. With the RETURN statement, you can immediately exit a stored procedure, returning an integer error code to the user. Using the PRINT statement, you can output character data to the user, enabling you to output simple information. The RAISERROR statement enables you to return complex error messages to the user, making the messages look like server errors. Lastly, we looked at OUTPUT parameters.

Creating Stored Procedures that Insert Data

IN THIS CHAPTER

So far, the stored procedures we've looked at and worked with have dealt only with getting data out of the database using SELECT statements. There is much more to stored procedures than that. Stored procedures can also be used to INSERT data into your tables. When adding data to your tables using stored procedures, you need to consider several things. We cover all these considerations in this chapter.

In this chapter, we cover the following:

- Inserting data
- Inserting data into a view
- Inserting data based on a SELECT statement
- Minimizing blocking conditions
- Automating the creation of the code

Inserting Data with the INSERT Statement

As you know, databases aren't used only for querying data. Databases are also used for storing data. Adding data to a database is done through the use of the INSERT statement, which adds rows to a single table that you specify. For review, the following is the syntax and an explanation of the INSERT statement:

```
INSERT [INTO]
    {
      table_name WITH ( <table_hint_limited> [...n])
      | view_name
      | rowset_function_limited
    }
    {    [(column_list)]
        { VALUES ( {    DEFAULT
                        |   NULL
                        |   expression
                    }[,...n]
            )
        | derived_table
        | execute_statement
        }
    }
    | DEFAULT VALUES

<table_hint_limited> ::=
    {    INDEX(index_val [,...n])
        | FASTFIRSTROW
        | HOLDLOCK
        | PAGLOCK
```

```
    |  READCOMMITTED
    |  REPEATABLEREAD
    |  ROWLOCK
    |  SERIALIZABLE
    |  TABLOCK
    |  TABLOCKX
}
```

Table 7.1 describes each element in this syntax.

TABLE 7.1   INSERT Options

Keyword/Option	Description
INSERT	Tells SQL Server that you want to add a row to a table or a view.
INTO	Separates the name of the table or view from the INSERT keyword. The brackets in the syntax indicate that this keyword is optional.
table_name	Indicates the name of the table to which you are going to add data. You can add data to only one table or view at a time.
WITH	Specifies that you are going to use some sort of table hint.
<table_hint_limited>	Specifies the table hint that you are going to use.
[...n]	Specifies that you can use more than one table hint. Some hints are exclusive of other hints, so ensure that all hints you use are compatible.
view_name	Indicates the name of the view into which you are optionally specifying that you INSERT data. This view must be updatable. If the view into which you are adding data contains multiple tables, you can add data to only one at a time.
rowset_function_limited	A placeholder for either the OPENQUERY or OPENRECORDSET function. For more information on these functions, query SQL Server Books Online.
(column_list)	Indicates the list of columns into which you are going to add data. This isn't a required option if you are adding data to all the columns in the table. If you don't want to add data to all the columns in the table, you can list the individual columns, separated by commas and enclosed in parentheses, to which you want to add data. If you specify a column in this list, SQL Server has to define a value for

continues

7

TABLE 7.1 Continued

Keyword/Option	Description
	that column or the row can't be added to the database. If a value isn't specified, SQL Server provides a value for the column if the column meets any of the following criteria: the column has an IDENTITY property defined; the column has a default value defined on it; the column is of the TIMESTAMP data type; or the column is defined as nullable.
VALUES	Specifies that you are going to list the values that will be added to the table or view. There must be one value for each column that you specified in the *column_list*, if you specified columns, or one value for each column in the table. Each value you specify must be of the same data type as that of the column into which you are inserting the value. The values are separated by commas and enclosed in parentheses.
DEFAULT	Forces SQL Server to insert the default value for a particular column. If a default value exists on that column, that value is inserted into the column. If no default exists and the column allows NULL values, NULL will be inserted into the column. If the data type of the column is TIMESTAMP, SQL Server will insert the next valid timestamp.
NULL	Specifies that you are going to insert the NULL value into the corresponding column. If the column isn't nullable, an error will be produced and the row won't be added to the table.
expression	Specifies a constant, variable, or expression. The expression can't be a SELECT or EXECUTE statement.
[, ...*n*]	Symbolizes that you are going to specify multiple values for the row.
derived_table	Holds the place for a SELECT statement that will return multiple rows that can be returned and added to a table.
execute_statement	Executes a specified stored procedure that returns data using a SELECT statement or READTEXT function. When data is returned from the execution of a stored procedure, you must make sure that all columns returned are compatible with the columns in the table into which you are adding data.

Keyword/Option	Description
DEFAULT VALUES	Adds a row to the table using all DEFAULT VALUES defined on the table.
INDEX(index_val [,...n])	Specifies the name or ID of the index you want SQL Server to use when processing the statement.
FASTFIRSTROW	Specifies that the query is optimized for the retrieval of one row.
HOLDLOCK	Specifies that SQL Server will hold the lock that was acquired on the row for the length of the entire transaction.
PAGLOCK	Specifies that SQL Server should take shared page locks instead of a shared table lock.
READCOMMITTED	Specifies that the locks acquired during the modification are held only for the time of the insert but downgrades the lock before the end of the transaction so that it can be read by other users.
REPEATABLEREAD	Specifies that locks are placed on all data used in the query, keeping any users from updating the rows, but new rows can be inserted and will be included in later reads from the database.
ROWLOCK	Specifies that a row lock should be acquired when a page lock or a table lock would normally be acquired.
SERIALIZABLE	Similar in functionality to the HOLDLOCK option; specifies that SQL Server will hold the lock that was acquired on the row for the length of the entire transaction.
TABLOCK	Specifies that a table lock should be taken where any other type of lock would normally be taken. This lock is held until the end of the statement.
TABLOCKX	Specifies that an exclusive table lock is acquired and held on the table when any other type of lock would normally be taken. This lock is held until the end of the statement.

For the most part, the table hints, also called *optimizer hints*, won't be used. You will primarily use the straight INSERT statement. The following code is a simple INSERT statement that adds a single row to the authors table in the pubs database:

```
INSERT INTO authors
VALUES ('111-11-1111', 'Jones', 'Billy', '777-555-1212', '123 5th St.',
     ➥'Anytown', 'KS', '55555', 1)
GO
```

This statement adds one row to the `authors` table with a value in each column. If you don't want to add a value to each column, you can list the individual columns, as follows:

```
INSERT INTO authors (au_id, au_lname, au_fname, phone, contract)
VALUES ('222-22-2222', 'Smith', 'Brian', '555-777-1212', 1)
GO
```

This statement inserts a row into the `authors` table without adding values to the address, city, state, or zip columns.

Inserting Data into Views

As mentioned previously, you can insert data into a view. The view has to be created in a specific way to handle data insertion. Several rules also must be followed to make these types of inserts work:

- The `SELECT` statement used to make the view cannot contain any aggregate functions.
- The `SELECT` statement used to make the view cannot contain `GROUP BY`, `TOP`, `UNION`, or `DISTINCT` statements.
- Aggregate functions can be used in the `FROM` clause of the `SELECT` statement as long as the values returned by the function aren't modified.
- The `SELECT` statement cannot contain any derived columns. In a view, a *derived column* is created by anything other than a single value from a column. This can be done by using functions, mathematical operators, or concatenation of columns.
- The `FROM` clause in the `SELECT` statement that's used to create the view must contain at least one table.
- If the `FROM` clause contains more than one table, you can insert rows into only one table at a time.

The rules for inserting data into a view are rather simple, but because of the restrictions on inserting data into multiple tables, using views makes things very difficult. First, look at the code in Listing 7.1. In this code, a single table view is created and data is inserted into it.

LISTING 7.1   Inserting into a View

```
CREATE TABLE ViewTableTest
(
    TestID      INT,
    TestName    VARCHAR(32)
)
GO
```

```
CREATE VIEW TestingView
AS
SELECT      TestID, TestName
FROM    ViewTableTest
GO


INSERT ViewTableTest (TestID, TestName) VALUES (1, 'Direct Insert Into Table')
GO


SELECT      TestID, TestName
FROM    TestingView
GO


INSERT INTO TestingView (TestID, TestName) VALUES (2, 'Insert Using View')
GO


SELECT  TestID, TestName
FROM    TestingView
GO
```

This INSERT statement works well as only one table is affected. The problem comes when you have a view that contains more than one table, as most do. These tables are usually joined on a column. Every table will have that column, but it will be displayed in the view only one time. The code in Listing 7.2 shows the types of problems that you will encounter.

LISTING 7.2   Inserting Into Multitable Views

```
CREATE TABLE ViewTableNames
(
    PersonalID   INT,
    FirstName    VARCHAR(32),
    LastName     VARCHAR(32)
)


CREATE TABLE ViewTableAddresses
(
    PersonalID   INT,
    Address      VARCHAR(64),
    City         VARCHAR(32),
    State        CHAR(2),
    Zip          CHAR(5)
)
```

continues

Listing 7.2   Continued

```
CREATE TABLE ViewTablePhone
(
    PersonalID    INT,
    PhoneType     VARCHAR(32),
    PhoneNumber   VARCHAR(13)
)
GO

INSERT INTO ViewTableNames VALUES (101, 'Misty', 'Pfeifer')
INSERT INTO ViewTableAddresses VALUES (101, '123 4th St.',
        ➥'Anycity', 'KS', '66777')
INSERT INTO ViewTablePhone VALUES (101, 'Home', '123-456-7890')
GO

CREATE VIEW NamesView
AS
SELECT    VTN.PersonalID, LastName, FirstName, Address, City, State, Zip,
          PhoneType, PhoneNumber
FROM    ViewTableNames VTN INNER JOIN ViewTableAddresses VTA
    ON (VTN.PersonalID = VTA.PersonalID)
    INNER JOIN ViewTablePhone VTP ON
    (VTN.PersonalID = VTP.PersonalID)
GO

INSERT INTO NamesView (PersonalID, LastName, FirstName) VALUES (102,
        ➥'Jones', 'Bill')
GO

INSERT INTO NamesView (PersonalID, Address, City, State, Zip) VALUES
        ➥(102, '234 5th St.', 'Anycity', 'KS', '66777')
GO

INSERT INTO NamesView (PersonalID, PhoneType, PhoneNumber) VALUES (102,
        ➥'Cellular', '234-567-8901')
GO
```

When you run this code, you can insert data into the view that is placed in the ViewTableNames table. When the other two inserts run, SQL Server generates an error message telling you that you are trying to insert data into two tables and it doesn't work. You can fix this by using INSTEAD OF triggers, which are discussed in Chapter 15, "Writing Triggers."

Inserting Data Based on a SELECT Statement

One feature of the INSERT statement that you will use quite a bit is the ability to insert data into a table based on a SELECT statement. This action enables you to add multiple rows into a table very easily. When you INSERT large amounts of data into a table by using a SELECT statement, the entire process is a single transaction. This enables you to roll back the entire thing if something out of the ordinary happens. The process of adding data to a table based off a SELECT statement can be slightly difficult at first. The two main things that you have to remember are that you don't use the VALUES keyword and don't enclose the SELECT statement in parentheses. If you forget either of these, SQL Server returns an error and won't add any data to the table. The code in Listing 7.3 outlines the addition of rows to a new table based on a SELECT statement.

LISTING 7.3   Inserting by Using a SELECT Statement

```
CREATE TABLE AuthorInformation
(
    AuthorName    CHAR(32),
    PhoneNumber   CHAR(13),
    AddressLine1  VARCHAR(64),
    AddressLine2  VARCHAR(64)
)
GO

INSERT INTO AuthorInformation
    SELECT   au_lname + ', ' + au_fname, phone, address, city + ', '
             ➥ + state + ' ' + zip
    FROM     authors
    ORDER    BY 1
GO

SELECT * FROM AuthorInformation
GO
```

Inserting Data with an EXECUTE Statement

Another option at your disposal is to INSERT data into a table based on the execution of a stored procedure. This enables you to use this data for any other queries or to store the data for later analysis. Other than for storing data for later analysis, you will rarely use this functionality as there are much more efficient ways of storing data for use in other queries. Listing 7.4 shows an example of adding data to a table by using an EXECUTE statement.

LISTING 7.4   Inserting Data Based on Stored Procedure Execution

```
CREATE TABLE TempSPWHO2
(
    SPID1        INT,
    Status       VARCHAR(60),
    Login        VARCHAR(16),
    Hostname     VARCHAR(256),
    BlkBy        VARCHAR(3),
    DBName       VARCHAR(256),
    Command      VARCHAR(32),
    CPUTime      INT,
    DiskIO       INT,
    LastBatch    VARCHAR(16),
    ProgramName  VARCHAR(256),
    SPID2        INT
)
GO

INSERT INTO TempSPWHO2
    EXEC sp_who2
GO

SELECT      *
FROM        TempSPWHO2
GO
```

As with the INSERT using a SELECT statement, don't use the VALUES keyword or enclose the code in parentheses. Doing so will cause an error.

Minimizing Blocking Conditions

One problem that you can run into when you insert data into a table is blocking due to large amounts of locks. Locks are used to keep multiple users from changing the same data at the same time. For more information on locks, see Chapter 16, "Consideration When Using Stored Procedures and Triggers." A block occurs when one user holds a lock on a resource and other users require that resource. This results in one user being placed in a wait state, or being blocked, until the other user releases the lock. If the lock is being held on a table and the query is long running, this can result in huge amounts of time that users have to wait.

You can minimize locking conditions in several ways. First, use good judgment when writing your queries and applications. Try to ensure that the activity in the database is kept to as short a time as possible. If you can't minimize the amount of time that your queries are in the database, you should try to limit the number of rows that you access in any one table at a time. You can do this through the use of cursors. With cursors, you can create a recordset that can be looped through and accessed one record at a time. This minimizes the number and size of the locks that your query holds at any point.

To create a script that uses a cursor to eliminate blocking, first determine which rows you are going to affect using a SELECT statement into a cursor. Then, as you loop through the cursor with the FETCH statement, you can modify one row at a time. The code in Listing 7.5 shows how this works.

LISTING 7.5   Using a Cursor to Eliminate Blocking

```
CREATE TABLE CursorTest
(
    RowID    INT,
    RowText  CHAR(4)
)
GO

CREATE TABLE CursorTestOdd
(
    RowID    INT,
    RowText  CHAR(4)
)
GO

SET NOCOUNT ON

DECLARE @intCounter    INT
DECLARE @chrTextOdd    CHAR(4)
DECLARE @chrTextEven   CHAR(4)

SELECT    @intCounter = 1
SELECT    @chrTextOdd = 'Odd'
SELECT    @chrTextEven = 'Even'

WHILE (@intCounter <= 200000)
BEGIN
    IF (@intCounter % 2) = 0
    BEGIN
        INSERT INTO CursorTest VALUES (@intCounter, @chrTextEven)
    END ELSE
    BEGIN
        INSERT INTO CursorTest VALUES (@intCounter, @chrTextOdd)
    END
    SELECT @intCounter = @intCounter + 1
END
```

continues

LISTING 7.5   Continued

```
GO

DECLARE    @intRowID    INT

DECLARE curOddRows CURSOR FOR
    SELECT  RowID
    FROM    CursorTest
    WHERE   RowID % 2 = 1

OPEN    curOddRows

FETCH NEXT FROM curOddRows INTO @intRowID

WHILE (@@FETCH_STATUS <> -1)
BEGIN
    BEGIN TRANSACTION
        INSERT INTO CursorTestOdd
            SELECT  *
            FROM    CursorTest
            WHERE   RowID = @intRowID

        DELETE  CursorTest
        WHERE   RowID = @intRowID
    COMMIT
    FETCH NEXT FROM curOddRows INTO @intRowID
END

CLOSE       curOddRows
DEALLOCATE  curOddRows
GO

SELECT TOP 1000 * FROM CursorTest
SELECT TOP 1000 * FROM CursorTestOdd
GO

DROP TABLE CursorTest
DROP TABLE CursorTestOdd
GO
```

First, this script creates a temporary table that contains 200,000 rows. Then, it creates a cursor that contains the odd-numbered rows. As the script loops through the cursor, it inserts these rows into one table and deletes them from the other. If you performed this as a single operation, it would lock both tables for the entire length of the operation. When you do it in this manner, you instead lock a single row at a time.

> **NOTE**
>
> This query will run for quite a while. It shouldn't be run on a production server because it can use a great deal of system resources.

As you can see, this forces SQL Server to affect one row at a time in the database. This means SQL Server will lock only a single row at a time in each table.

Automating the Creation of the Code

One great thing about stored procedures is that they can save time. One stored procedure that I needed would write the code that, when executed, would be a stored procedure that would insert rows into a table. This stored procedure can be seen in Listing 7.6.

LISTING 7.6 Automatic Creation of Stored Procedure Code

```
CREATE PROCEDURE usp_create_insert_proc
    @vchTableName    VARCHAR(64)
AS

SET NOCOUNT ON

-- Declare the variables

DECLARE @vchCurrentLine     VARCHAR(128)
DECLARE @vchColumnName      VARCHAR(32)
DECLARE @vchColumnType      VARCHAR(16)
DECLARE @intColumnLength    INT
DECLARE @bitNullable        BIT
DECLARE @intColNameLength   INT
DECLARE @intColCounter      INT
DECLARE @vchVariableName    VARCHAR(32)

-- Creates and prints the CREATE PROCEDURE command

SELECT    @vchCurrentLine = 'CREATE PROCEDURE usp_insert_' + @vchTableName
PRINT     @vchCurrentLine

-- Creates the temporary table used to determine the datatypes, nullability
-- and primary key participation for each column
```

continues

LISTING 7.6 Continued

```
CREATE TABLE TempColumnInfo
(
    ColumnName      VARCHAR(32) NOT NULL,
    Type            VARCHAR(16) NOT NULL,
    Length          INT NOT NULL,
    Nullable        BIT,
    IsPrimaryKey    BIT
        DEFAULT 0,
    VariableName    VARCHAR(32) NULL
)

-- Inserts the name, data type, length and nullability of each column into
-- temporary table.  If the data type is any character data type, then the
-- length is set for that data type.  Otherwise, the length is set to -1.

INSERT INTO TempColumnInfo (ColumnName, Type, Length, Nullable)
    SELECT      'Column_name' = CONVERT(VARCHAR(32), name),
        'Type' = CONVERT(VARCHAR(16), TYPE_NAME(xusertype)),
        'Length' = CASE
                    WHEN xtype IN (165, 167, 173, 175, 231, 239)
                        ➡AND xtype = xusertype THEN CONVERT(INT, length)
                    ELSE -1
                END,
        'Nullable' = isnullable
    FROM    syscolumns
    WHERE   id = (SELECT OBJECT_ID(@vchTableName)) AND
        number = 0
    ORDER   BY colid

-- Initialize the @intColCounter variable

SELECT @intColCounter = 0

-- Creates a cursor that contains information from the temporary
-- table.  This is used to determine the variable name that will
-- be used in the stored procedure.

DECLARE curColumnInfo INSENSITIVE CURSOR FOR
    SELECT ColumnName, Type, Length, Nullable
    FROM TempColumnInfo

OPEN curColumnInfo
```

```
FETCH NEXT FROM curColumnInfo INTO @vchColumnName, @vchColumnType,
    ➥@intColumnLength, @bitNullable
WHILE (@@FETCH_STATUS <> -1)
BEGIN
    SELECT @vchCurrentLine =
        CASE
            WHEN @vchColumnType = 'int' THEN '@int'
            WHEN @vchColumnType = 'smallint' THEN '@ins'
            WHEN @vchColumnType = 'tinyint' THEN '@iny'
            WHEN @vchColumnType = 'float' THEN '@flt'
            WHEN @vchColumnType = 'real' THEN '@rel'
            WHEN @vchColumnType = 'numeric' THEN '@num'
            WHEN @vchColumnType = 'decimal' THEN '@dec'
            WHEN @vchColumnType = 'money' THEN '@mny'
            WHEN @vchColumnType = 'smallmoney' THEN '@mns'
            WHEN @vchColumnType = 'bit' THEN '@bit'
            WHEN @vchColumnType = 'datetime' THEN '@dtm'
            WHEN @vchColumnType = 'smalldatetime' THEN '@dts'
            WHEN @vchColumnType = 'char' THEN '@chr'
            WHEN @vchColumnType = 'varchar' THEN '@chv'
            WHEN @vchColumnType = 'binary' THEN '@bny'
            WHEN @vchColumnType = 'varbinary' THEN '@bnv'
            WHEN @vchColumnType = 'text' THEN '@txt'
            WHEN @vchColumnType = 'image' THEN '@img'
            ELSE '@'
        END

    SELECT @vchCurrentLine = @vchCurrentLine + UPPER(LEFT(@vchColumnName, 1))
    SELECT @intColNameLength = LEN(@vchColumnName)
    SELECT @vchCurrentLine = @vchCurrentLine + SUBSTRING(@vchColumnName, 2,
                             ➥@intColNameLength)

-- Updates the temp tables with the variable name information.

    UPDATE  TempColumnInfo
    SET     VariableName = @vchCurrentLine
    WHERE   ColumnName = @vchColumnName

-- Begins formatting the datatype output

    SELECT @vchCurrentLine = @vchCurrentLine + '       '
    SELECT @vchCurrentLine = @vchCurrentLine + @vchColumnType

-- If the length is not -1, print the column length.
```

continues

LISTING 7.6   Continued

```
    IF (@intColumnLength <> -1)
    BEGIN
        SELECT @vchCurrentLine = @vchCurrentLine + '(' + CONVERT(VARCHAR(4),
                            ➡@intColumnLength) + ')'
    END

-- If the nullable bit is 1, then print the null option for that column

    IF (@bitNullable = 1)
    BEGIN
        SELECT @vchCurrentLine = @vchCurrentLine + ' = NULL'
    END

-- If the column is a primary key, update that column and save the
-- information for future use.

    IF (@intColCounter IN (SELECT colid FROM sysconstraints
        ➡WHERE id = OBJECT_ID(@vchTableName) AND status = 2593))
    BEGIN
        UPDATE TempColumnInfo SET IsPrimaryKey = 1
            ➡WHERE ColumnName = @vchColumnName
    END

-- Fetch the next column and print that information

    FETCH NEXT FROM curColumnInfo INTO @vchColumnName, @vchColumnType,
                                ➡@intColumnLength, @bitNullable
    IF (@@FETCH_STATUS <> 0)
    BEGIN
        PRINT @vchCurrentLine
    END ELSE
    BEGIN
        SELECT @vchCurrentLine = @vchCurrentLine + ','
        PRINT @vchCurrentLine
    END

    SELECT @intColCounter = @intColCounter + 1

END
CLOSE curColumnInfo
DEALLOCATE curColumnInfo

-- Indicate the beginning of the actual code
```

```
PRINT ''
PRINT 'AS'
PRINT ''

-- Open a cursor that contains all primary keys

DECLARE curPrimaryKeys INSENSITIVE CURSOR FOR
    SELECT  ColumnName, VariableName
    FROM    TempColumnInfo
    WHERE   IsPrimaryKey = 1

OPEN curPrimaryKeys

-- Print code that checks the primary keys to see if they exist in
-- the table.

FETCH NEXT FROM curPrimaryKeys INTO @vchColumnName, @vchVariableName
WHILE (@@FETCH_STATUS <> -1)
BEGIN
    SELECT  @vchCurrentLine = 'IF ' + @vchVariableName + ' IN (SELECT ' +
            ➥@vchColumnName + ' FROM ' + @vchTableName + ')'
    PRINT   @vchCurrentLine
    SELECT  @vchCurrentLine = 'BEGIN'
    PRINT   @vchCurrentLine
    SELECT  @vchCurrentLine = '    RAISERROR(' + CHAR(39) +
            ➥'Cannot insert a duplicate row in this table.'
    SELECT  @vchCurrentLine = @vchCurrentLine + CHAR(39) + ', 0, 1)'
    PRINT   @vchCurrentLine
    SELECT  @vchCurrentLine = '    RETURN (100)'
    PRINT   @vchCurrentLine
    SELECT  @vchCurrentLine = 'END'
    PRINT   @vchCurrentLine

    FETCH NEXT FROM curPrimaryKeys INTO @vchColumnName, @vchVariableName
END
CLOSE curPrimaryKeys
DEALLOCATE curPrimaryKeys

PRINT      ''

-- Print the code that performs the actual insert

SELECT     @vchCurrentLine = 'INSERT INTO     ' + @vchTableName
PRINT      @vchCurrentLine
SELECT     @vchCurrentLine = 'VALUES     ('
```

continues

LISTING 7.6   Continued

```
-- Fetch the names of each variable and return them

DECLARE curVariables INSENSITIVE CURSOR FOR
    SELECT     VariableName
    FROM       TempColumnInfo

OPEN curVariables

FETCH NEXT FROM curVariables INTO @vchVariableName
WHILE (@@FETCH_STATUS <> -1)
BEGIN
    SELECT @vchCurrentLine = @vchCurrentLine + @vchVariableName
    FETCH NEXT FROM curVariables INTO @vchVariableName
    IF (@@FETCH_STATUS = 0)
    BEGIN
        SELECT @vchCurrentLine = @vchCurrentLine + ', '
    END
END

CLOSE curVariables
DEALLOCATE curVariables

-- Close the parenthesis and print a GO to end the procedure

SELECT     @vchCurrentLine = @vchCurrentLine + ')'
PRINT      @vchCurrentLine
SELECT     @vchCurrentLine = 'GO'
PRINT      ' '
PRINT      @vchCurrentLine

-- Drop the table

DROP TABLE TempColumnInfo
```

The first thing that this stored procedure does is create a table that will store information about all the columns in the table that the insert stored procedure will be hitting against. Then, information about all the tables is inserted into the temporary table. After the information about the columns is added to the table, the stored procedure opens a cursor that begins building the stored procedure. First, the stored procedure begins by declaring the variables and determining the defaults for the columns. If the column is nullable in the table, the default for the variable will be null. Otherwise, no null value is declared for the variable. After the variables are declared, the stored procedure looks to see whether there's a primary key on the table. If a primary key does exist, the stored procedure will add code that checks to see whether the same value already exists in the table. This code specifies that, if the value does exist in the table, the new stored procedure will return an error and then exit. If there are no duplicates, the new stored procedure will insert the row into the database. After the code for the new stored procedure has been created, this stored procedure performs cleanup operations and exits.

This stored procedure, when run on the authors table, will create the code as seen in Listing 7.7. The syntax for this is as follows:

```
usp_create_insert_proc authors, au_id
```

LISTING 7.7   The Results from Listing 7.6

```
CREATE PROCEDURE usp_insert_authors
@Au_id      id,
@chvAu_lname      varchar(40),
@chvAu_fname      varchar(20),
@chrPhone      char(12),
@chvAddress      varchar(40) = NULL,
@chvCity      varchar(20) = NULL,
@chrState      char(2) = NULL,
@chrZip      char(5) = NULL,
@bitContract      bit

AS

IF @Au_id IN (SELECT au_id FROM authors)
BEGIN
    RAISERROR('Cannot insert a duplicate row in this table.', 0, 1)
    RETURN (100)
END

INSERT INTO      authors
VALUES      (@Au_id, @chvAu_lname, @chvAu_fname, @chrPhone, @chvAddress,
            ➥@chvCity, @chrState, @chrZip, @bitContract)

GO
```

An example of the execution of this stored procedure is as follows:

```
usp_insert_authors '111-11-1111', 'Test', 'Author', '555-555-5555',
                    ➥'123 4th St.', 'Anytown', 'KS', '66789', 1
```

Conclusion

In this chapter, you saw how to use stored procedures to add data to tables within your database. First, you saw an overview of the INSERT command and how to use it with the SELECT and EXECUTE statements. After that, you saw how to use cursors to help you eliminate blocking situations. Last, you saw how to create a stored procedure that will assist you in the creation of INSERT stored procedures.

Creating Stored Procedures that Modify Data

IN THIS CHAPTER

In the previous two chapters, you've seen the ins and outs of creating stored procedures that query and add data to your database tables. In this chapter, you see how to create stored procedures that modify data. You see some pitfalls of creating stored procedures, such as verifying the data that is to be modified and maintaining relationships between tables when you make changes to table keys.

The following subjects are covered in this chapter:

- Verifying data to be modified
- Creating procedures to delete data
- Automating the creation of the code

Verifying the Data to Be Modified

When you add data into your database tables, you frequently check the data that you are adding to ensure that the added data falls in the ranges accepted in your database and your applications. You perform similar steps when you modify data in your database. It is much more important to perform data verification and validation because existing data is often referenced in some way by other tables in the database. If you don't check to see what data is being referenced and how, you can run into major problems. If some piece of data that's being referenced is changed, and you don't check to see whether that data is being referenced, the reference is broken and an orphan is created. An *orphan* is a piece of data in the database that was referenced at one point but isn't referenced any longer. The broken reference makes that piece of data useless in the database.

Of course, the argument can be made that primary key and foreign key relationships can solve this problem. These relationships can maintain the integrity of the data, but they return somewhat cryptic errors to the calling application and the user. Look at the following statement:

```
UPDATE authors
SET   au_id = '112-23-3444'
WHERE au_id = '172-32-1176'
```

The error message returned from this statement is as follows:

```
Server: Msg 547, Level 16, State 1, Line 1
DELETE statement conflicted with COLUMN REFERENCE constraint
      'FK__titleauth__au_id__164452B1'.
The conflict occurred in database 'pubs', table 'titleauthor', column 'au_id'.
The statement has been terminated.
```

As an application developer, you want to create better error messages to pass back to your users. To do this, you must check any tables that reference the table you are changing. To do this, you must know how the data in the tables is stored and how the application uses that data.

The stored procedure in Listing 8.1 performs all these checks and returns better error messages to the calling user or application.

> **CAUTION**
>
> Be extremely careful when implementing the type of code in Listing 8.1. For this code to work, you must remove all foreign keys so that you can make any necessary updates to the key values. Primary/foreign key relationships are a wonderful tool that you can use to ensure that all the data in your tables remains consistent and that you have no orphan records in the tables. The only time that you should consider using this approach is if you are using stored procedures as a security method, as outlined in Chapter 9, "Providing Security for Stored Procedures." With this method, you block your users from accessing the tables in your database directly and allow them to access the tables only through the procedures. If you don't subscribe to this level of security, don't consider using this type of code in your stored procedures.

LISTING 8.1 Update Stored Procedure

```
ALTER TABLE titleauthor
    DROP CONSTRAINT FK__titleauth__au_id__164452B1
GO

CREATE PROCEDURE usp_8_2
    @vchKeyValue    VARCHAR(11) = NULL,
    @vchNewAuID     VARCHAR(11) = '%',
    @vchNewAuLName    VARCHAR(40) = '%',
    @vchNewAuFName    VARCHAR(20) = '%',
    @chrNewPhone    CHAR(12) = '%',
    @vchNewAddress    VARCHAR(40) = '%',
    @vchNewCity    VARCHAR(20) = '%',
    @chrNewState    CHAR(2) = '%',
    @chrNewZip    CHAR(5) = '%',
    @bitNewContract    BIT = NULL
AS

SET NOCOUNT ON

/* Declare the variables */

DECLARE    @vchErrorMessage    VARCHAR(128)
DECLARE @bitUseNewKey        BIT
```

continues

LISTING 8.1   Continued

```
SELECT    @bitUseNewKey = 0

/* Return an error if the user did not provide a key value */

IF (@vchKeyValue = NULL)
BEGIN
    SELECT @vchErrorMessage =
    'A key value must be passed in. The key column for the %s table is %s.'
    RAISERROR(@vchErrorMessage, 12, 1, 'authors', 'au_id')
    RETURN 101
END

/* Check to see if the key value exists */

IF (SELECT COUNT(*) FROM authors WHERE au_id = @vchKeyValue) = 0
BEGIN
    SELECT @vchErrorMessage =
    'The key value passed in was not found in the database.'
    RAISERROR(@vchErrorMessage, 12, 1)
    RETURN 101
END

/* Check the validity of the new value and update the keys if */
/* it is valid */

IF      (@vchNewAuID != '%')
BEGIN
    IF (SELECT COUNT(*) FROM authors WHERE au_id = @vchNewAuID) > 0
    BEGIN
        SELECT @vchErrorMessage =
        'You cannot update the %s column with the %s value.
        ➡The new value already exists in the table.'
        RAISERROR(@vchErrorMessage, 12, 1, 'au_id')
        RETURN 102
    END ELSE
    BEGIN
        BEGIN TRANSACTION

        UPDATE      titleauthor
        SET     au_id = @vchNewAuID
        WHERE       au_id = @vchKeyValue

        UPDATE      authors
        SET     au_id = @vchNewAuID
        WHERE       au_id = @vchKeyValue
```

```
        IF (@@ROWCOUNT) = 0
        BEGIN
            SELECT @vchErrorMessage = 'An error occurred in the update of
                  ➡the %s column of the %s table.'
            RAISERROR(@vchErrorMessage, 12, 1, 'au_id', 'authors')
            ROLLBACK TRANSACTION
            RETURN 103
        END

        SELECT    @bitUseNewKey = 1

        COMMIT TRANSACTION
    END
END

/* Update the last name if it exists */

IF    (@vchNewAuLName != '%')
BEGIN
    IF @bitUseNewKey = 0
    BEGIN
        UPDATE    authors
        SET     au_lname = @vchNewAuLName
        WHERE     au_id = @vchKeyValue
    END ELSE
    BEGIN
        UPDATE    authors
        SET     au_lname = @vchNewAuLName
        WHERE     au_id = @vchNewAuID
    END
END

/* Update the first name if it exists */

IF    (@vchNewAuFName != '%')
BEGIN
    IF @bitUseNewKey = 0
    BEGIN
        UPDATE    authors
        SET     au_fname = @vchNewAuFName
        WHERE     au_id = @vchKeyValue
    END ELSE
    BEGIN
        UPDATE    authors
        SET     au_lname = @vchNewAuFName
        WHERE     au_id = @vchNewAuID
    END
```

8

CREATING STORED
PROCEDURES THAT
MODIFY DATA

continues

LISTING 8.1   Continued

```
END

/* Update the phone number if it exists */

IF    (@chrNewPhone != '%')
BEGIN
    IF @bitUseNewKey = 0
    BEGIN
        UPDATE    authors
        SET    phone = @chrNewPhone
        WHERE    au_id = @vchKeyValue
    END ELSE
    BEGIN
        UPDATE    authors
        SET    phone = @chrNewPhone
        WHERE    au_id = @vchNewAuID
    END
END

/* Update the address if it exists */

IF    (@vchNewAddress != '%')
BEGIN
    IF @bitUseNewKey = 0
    BEGIN
        UPDATE    authors
        SET    address = @vchNewAddress
        WHERE    au_id = @vchKeyValue
    END ELSE
    BEGIN
        UPDATE    authors
        SET    address = @vchNewAddress
        WHERE    au_id = @vchNewAuID
    END
END

/* Update the city if it exists */

IF    (@vchNewCity != '%')
BEGIN
    IF @bitUseNewKey = 0
    BEGIN
        UPDATE    authors
        SET    city = @vchNewCity
        WHERE    au_id = @vchKeyValue
    END ELSE
```

```
    BEGIN
        UPDATE    authors
        SET     city = @vchNewCity
        WHERE    au_id = @vchNewAuID
    END
END

/* Update the state if it exists */

IF    (@chrNewState != '%')
BEGIN
    IF @bitUseNewKey = 0
    BEGIN
        UPDATE    authors
        SET     state = @chrNewState
        WHERE    au_id = @vchKeyValue
    END ELSE
    BEGIN
        UPDATE    authors
        SET     state = @chrNewState
        WHERE    au_id = @vchNewAuID
    END
END

/* Update the zip if it exists */

IF    (@chrNewZip != '%')
BEGIN
    IF @bitUseNewKey = 0
    BEGIN
        UPDATE    authors
        SET     zip = @chrNewZip
        WHERE    au_id = @vchKeyValue
    END ELSE
    BEGIN
        UPDATE    authors
        SET     zip = @chrNewZip
        WHERE    au_id = @vchNewAuID
    END
END

/* Update the contract if it exists */

IF    (@bitNewContract != NULL)
BEGIN
    IF @bitUseNewKey = 0
```

8

CREATING STORED
PROCEDURES THAT
MODIFY DATA

continues

LISTING 8.1   Continued

```
BEGIN
    UPDATE     authors
    SET        contract = @bitNewContract
    WHERE      au_id = @vchKeyValue
END ELSE
BEGIN
    UPDATE     authors
    SET        contract = @bitNewContract
    WHERE      au_id = @vchNewAuID
    END
END
```

The first portion of this script drops the foreign key from the `titleauthor` table. If this key remains on the table, this stored procedure won't work. The first thing that the stored procedure does is declare all the parameters that can be passed in. All these parameters have default values of % or NULL. After the parameters are declared, any other variable needed during the execution of the stored procedure is declared. The procedure first checks that a key value was passed in. This key value is the value that's the unique value in the table—in this case, the author ID. Next, the stored procedure checks to see whether the passed-in key value is valid and is contained in the `authors` table. After the key value is determined to be valid, the stored procedure checks to see whether a new author ID is being passed in. If it is, the stored procedure makes several checks:

1. Sees whether the value to which the author ID is being changed already exists in the table.

2. If it exists, the stored procedure returns an error and then exits. If the value doesn't exist, the stored procedure updates the `authors` and `titleauthor` tables.

3. This portion of the stored procedure maintains the relationships between the tables. If the author ID is changed, the stored procedure changes a flag that is checked later in the stored procedure to see which author ID to use.

4. Sees whether any of the other parameters contain values. If they do, the procedure updates each value in the table.

You can modify this stored procedure for use in any table. If you have multiple key values in a table, you have to perform multiple checks on those values to make sure that they are contained in the table and any other tables that are referenced.

Creating Procedures to Delete Data

As with procedures that update data, you should check to see whether there are relationships that need to be checked and maintained in the database. There are two ways to do this:

- Use triggers that are fired when a delete statement is run against the table. These triggers can then perform the required deletions in other tables. There can be issues with this approach, especially when the delete statement recursively fires many other triggers. For more information on this, see Chapter 15, "Writing Triggers."

- Use stored procedures to perform this functionality. This way, you can delete any other rows from other tables referenced by the table from which you are deleting. Listing 8.2 shows the code for this type of procedure.

LISTING 8.2   Delete Stored Procedure

```
CREATE PROCEDURE usp_8_3
    @vchKeyValue     VARCHAR(11) = NULL
AS

SET NOCOUNT ON

DECLARE     @vchErrorMessage     VARCHAR(128)

IF (@vchKeyValue = NULL)
BEGIN
    SELECT @vchErrorMessage = 'A key value must be passed in.
                        ➥The key column for the %s table is %s.'
    RAISERROR(@vchErrorMessage, 12, 1, 'authors', 'au_id')
    RETURN 101
END

IF (SELECT COUNT(*) FROM authors WHERE au_id = @vchKeyValue) = 0
BEGIN
    SELECT @vchErrorMessage = 'The key value passed in was not
                        ➥found in the database.'
    RAISERROR(@vchErrorMessage, 12, 1)
    RETURN 102
END

BEGIN TRAN

    DELETE     titleauthor
    WHERE     au_id = @vchKeyValue
```

continues

LISTING 8.2   Continued

```
DELETE    authors
WHERE     au_id = @vchKeyValue

IF (SELECT @@ROWCOUNT) = 0
BEGIN
    SELECT @vchErrorMessage = 'An error occurred in the delete from the
                           ➥ %s table.'
    RAISERROR(@vchErrorMessage, 12, 1, 'authors')
    ROLLBACK TRANSACTION
    RETURN 103
END

COMMIT TRANSACTION
```

Like the previous stored procedure, this procedure requires that the foreign key relationship between the authors and titleauthor tables is dropped. It starts by declaring the parameters that can be passed in. For this procedure, this is the key value in the table. The procedure then checks to see whether a key value has been passed in and that the key value exists in the database. If this checks out, the stored procedure deletes from both the authors and titleauthor tables.

Automating Code Creation

In the previous chapter, I gave you code that you can run to create a stored procedure that creates a stored procedure that inserts data into the table that you specify. The stored procedure in Listing 8.3 creates the code that can be run to create a stored procedure that updates any table that you pass in.

LISTING 8.3   Creating an Update Procedure

```
CREATE  PROC usp_create_update_proc
    @vchTable varchar(30),
    @vchKey varchar(30)
AS

SET NOCOUNT ON

/* Declare the variable */
DECLARE    @vchName      varchar(30)
DECLARE    @intType      int
DECLARE    @vchNameType     varchar(255)
DECLARE    @vchPrint     varchar(255)
```

```
DECLARE    @vchName2       varchar(30)
DECLARE    @vchNameType2 varchar(255)
DECLARE    @vchMessage     varchar(255)
DECLARE    @intReturnVal int
DECLARE    @vchDBName      varchar(30)

/*  Check to see if the key value and the table exist */

IF NOT EXISTS(
    SELECT    *
    FROM     sysobjects so INNER JOIN syscolumns sc ON (so.id = sc.id)
    WHERE     so.name = @vchTable AND
        sc.name = @vchKey)
BEGIN
    SELECT    @intReturnVal = 1
    SELECT    @vchMessage = 'Either table ''%s'' or column ''%s''' +
              ➥' does not exist in the database ''%s''.'
    SELECT    @vchDBName = DB_NAME()
    RAISERROR (@vchMessage, 10, -1, @vchTable, @vchKey, @vchDBName)
    RETURN     @intReturnVal
END

/*  Gather information on all of the columns */

DECLARE crColumnTypes SCROLL CURSOR FOR
    SELECT    sc.name AS name,
        TYPE_NAME(xusertype) +
        CASE
            WHEN sc.type IN (37,45,39,47) AND xusertype = xtype
                THEN '(' + RTRIM(CONVERT(varchar(10),sc.length)) + ') '
            WHEN sc.type IN (55, 63)
                THEN '(' + RTRIM(CONVERT(varchar(10),sc.prec)) + ', ' +
                ➥RTRIM(CONVERT(varchar(10),sc.scale)) + ') '
            ELSE ' '
        END +
        CASE sc.status & 8
            WHEN 0 THEN ''
            WHEN 8 THEN ' = NULL'
        END AS type
    FROM     syscolumns sc
    WHERE     id = OBJECT_ID(@vchTable)
    ORDER BY  sc.colid

DECLARE crColumns SCROLL CURSOR FOR
    SELECT  sc.name AS name,
        CASE
```

8

CREATING STORED
PROCEDURES THAT
MODIFY DATA

continues

LISTING 8.3   Continued

```
            WHEN st2.type IN (37,45) THEN
                CASE
                WHEN sc.status & 8 = 8 THEN 1
                WHEN sc.status & 8 = 0 THEN 8
                END
            WHEN st2.type IN (39,47) THEN
                CASE
                WHEN sc.status & 8 = 8 THEN 2
                WHEN sc.status & 8 = 0 THEN 9
                END
            WHEN st2.type IN (38, 106, 108, 109, 110) THEN 3
            WHEN st2.type = 111 THEN 4
            WHEN st2.type IN (48, 52, 55, 56, 59, 60, 62, 63, 122) THEN 5
            WHEN st2.type = 50 THEN 6
            WHEN st2.type IN (58, 61) THEN 7
            END AS type
    FROM    syscolumns sc
        JOIN systypes st2 ON sc.type=st2.type
    WHERE   id = OBJECT_ID(@vchTable)
    AND     st2.usertype < 100
    AND     st2.name NOT IN ('sysname','timestamp')
    ORDER BY  sc.colid

/* Begin outputting the stored procedure */

SELECT    @vchPrint='CREATE PROC usp_update_' + @vchTable

PRINT    @vchPrint

OPEN crColumnTypes

/* Return the information from the cursor about the datatypes */

FETCH NEXT FROM crColumnTypes INTO @vchName, @vchNameType
IF (@@FETCH_STATUS <> -1)
BEGIN
    WHILE 1 = 1
    BEGIN
        FETCH RELATIVE 0 FROM crColumnTypes INTO @vchName, @vchNameType
        FETCH RELATIVE 1 FROM crColumnTypes INTO @vchName2, @vchNameType2
        SELECT    @vchName2 = @vchName,
            @vchNameType2 = @vchNameType
        SELECT    @vchPrint = '@' + @vchName2 + SPACE(34 -
                ➥DATALENGTH(@vchName2)) + @vchNameType2
```

```
            IF (@@FETCH_STATUS <> -1)
            BEGIN
                SELECT @vchPrint = '      ' + @vchPrint + ', '
                PRINT @vchPrint
            END
            ELSE
            BEGIN
                SELECT @vchPrint = '      ' + @vchPrint
                PRINT @vchPrint
            BREAK
            END
        END
END

CLOSE crColumnTypes

/* Continue outputting data */

PRINT    'AS'
PRINT    ''

/* Output information on the column types */

OPEN crColumnTypes
FETCH NEXT FROM crColumnTypes INTO @vchName, @vchNameType

WHILE (@@FETCH_STATUS <> -1)
BEGIN
    IF (@@FETCH_STATUS <> -2)
    BEGIN
        SELECT      @vchPrint = 'DECLARE      @' + @vchName + '2' +
                    ➥SPACE(33 - DATALENGTH(@vchName)) + @vchNameType
        IF (CHARINDEX('=', @vchPrint))<> 0
        BEGIN
            SELECT      @vchPrint = LEFT(@vchPrint, DATALENGTH(@vchPrint) -7)
        END
        PRINT      @vchPrint
    END
    FETCH NEXT FROM crColumnTypes INTO @vchName, @vchNameType
END

CLOSE crColumnTypes
```

continues

LISTING 8.3 Continued

```
/* Print control information */

PRINT    'DECLARE    @intReturnVal                    int'
PRINT    'DECLARE    @vchMessage                      varchar(255)'
PRINT    'DECLARE    @tinCount                        tinyint'
PRINT    ''
PRINT    'SELECT     @intReturnVal = 0'
PRINT    'SELECT '

/* Print the variable declaration information */

OPEN crColumnTypes

FETCH NEXT FROM crColumnTypes INTO @vchName, @vchNameType
IF (@@FETCH_STATUS <> -1)
BEGIN
    WHILE 1 = 1
    BEGIN
        FETCH RELATIVE 0 FROM crColumnTypes INTO @vchName, @vchNameType
        FETCH RELATIVE 1 FROM crColumnTypes INTO @vchName2, @vchNameType2
        SELECT    @vchName2 = @vchName,
            @vchNameType2 = @vchNameType
        SELECT    @vchPrint = '    @' + @vchName2 + '2 = ' + @vchName2
        IF (@@FETCH_STATUS <> -1)
        BEGIN
            SELECT    @vchPrint = @vchPrint + ','
            PRINT     @vchPrint
        END
        ELSE
        BEGIN
            PRINT     @vchPrint
            BREAK
        END
    END
END

CLOSE crColumnTypes

SELECT    @vchPrint = 'FROM     ' + @vchTable
PRINT     @vchPrint
SELECT    @vchPrint = 'WHERE    ' + @vchKey + ' = @' + @vchKey
PRINT     @vchPrint
PRINT     ''
PRINT     'IF @@ROWCOUNT = 0'
```

```
PRINT       'BEGIN'
PRINT       '    SELECT @intReturnVal = -1'
SELECT      @vchPrint= '    SELECT @vchMessage = ''' + @vchTable +
            ➥' with Id of '' + ' + '
            ➥RTRIM(CONVERT(varchar(10), @' + @vchKey + ')) +
            ➥' + ''' was not found.'''
PRINT       @vchPrint
PRINT       '    PRINT @vchMessage'
PRINT       '    RETURN @intReturnVal'
PRINT       'END'
PRINT       ''
PRINT       'SELECT    @tinCount = 0'
PRINT       ''
PRINT       'BEGIN TRAN'
PRINT       ''

/* Comparison information on the different columns */

OPEN crColumns

FETCH NEXT FROM crColumns INTO @vchName, @intType

WHILE (@@FETCH_STATUS <> -1)
BEGIN
    IF (@@FETCH_STATUS <> -2)
    BEGIN
        IF @vchName <> @vchKey
        BEGIN
        IF @intType = 1
            SELECT    @vchPrint = 'IF COALESCE(@' + @vchName + '2, 0x0)
                      ➥<> COALESCE(@' + @vchName + ', 0x0)'
        ELSE IF @intType = 2
            SELECT    @vchPrint = 'IF COALESCE(@' + @vchName + '2, '''')
                      ➥ <> COALESCE(@' + @vchName + ', '''')'
        ELSE IF @intType = 3
            SELECT    @vchPrint = 'IF COALESCE(@' + @vchName + '2, 0)
                      ➥ <> COALESCE(@' + @vchName + ', 0)'
        ELSE IF @intType = 4
            SELECT     @vchPrint = 'IF COALESCE(@' + @vchName + '2,
                       ➥''1/1/1900'') <> COALESCE(@' + @vchName + ',
                       ➥''1/1/1900'')'
        ELSE
            SELECT    @vchPrint = 'IF @' + @vchName + '2 <> @' + @vchName
            PRINT     @vchPrint
            PRINT     'BEGIN'
            PRINT     '    SELECT    @tinCount = @tinCount + 1'
```

continues

8

CREATING STORED
PROCEDURES THAT
MODIFY DATA

LISTING 8.3   Continued

```
            SELECT    @vchPrint = '    UPDATE    ' + @vchTable
            PRINT     @vchPrint
            SELECT    @vchPrint = '    SET    ' + @vchName + ' = @' + @vchName
            PRINT     @vchPrint
            SELECT    @vchPrint = '    WHERE    ' + @vchKey + ' = @' + @vchKey
            PRINT     @vchPrint
            PRINT     'END'
            PRINT     ' '
        END
    END
    FETCH NEXT FROM crColumns INTO @vchName, @intType
END

CLOSE crColumns
DEALLOCATE crColumns
DEALLOCATE crColumnTypes

/* Check for changes.  If none exist, report that. */

PRINT 'IF @tinCount = 0'
PRINT 'BEGIN'
PRINT '    ROLLBACK TRAN'
PRINT '    SELECT    @intReturnVal = 1'
PRINT '    SELECT    @vchMessage =
                ➥''No changes were detected. No changes were made.'''
PRINT '    PRINT    @vchMessage'
PRINT '    RETURN    @intReturnVal'
PRINT 'END'
PRINT 'ELSE'
PRINT 'BEGIN'
PRINT '    COMMIT TRAN'
PRINT '    RETURN @intReturnVal'
PRINT 'END'

SET NOCOUNT OFF
```

This code really gathers only one set of information in the database in which the stored procedure is run—the column names and associated types from the syscolumns table. The rest of the stored procedure is spent looping through that information, formatting and outputting it in a way that creates the code for the stored procedure. Listing 8.4 shows the code created by the stored procedure in Listing 8.3. This procedure was created by running Listing 8.3 on the authors table.

LISTING 8.4   The Results from Listing 8.3

```
CREATE PROC usp_update_authors
    @au_id                      id ,
    @au_lname                   varchar(40),
    @au_fname                   varchar(20),
    @phone                      char(12),
    @address                    varchar(40) = NULL,
    @city                       varchar(20) = NULL,
    @state                      char(2) = NULL,
    @zip                        char(5) = NULL,
    @contract                   bit
AS

DECLARE     @au_id2                     id
DECLARE     @au_lname2                  varchar(40)
DECLARE     @au_fname2                  varchar(20)
DECLARE     @phone2                     char(12)
DECLARE     @address2                   varchar(40)
DECLARE     @city2                      varchar(20)
DECLARE     @state2                     char(2)
DECLARE     @zip2                       char(5)
DECLARE     @contract2                  bit
DECLARE     @intReturnVal               int
DECLARE     @vchMessage                 varchar(255)
DECLARE     @tinCount                   tinyint

SELECT      @intReturnVal = 0
SELECT
    @au_id2 = au_id,
    @au_lname2 = au_lname,
    @au_fname2 = au_fname,
    @phone2 = phone,
    @address2 = address,
    @city2 = city,
    @state2 = state,
    @zip2 = zip,
    @contract2 = contract
FROM    authors
WHERE    au_id = @au_id

IF @@ROWCOUNT = 0
BEGIN
    SELECT @intReturnVal = -1
    SELECT @vchMessage = 'authors with Id of ' +
        ➡RTRIM(CONVERT(varchar(10), @au_id)) + ' was not found.'
```

continues

LISTING 8.4   Continued

```
    PRINT   @vchMessage
    RETURN @intReturnVal
END


SELECT    @tinCount = 0

BEGIN TRAN

IF @au_lname2 <> @au_lname
BEGIN
    SELECT  @tinCount = @tinCount + 1
    UPDATE  authors
    SET     au_lname = @au_lname
    WHERE   au_id = @au_id
END


IF @au_lname2 <> @au_lname
BEGIN
    SELECT  @tinCount = @tinCount + 1
    UPDATE  authors
    SET     au_lname = @au_lname
    WHERE   au_id = @au_id
END


IF @au_lname2 <> @au_lname
BEGIN
    SELECT  @tinCount = @tinCount + 1
    UPDATE  authors
    SET     au_lname = @au_lname
    WHERE   au_id = @au_id
END


IF @au_fname2 <> @au_fname
BEGIN
    SELECT  @tinCount = @tinCount + 1
    UPDATE  authors
    SET     au_fname = @au_fname
    WHERE   au_id = @au_id
END


IF @au_fname2 <> @au_fname
BEGIN
    SELECT  @tinCount = @tinCount + 1
    UPDATE  authors
```

```
    SET     au_fname = @au_fname
    WHERE   au_id = @au_id
END

IF @au_fname2 <> @au_fname
BEGIN
    SELECT  @tinCount = @tinCount + 1
    UPDATE  authors
    SET     au_fname = @au_fname
    WHERE   au_id = @au_id
END

IF @phone2 <> @phone
BEGIN
    SELECT  @tinCount = @tinCount + 1
    UPDATE  authors
    SET     phone = @phone
    WHERE   au_id = @au_id
END

IF @phone2 <> @phone
BEGIN
    SELECT  @tinCount = @tinCount + 1
    UPDATE  authors
    SET     phone = @phone
    WHERE   au_id = @au_id
END

IF COALESCE(@address2, '') <> COALESCE(@address, '')
BEGIN
    SELECT  @tinCount = @tinCount + 1
    UPDATE  authors
    SET     address = @address
    WHERE   au_id = @au_id
END

IF COALESCE(@address2, '') <> COALESCE(@address, '')
BEGIN
    SELECT  @tinCount = @tinCount + 1
    UPDATE  authors
    SET     address = @address
    WHERE   au_id = @au_id
END
```

8

CREATING STORED
PROCEDURES THAT
MODIFY DATA

continues

LISTING 8.4   Continued

```
IF COALESCE(@address2, '') <> COALESCE(@address, '')
BEGIN
    SELECT  @tinCount = @tinCount + 1
    UPDATE  authors
    SET     address = @address
    WHERE   au_id = @au_id
END

IF COALESCE(@city2, '') <> COALESCE(@city, '')
BEGIN
    SELECT  @tinCount = @tinCount + 1
    UPDATE  authors
    SET     city = @city
    WHERE   au_id = @au_id
END

IF COALESCE(@city2, '') <> COALESCE(@city, '')
BEGIN
    SELECT  @tinCount = @tinCount + 1
    UPDATE  authors
    SET     city = @city
    WHERE   au_id = @au_id
END

IF COALESCE(@city2, '') <> COALESCE(@city, '')
BEGIN
    SELECT  @tinCount = @tinCount + 1
    UPDATE  authors
    SET     city = @city
    WHERE   au_id = @au_id
END

IF COALESCE(@state2, '') <> COALESCE(@state, '')
BEGIN
    SELECT  @tinCount = @tinCount + 1
    UPDATE  authors
    SET     state = @state
    WHERE   au_id = @au_id
END

IF COALESCE(@state2, '') <> COALESCE(@state, '')
BEGIN
    SELECT  @tinCount = @tinCount + 1
    UPDATE  authors
```

```
    SET      state = @state
    WHERE    au_id = @au_id
END

IF COALESCE(@state2, '') <> COALESCE(@state, '')
BEGIN
    SELECT   @tinCount = @tinCount + 1
    UPDATE   authors
    SET      state = @state
    WHERE    au_id = @au_id
END

IF COALESCE(@zip2, '') <> COALESCE(@zip, '')
BEGIN
    SELECT   @tinCount = @tinCount + 1
    UPDATE   authors
    SET      zip = @zip
    WHERE    au_id = @au_id
END

IF COALESCE(@zip2, '') <> COALESCE(@zip, '')
BEGIN
    SELECT   @tinCount = @tinCount + 1
    UPDATE   authors
    SET      zip = @zip
    WHERE    au_id = @au_id
END

IF COALESCE(@zip2, '') <> COALESCE(@zip, '')
BEGIN
    SELECT   @tinCount = @tinCount + 1
    UPDATE   authors
    SET      zip = @zip
    WHERE    au_id = @au_id
END

IF @contract2 <> @contract
BEGIN
    SELECT   @tinCount = @tinCount + 1
    UPDATE   authors
    SET      contract = @contract
    WHERE    au_id = @au_id
END
```

8

CREATING STORED
PROCEDURES THAT
MODIFY DATA

continues

LISTING 8.4   Continued

```
IF @tinCount = 0
BEGIN
    ROLLBACK TRAN
    SELECT  @intReturnVal = 1
    SELECT  @vchMessage =     'No changes were detected. No changes were made.'
    PRINT   @vchMessage
    RETURN  @intReturnVal
END
ELSE
BEGIN
    COMMIT TRAN
    RETURN @intReturnVal
END
```

This stored procedure checks all the passed-in parameters to see whether they are already contained in the table. If the value is there, no data is changed. Otherwise, the stored procedure makes the change and then exits.

Conclusion

In this chapter, you learned to create a stored procedure that modifies data in your database tables. First, you saw how important it is to maintain relationships between your database tables. Then, you saw how to create a stored procedure that updates tables. This stored procedure checks all relationships on related tables and then makes the changes. Next, you learned to create a stored procedure that deletes data from your table. As does the first procedure, this procedure checks relationships and deletes data based on that. Last, you saw how to create a stored procedure that generates the code that makes a stored procedure that updates the table that you pass in.

Security and Advanced Procedure Development

IN THIS PART

Providing Security for Stored Procedures

IN THIS CHAPTER

Most developers start to think about security after they design and code their applications. Although providing security for your applications is always important, starting to do so after you design the application isn't the best time. You should start thinking about security during the design process. If you start early, your application will be designed in a way that enables you to provide security easily. This chapter concentrates on providing security for your application by covering the following points:

- SQL Server security
- Stored procedures as a security mechanism
- Application security
- Ownership chains

Security Basics

There are really three ways to provide security for your applications:

- You can rely on SQL Server to provide security for your application. This method is one of the simplest and allows you to have a single place to manage the security.
- You can use stored procedures as a security mechanism. With this method, you can create stored procedures that perform all the modifications to the tables in your database. You then apply security to the stored procedures.
- You can use a special security model in which you specify an application security context. This forces all your users to use a specific application to access the data. No other application works.

SQL Server Security

As a part of any real relational database management system, the ability to control who has access to what data is very important. There is certain data that you want only a couple of people to see. Whether it's company confidential information such as product formulas and client lists or HR data such as salaries, you have to be able to control who sees what. SQL Server enables you to do this through the use of logins, users, roles, and permissions.

Logins

A login is the first step to gaining access to a SQL Server. A login ID is the credential you must supply to the SQL Server when you try to establish a connection. If the SQL Server can't verify the supplied login ID, the connection is refused and the person trying to access the server is rejected.

The process of logging in to the server is known as *authentication*. Two types of authentication can be used with SQL Server 2000:

- **SQL Server Authentication**—With SQL Server authentication, someone in the sysadmin fixed server role must create a login ID for every user who will connect to the server. In this case, the person logging in has to supply a login and password every time he needs to connect to the SQL Server. This login ID might not be related to the Windows NT user ID used to log in to the network.

- **Windows NT Authentication**—With Windows NT authentication, the user trying to access the server doesn't have to pass in a user ID and password. In this case, a member of the sysadmin fixed server role must specify the usernames or group names of the Windows NT resources that have access to the server. The Windows NT user or group account controls access to the SQL Server. If a user hasn't successfully logged in to the Windows NT network, any connection he attempts to make to the server is refused. In this case, the SQL Server doesn't have anything to do with the authentication of users. It relies on Windows NT to provide all that.

If you've installed SQL Server on a Windows NT server, two options are available to you for security modes:

- **Windows NT Authentication Mode**—With Windows NT Authentication mode, only Windows NT Authentication is allowed. SQL Server user IDs aren't allowed.

- **Mixed Authentication Mode**—With Mixed Authentication, both SQL Server Authentication and Windows NT Authentication can be used.

If SQL Server has been installed on a Windows 95/98 machine, only SQL Server authentication is available.

Users

After a user is authenticated into the server, he or she can do very little unless a member of the db_owner fixed database role has assigned a user ID in one of the databases on the server to the login ID that was used to authenticate into the database. A user ID defines a user in the context of the database and is mapped to a login ID. User IDs are unique only within the context of a single database. Because of this, it might be possible to have a user called MyUserID that is assigned to one login ID in the pubs database and another user called MyUserID that is assigned to a different login ID in the Northwind database. Under normal circumstances, the login ID and the user ID are the same, but it's not required.

All login IDs must be associated with a user ID in a database before the user who connected with that login ID can access any of the objects in the database. If a login hasn't been assigned to a user ID in a database, the user is associated with the guest login in the database, if one exists. By default, a guest account doesn't exist in any database on the server.

Roles

The concept of SQL Server roles was introduced in SQL Server 7.0. Roles are basically the same thing as groups were in previous versions of the software. The primary functionality that a role provides is the ability to collect users in functional and logical groups and then assign permissions to the collections instead of individual users. Four types of roles are available to you on the server:

- **Predefined Server Roles**—These roles are created when SQL Server is installed and provide a way to assign server-wide permissions to users.

- **Predefined Database Roles**—These roles are created whenever a new database is created. These roles provide a way to assign permission to users at a database level.

- **The Public Role**—The public group is a special group that's created in each database on the server and is used to create a default set of permissions for all users.

- **Custom Roles**—Custom roles are roles that you create and to which you assign permissions. These are usually functional and logical groupings of users. For example, you might group all users in the Accounting department into one role because they probably all need the same access in a database.

Predefined Server Roles

When you set up SQL Server, several server roles are automatically created so that you can offload some of the system administration tasks to other users. These roles can be extremely powerful and you should be very careful when using them. Novice users assigned to these roles can cause havoc on the server if they attempt to perform the wrong operation at the wrong time. You can use seven predefined server roles:

- sysadmin—Members of this server role can perform any action on the server. This is the most powerful of all the server roles and is analogous to the sa account in previous versions of SQL Server.

- serveradmin—Members of this role can perform any configuration to server-wide settings.

- setupadmin—Members of this server role can add and remove linked servers and execute some system stored procedures, such as sp_serveroption.

- securityadmin—Members of this group can manage SQL Server logins.

- processadmin—Members of this group can manage any process that's running on the SQL Server. Membership in this group allows users to run commands such as KILL.

- dbcreator—This server group has the rights to create databases on the server.

- diskadmin—This server group has the rights to create and manage disk files.

Predefined Database Roles

As with the predefined server roles, SQL Server also creates several predefined database roles in every database that you create. Some of these roles enable you to offload administrative duties to other users, whereas others enable you to assign permissions on all objects in the database. There are nine predefined server roles that you can use:

- db_owner—Members of this group are considered to be the database owner. These users can perform the activities of all database roles, as well as other maintenance and configuration activities in the database.
- db_accessadmin—Membership in this group enables the user to add and remove Windows NT and SQL Server users in the database.
- db_datareader—The members of this group can see all data from all user tables in the database.
- db_datawriter—The members of this group have permission to add, change, and delete data from all user tables in the database.
- db_ddladmin—Membership in this group enables a user to add, modify, and drop objects in the database.
- db_securityadmin—The members of this group can manage roles and members of SQL Server database roles, and can manage statement and object permissions in the database.
- db_backupoperator—The members in this role have permissions to back up the database.
- db_denydatareader—Members in this group can't see any data in the database at all.
- db_denydatawriter—Members in this group have no permissions whatsoever to change data in the database.

The Public Role

The public role is a special database role, of which every user in the database is a member. This role is created in every database. As administrator, you can't make any changes to the properties of the public role, and you can't add or remove users from that role.

The usefulness of the public role comes when you need to supply a default set of permissions that all users have. For example, if you want every user in the database to have SELECT permissions on a specific table, assign those permissions to the public role and all users have those permissions unless their accounts specifically revoke them.

Custom Roles

Custom roles are roles that you create at a database level. As mentioned previously, this type of role is used to group the users of your applications into logical collections. This enables you to assign permissions to all the users in that role at the same time by assigning permissions to the

9

role instead of the users. When a new user is added to the system, all you have to do is add the new user to the corresponding group. In this way, you don't have to worry about assigning permissions to individual users. A few rules apply to custom database roles:

- Custom database roles are created within the context of a database and can't span across multiple databases.
- Users can't belong to more than one custom database role at a time.
- Custom roles can contain Windows NT login IDs, SQL Server login IDs, and other SQL Server roles.

Permissions

You assign permissions to allow users to do some action at either the server or database level. Three types of permissions are available in SQL Server. Two of these types, statement and object permissions, are assigned to users either at a server level or at a database level. The third type, implied permissions, are available only when you add users to specific groups on the server.

Statement Permissions

Statement permissions are usually given only to users who need the ability to create or modify objects within the database, perform database backups, or perform transaction log backups. These types of permissions are very powerful and, under normal circumstances, there are very few people who need to be assigned these permissions. Usually, only database developers and any user who is assisting with the administration of the server requires any statement permissions. It's important to realize that all these permissions are assigned at the database level, and it's not possible to have permissions that span multiple databases. The statement permissions include the following:

- CREATE DATABASE—Users assigned this permission can create new databases on the server. This permission resides only in the master database.
- CREATE DEFAULT—Users assigned this permission can create defaults in the current database.
- CREATE PROCEDURE—This permission enables users to create stored procedures in the current database.
- CREATE RULE—This permission enables users to create rules in the current database.
- CREATE TABLE—Users who have this permission can create tables in the current database.
- CREATE VIEW—This permission enables users to create views in the current database.

- BACKUP DATABASE—This permission enables users to create backups of the database on which they have been given the permission.
- BACKUP LOG—This permission enables users to create backups of the transaction log of the database on which they have been given the permission.

The statement-level permissions rarely have to be assigned. This is because the predefined server and database roles enable you to provide the same functionality by simply assigning a user to a role.

Object Permissions

Object permissions enable users to access and work with preexisting objects in the database. Without these permissions, your users wouldn't be able to use any of the objects in the database. The available object permissions are as follows:

- SELECT is assigned to a user on a specific table in the database and enables the user to view any of the data stored in that table.
- INSERT is assigned to a user on a specific table in the database and enables the user to add new data to that table.
- UPDATE is assigned to a user on a specific table in the database and enables the user to modify existing data in that table.
- DELETE is assigned to a user on a specific table in the database and enables the user to delete data from that table.
- EXECUTE is assigned to a user on a stored procedure and enables the user to execute the stored procedure.
- REFERENCES enables a user to link two tables by using a primary key/foreign key relationship. Under normal circumstances, your users won't have to use this type of permission because the database developer predefines the primary key/foreign key relationships.

Implied Permissions

Implied permissions are assigned to users when they are added to any of the predefined system and database roles. These roles enable the administrator to add users without worrying about individually assigning them permissions.

Permission States

When working with SQL Server permissions, a permission can be in three states for a specific user or role. These states determine whether a user can perform the specific function that the permission specifies.

9

SECURITY FOR
STORED
PROCEDURES

> **NOTE**
>
> When permissions are granted or revoked to a role, the users in that role inherit those permissions. Even if a user has been granted or revoked a permission directly, if he is a member of a role that has been revoked or granted that same permission, the role permission overrides the direct permission.

Deny

A denied permission is the strongest permission level. A permission that has been denied to a user, no matter the level, denies the user access to it even if the user is granted access at a different level.

Revoke

When a permission is revoked, it simply removes the deny or grant that was previously applied to that permission for that user. If that same permission is granted or denied at another level, it still applies.

Grant

A granted permission removes the previous denied or revoked permission and allows the user to perform the function. If the same permission is denied at any other level, the user can't perform the function. If the permission is revoked at another level, the user can perform the function.

Assigning Permissions

There are two ways to assign permissions to a user. The simplest way to do this is to use Enterprise Manager. Because this book is targeted at more advanced users, I assume that you already know how to do that. Instead, in this section, you learn how to assign permissions from within a query tool, such as Query Analyzer. To assign permissions using Query Analyzer, you use the GRANT, REVOKE, and DENY commands. The syntaxes for these commands are as follows:

```
GRANT permission_name TO account_name [WITH GRANT OPTION]

REVOKE [GRANT OPTION FOR] permission_name FROM account_name [CASCADE]

DENY permission_name TO account_name [CASCADE]
```

Table 9.1 describes the options available for each command.

TABLE 9.1   GRANT, REVOKE, and DENY Options

Option	Description
permission_name	The name of the permission that you are going to GRANT, REVOKE, or DENY.
account_name	The account that you are going to GRANT TO, REVOKE FROM, or DENY TO.
[WITH GRANT OPTION]	Used with the GRANT statement only. This means that the user to whom this is assigned can assign this permission to other users.
[GRANT OPTION FOR]	Used with the REVOKE statement only. This removes the ability to regrant permissions to other users.
[CASCADE]	Used with both the DENY and REVOKE statements. If you specify the CASCADE option, any user granted permissions by the user from whom the permission is being removed also has his permissions removed.

Adding Logins and Users

There are several ways to add logins and users to a SQL Server. The easiest way is to add them by using Enterprise Manager. It's assumed that you already know how to do this. In this section, I discuss adding logins and users by using stored procedures from within SQL Query Analyzer.

To add a user who will be authenticated using Windows NT Authentication, you use the sp_grantlogin system stored procedure. The syntax of the sp_grantlogin system stored procedure is as follows:

```
sp_grantlogin [@loginame =] 'login'
```

In this syntax, the option is the name of the Windows NT user, plus the domain in which the user is contained. For example, if you want to add a user named Joe from the Accounting domain, you would execute the following:

```
sp_grantlogin 'Accounting\Joe'
```

If your server is set up to allow SQL Server authentication, you can add a SQL Server user by using the sp_addlogin system stored procedure. The syntax for this procedure is as follows:

```
sp_addlogin [@loginame =] 'login'
    [,[@passwd =] 'password']
    [,[@defdb =] 'database']
    [,[@deflanguage =] 'language']
    [,[@sid =] 'sid']
    [,[@encryptopt =] 'encryption_option']
```

9

SECURITY FOR
STORED
PROCEDURES

Table 9.2 lists the options for this procedure.

TABLE 9.2   sp_addlogin Options

Option	Description
@loginame = 'login'	The name of the login ID that you are adding to the server.
@passwd = 'password'	The password for the login ID you are adding.
@defdb = 'database'	The default database for the user you are adding. A default database is one the user will automatically use when he logs in to the server. Even if you set this, you still must assign the user permission to use that database.
@deflanguage = 'language'	The default language for the user. It's possible to have multiple languages installed on the server, allowing the user to receive error and informational messages from SQL Server in her own language.
@sid = 'sid'	A security ID number that can be assigned to the user. This option isn't normally used.
@encryptopt = 'encryption_option'	Tells SQL Server whether to encrypt the password that you pass into it. It's not a good plan to not encrypt the passwords. This option isn't normally used.

For example, to add a user named Bill to the database with a password of thecat and a default database of Northwind, you execute the following:

```
sp_adduser 'Bill', 'thecat', 'Northwind'
```

After you add a login to the server, you must then add a user ID to the databases that the person using that login ID may access. Without this, the user won't be able to access the databases. To do this, you use the sp_grantdbaccess system stored procedure. The syntax of this stored procedure is as follows:

```
sp_grantdbaccess [@loginame =] 'login'
    [,[@name_in_db =] 'name_in_db'
```

where the options are as follows:

Option	Description
@loginame = 'login'	The name of a login ID that has already been added to the server.

| @name_in_db = 'name_in_db' | The name that the login ID you are passing in is associated with in the database. Normally, you want the login ID and the user ID to be the same, but this isn't required. |

After you add the login ID and user ID, you assign permissions to the user in the database. If you don't explicitly assign the user permissions, that user will inherit the permissions assigned to the public group, if any.

Stored Procedures as a Security Mechanism

Using stored procedures as a security mechanism is one way you can provide security for your application. As with all database applications, you first have to create the tables that will track your data. When the tables are created, you must then create stored procedures for every data action that you will make on those tables. For example, if you have a table from which you will always insert and delete data, you must create one stored procedure that inserts data and one stored procedure that deletes data. After you create all the requisite stored procedures, you give your users permissions to execute those stored procedures and revoke all INSERT, UPDATE, and DELETE privileges to the underlying tables. This method allows your users to access the data through the application and the stored procedures, but not through the tables directly. This keeps your users from accessing any data from other applications such as Microsoft Access or Crystal Reports, unless they tie directly into the stored procedures you've created.

Listing 9.1 outlines one example of using stored procedures as a security mechanism. When you execute this script, be sure to do it in three parts, as noted in the code.

LISTING 9.1   Stored Procedures as a Security Mechanism

```
SETUSER
DROP TABLE ProcSecurity
DROP PROC uspSelectProcSecurity
DROP PROC uspInsertProcSecurity
DROP PROC uspUpdateProcSecurity
DROP PROC uspDeleteProcSecurity
GO

SET NOCOUNT ON
GO

CREATE TABLE ProcSecurity
(
    ColumnID    INT
        IDENTITY (1, 1),
```

9

SECURITY FOR
STORED
PROCEDURES

continues

LISTING 9.1   Continued

```
    StoredInfo     VARCHAR(32)
)
GO

INSERT INTO ProcSecurity(StoredInfo) VALUES ('First')
INSERT INTO ProcSecurity(StoredInfo) VALUES ('Second')
INSERT INTO ProcSecurity(StoredInfo) VALUES ('Third')
INSERT INTO ProcSecurity(StoredInfo) VALUES ('Fourth')
INSERT INTO ProcSecurity(StoredInfo) VALUES ('Fifth')
INSERT INTO ProcSecurity(StoredInfo) VALUES ('Sixth')
INSERT INTO ProcSecurity(StoredInfo) VALUES ('Seventh')
INSERT INTO ProcSecurity(StoredInfo) VALUES ('Eighth')
INSERT INTO ProcSecurity(StoredInfo) VALUES ('Ninth')
INSERT INTO ProcSecurity(StoredInfo) VALUES ('Tenth')
GO

sp_addlogin 'Security', 'test'
GO

sp_grantdbaccess 'Security', 'Security'
GO

CREATE PROC uspSelectProcSecurity
    @intColumnID INT = NULL
AS
IF (ISNULL(@intColumnID, -1) = -1)
BEGIN
    SELECT     *
    FROM    ProcSecurity
END ELSE
BEGIN
    SELECT     *
    FROM    ProcSecurity
    WHERE    ColumnID = @intColumnID
END
GO

CREATE PROC uspInsertProcSecurity
    @vchStoredInfo    VARCHAR(32)
AS
INSERT INTO ProcSecurity(StoredInfo) VALUES (@vchStoredInfo)
GO
```

```
CREATE PROC uspUpdateProcSecurity
    @intColumnID    INT,
    @vchStoredInfo    VARCHAR(32)
AS
UPDATE    ProcSecurity
SET    StoredInfo = @vchStoredInfo
WHERE    ColumnID = @intColumnID
GO


CREATE PROC uspDeleteProcSecurity
    @intColumnID    INT
AS
DELETE
FROM    ProcSecurity
WHERE    ColumnID = @intColumnID
GO


GRANT EXECUTE ON uspSelectProcSecurity TO Security
GRANT EXECUTE ON uspInsertProcSecurity TO Security
GRANT EXECUTE ON uspUpdateProcSecurity TO Security
GRANT EXECUTE ON uspDeleteProcSecurity TO Security
REVOKE SELECT, INSERT, UPDATE, DELETE ON ProcSecurity FROM Security
GO

-- Stop Executing Here --

-- The following code will all produce errors.

SETUSER 'Security'
GO

SELECT    *
FROM    ProcSecurity
GO

INSERT INTO ProcSecurity(StoredInfo) VALUES ('Eleventh')
GO

UPDATE    ProcSecurity
SET    StoredInfo = 'Not One Anymore'
WHERE    ColumnID = 1
GO

DELETE
FROM    ProcSecurity
WHERE    ColumnID = 5
GO
```

9

SECURITY FOR
STORED
PROCEDURES

continues

LISTING 9.1   Continued

```
-- Stop Executing Here --

-- The following code will all run successfully

uspSelectProcSecurity
GO

uspInsertProcSecurity 'Eleventh'
GO

uspUpdateProcSecurity 1, 'Not One Anymore'
GO

uspDeleteProcSecurity 5
GO

uspSelectProcSecurity
GO
```

The first action performed in this listing is to drop all objects created during the script's execution. This is done to revert the database to the state it was in before the script was run, if you run it more than once. The next step is all the objects that will be used are created. This includes the table and all the stored procedures that access that table. A user called Security is created, permissions allowing that user to execute the stored procedures are assigned, and all table-level permissions are revoked.

The SETUSER Function

The SETUSER function is used at the beginning of the Listing 9.1. This function can be run only by a user who is in the sysadmin or db_owner fixed server role; it resets the user context to any other user who has been created in the current database. At the beginning of the script, SETUSER is called without passing in any parameters. This resets the user context to the original context if SETUSER has been run. If SETUSER hasn't been run, SQL Server simply ignores the command.

Toward the end of Listing 9.1, SETUSER is run and the parameter 'Security' is passed in. This means that the logged-in user assumes all the SQL Server permissions and rights assigned to the Security user.

Although this function is extremely useful, use it with caution because Microsoft has decided to phase out support for it and might not support it in future releases of SQL Server.

The next section of the script shows that you can't access the tables directly as the Security user. First, the SETUSER command is executed, thereby allowing the current user to impersonate the Security user. After you assume the role of the Security user, several commands are executed directly against the ProcSecurity table. Because permissions allowing the Security user to do this have been revoked, all these commands result in errors.

The last section of the script shows that the same data access and modification statements can be run by the Security user, but just not directly against the tables. The same actions that were tried in the second section succeed when they are run through the stored procedures.

Listing 9.2 shows a more useful example of using stored procedures to provide security for your data. In Listing 9.2, two tables are created: one to track sales representatives and one to track clients. The sales representatives can see only those clients, and their respective commission rates, that are assigned to them. As with the code in Listing 9.1, be sure to run the code in Listing 9.2 in three parts.

LISTING 9.2   Another Use of Stored Procedure Security

```
SETUSER
DROP TABLE ClientInformation
DROP PROC uspSelectClientInformation
GO

SET NOCOUNT ON
GO

CREATE TABLE ClientInformation
(
    ClientID    INT
        IDENTITY (1, 1),
    RepID       INT,
    ClientName   VARCHAR(32),
    CommissionPct    NUMERIC(5, 2)
)
GO

INSERT INTO ClientInformation(RepID, ClientName, CommissionPct)
VALUES (1, 'The Computer Shop', 4.5)
INSERT INTO ClientInformation(RepID, ClientName, CommissionPct)
VALUES (3, 'The PC Place', 3.0)
INSERT INTO ClientInformation(RepID, ClientName, CommissionPct)
VALUES (2, 'Computer Wholesalers, Inc.', 5.0)
INSERT INTO ClientInformation(RepID, ClientName, CommissionPct)
VALUES (1, 'HackMiester''s', 3.5)
```

continues

9

SECURITY FOR
STORED
PROCEDURES

LISTING 9.2   Continued

```
INSERT INTO ClientInformation(RepID, ClientName, CommissionPct)
VALUES (2, 'Hard Drives ''n'' Stuff', 4.0)
INSERT INTO ClientInformation(RepID, ClientName, CommissionPct)
VALUES (3, 'Misty''s Motherboards', 4.75)
INSERT INTO ClientInformation(RepID, ClientName, CommissionPct)
VALUES (2, 'Bailey''s Bytes', 3.8)
INSERT INTO ClientInformation(RepID, ClientName, CommissionPct)
VALUES (3, 'Miranda''s Modem Shop', 3.75)
INSERT INTO ClientInformation(RepID, ClientName, CommissionPct)
VALUES (1, 'Colby''s Computer Supply', 2.5)
INSERT INTO ClientInformation(RepID, ClientName, CommissionPct)
VALUES (1, 'Computers by Christopher', 2.75)
GO

CREATE TABLE RepInformation
(
    RepID          INT
        IDENTITY (1, 1),
    RepName         VARCHAR(32)
)
GO

INSERT INTO RepInformation(RepName) VALUES ('RepTest1')
INSERT INTO RepInformation(RepName) VALUES ('RepTest2')
INSERT INTO RepInformation(RepName) VALUES ('RepTest3')
GO

sp_addlogin 'RepTest1'
GO

sp_addlogin 'RepTest2'
GO

sp_addlogin 'RepTest3'
GO

sp_grantdbaccess 'RepTest1', 'RepTest1'
GO

sp_grantdbaccess 'RepTest2', 'RepTest2'
GO

sp_grantdbaccess 'RepTest3', 'RepTest3'
GO
```

```
CREATE PROC uspSelectClientInformation
AS
DECLARE @vchRepName     VARCHAR(32)

SELECT @vchRepName = USER_NAME()

SELECT    ClientID, ClientName, CommissionPct
FROM      ClientInformation CI INNER JOIN
    RepInformation RI ON (CI.RepID = RI.RepID)
WHERE     RI.RepName = @vchRepName
GO

GRANT EXECUTE ON uspSelectClientInformation TO RepTest1
GRANT EXECUTE ON uspSelectClientInformation TO RepTest2
GRANT EXECUTE ON uspSelectClientInformation TO RepTest3
REVOKE SELECT, INSERT, UPDATE, DELETE ON ClientInformation FROM RepTest1
REVOKE SELECT, INSERT, UPDATE, DELETE ON ClientInformation FROM RepTest2
REVOKE SELECT, INSERT, UPDATE, DELETE ON ClientInformation FROM RepTest3
REVOKE SELECT, INSERT, UPDATE, DELETE ON RepInformation FROM RepTest1
REVOKE SELECT, INSERT, UPDATE, DELETE ON RepInformation FROM RepTest2
REVOKE SELECT, INSERT, UPDATE, DELETE ON RepInformation FROM RepTest3
GO

-- Stop Execution Here
-- The following code will fail due to lack of permissions

SETUSER 'RepTest1'

SELECT    *
FROM      ClientInformation
GO

SETUSER
GO

SETUSER 'RepTest2'

SELECT    *
FROM      ClientInformation
GO

SETUSER
GO

SETUSER 'RepTest3'
```

9

SECURITY FOR
STORED
PROCEDURES

continues

LISTING 9.2 Continued

```
SELECT    *
FROM      ClientInformation
GO

-- Stop Execution Here
-- The following code works fine

SETUSER
GO

SETUSER 'RepTest1'

EXEC uspSelectClientInformation
GO

SETUSER
GO

SETUSER 'RepTest2'

EXEC uspSelectClientInformation
GO

SETUSER
GO

SETUSER 'RepTest3'

EXEC uspSelectClientInformation
GO

SETUSER
GO
```

Listing 9.2 starts out much like Listing 9.1 by dropping any existing objects, creating the new ones, and assigning permissions to them. The stored procedure in this example gets the name of the user who is logged in and joins the RepInformation table with the ClientInformation table to return the list of clients to which the logged-in sales representative has access.

In the second section, each user is impersonated and SELECT statements are run. This is done to show that the users don't have access to the underlying tables directly. In the third section, each user is impersonated and the stored procedure that was created in the first section is run. As expected, only the data associated with that particular sales representative is returned.

Although using stored procedures to provide the required security for your application works very well, you could run into problems under some circumstances. Because the stored procedures—at least, the ones presented in Listing 9.1—don't contain any business logic, it becomes impossible for you to keep your users from doing things that go against your business rules. In this case, you would rely on your application to do this for you. If the user were to log in to the database by using the Query Analyzer or some other query tool, she could still make data modifications if she knows how the stored procedures work. The next section covers how you can keep your users in the context of your application.

Application Security

As mentioned previously, you will find certain circumstances when you don't want your users to access the data through any application other than the one that you create. In other words, you want to keep users from viewing or modifying data using Microsoft Access or Crystal Reports. With the release of SQL Server 7.0, Microsoft provides a way for developers to essentially lock up a database, with the developer's application as the only key. This new addition to SQL Server is an application role. The main functionality provided to you by an application role is as follows:

- Application roles don't contain any users. Instead, when a user logs in to the database through a specific application, the application invokes the application role. The user isn't a member of the role but can use the functionality provided by the role when he executes the application.

- An application role is inactive when a user logs in. It becomes active after an application executes the `sp_setapprole` system stored procedure and passes in the password required for that role. The `sp_setapprole` and its password are usually run by the application.

- When the application role is activated for the application, the connection loses all permissions assigned to the user or role that is logged in and gains the permissions associated with the application role. Application roles don't cross database boundaries. Therefore, if users need to access data that's stored in a different database, they have to access that data by using the guest account in that database. If the guest account doesn't exist in that database, that user can't access the database.

Ownership Chains

Stored procedures and views depend on other objects in the database such as tables, views, or other stored procedures. These dependencies are sometimes referred to as an *ownership chain*. In most situations, the user who owns the stored procedure or view also owns the underlying objects as well and, in most cases, all the underlying objects reside in the same database as the new object.

When a user accesses a view or a stored procedure, SQL Server won't check the permissions on the underlying objects if the same user owns all the objects and all the objects reside in the same database. It checks the permissions only on the stored procedure or view. If any of the objects are owned by different users or reside in different databases, the result is a broken ownership chain.

If a broken ownership chain occurs, SQL Server checks the permissions on each object in the chain whose next link isn't owned by the same user. The major problem with this is that the owner of the objects is the person who assigns the permissions on that object. That means every time permissions are changed on the upper-level object, the owners of all the other objects have to adjust the permissions on their objects. If they aren't changed, the new user can't access the underlying objects because of permissions issues.

To get around the problems of broken ownership chains, try to keep all the objects in the database owned by a single user, usually dbo. Although this forces you to think about security in a different way, you will see the results if you ever have to troubleshoot a broken ownership chain permission problem.

Conclusion

In this chapter, I covered the basics of security. First, you saw how SQL Server handles security. All users must jump through several hoops to gain access to the server. A user must gain access to the server by using a login ID. Then she must gain access to the database with a user ID and, finally, her user ID must be assigned permissions in the database. After you saw how SQL Server handles data and object security, you saw how you can use stored procedures to provide data security. This is done by creating stored procedures that your users can execute to gain access to the underlying tables, but by revoking their access to the tables themselves. Next, you saw how you can use application roles to provide application security for your data. Application roles ensure that no data in the database can be accessed except through the application that was intended to work with that database. Last, you saw the importance of keeping all your objects in the database under the same owner.

Programming Structures in SQL

IN THIS CHAPTER

A language isn't a programming language until it encompasses the basic fundamentals of logical operations. These operations include the mundane testing functions such as equal (=), less than (<), and greater than (>) and more complex operations such as looping and jumping. This makes T-SQL a programming language. Admittedly, T-SQL is nowhere near as powerful as some of its cousins such as C++, Visual Basic, or even COBOL. Another requirement for a programming language is the ability to call, create, and use functions. With SQL Server, you can use a number of built-in functions as well as create stored procedures and other user-defined functions.

In this chapter, I cover the following:

- Operators
- Looping structures
- Control-of-flow statements
- SQL Server functions

One thing that makes stored procedures so useful is that you can create extremely powerful applications with them. For the most part, you can use stored procedures to create the same functionality as any other programming language, minus the GUI abilities of more advanced programming languages. In this chapter, I cover all the things that make Transact-SQL a programming language. If you are already familiar with T-SQL and programmatical operators in general, you might want to skim over this chapter and keep it in mind for reference.

Operators

Operators are symbols that indicate that a specific action is to take place with one or more expressions. A great number of operators are available in SQL Server. Operators are divided into several categories, based on the operations they perform:

- Assignment
- Arithmetic
- Comparison
- Logical
- String concatenation
- Bitwise
- Unary

Assignment Operator

This operator—the equal sign (=)—is one of the most ubiquitous operators that you will run into. The assignment operator assigns a value to a variable or a column. An example of this is as follows:

```
SELECT @intValue = 1
```

Arithmetic Operators

Arithmetic operators are the same simple operations that you learned in grade school to add, subtract, multiple and divide numbers. These operators are used to perform said mathematical operations on two numeric expressions. Table 10.1 outlines the mathematical operators supported by SQL Server.

TABLE 10.1 Mathematical Operators

Operator	Meaning	Example
+	Addition. This operator takes two expressions and returns the combined sum of the two of them.	8 + 11 = 19
-	Subtraction. This operator takes two expressions and returns the difference between the two of them.	6 - 4 = 2
*	Multiplication. This operator takes two expressions and returns the result of the multiplication of the two.	4 * 7 = 28
/	Division. This operator takes two expressions and returns the dividend of the two.	12 / 4 = 3
%	Modulo. This operator takes two expressions and returns the remainder after the two numbers are divided.	5 % 2 = 1

Comparison Operators

Comparison operators can be used to check how one expression compares to another. These operators return TRUE, FALSE, or unknown, based on how the expression evaluates. Table 10.2 outlines the supported comparison operators.

TABLE 10.2   Comparison Operators

Operator	Meaning
=	Equal to. This operator checks to see whether the two values being compared are exactly equal. If the values are the same, the operator will return TRUE. Otherwise, it will return FALSE.
<>	Not equal to. This operator checks to see whether the two values being compared aren't equal. If the values aren't the same, the operator will return TRUE.
!=	Not equal to. This operator is the same as the preceding <> operator. It's not SQL-92 compliant, however, and might not be supported in future versions of SQL Server. Therefore, use the <> operator instead.
>	Greater than. This operator checks to see whether the value to the left of the operator is greater than the value to the right. If this tests out, the value TRUE is returned.
>=	Greater than or equal to. This operator checks to see whether the value on the left is greater than or equal to the value on the right.
!<	Not less than. This operator works in the same manner as the preceding >= operator. It isn't SQL-92 compliant and might not be included in future versions of SQL Server.
<	Less than. This operator evaluates whether the expression to the left of the operator is less than the expression to the right.
<=	Less than or equal to. This operator checks whether the expression on the left is less than or equal to the expression on the right.
!>	Not greater than. This operator is similar in function to the preceding <= operator. This operator isn't included in the SQL-92 standard and might not be supported in future versions of SQL Server.

Logical Operators

Logical operators test for a condition of truth between two expressions. These operators return a Boolean value that indicates a TRUE or FALSE value. These operators can be used to string together several comparison operators to return the combined TRUE or FALSE based off those values. Table 10.3 outlines the SQL Server–supported logical operators.

TABLE 10.3 Logical Operators

Operator	Meaning	Example
ALL	Compares a single scalar value with a column of values that are returned from a subquery. ALL returns TRUE if all the values in the returned column are true; otherwise, it returns FALSE.	5 > ALL (SELECT * FROM sales)
AND	Combines and compares two Boolean expressions to check whether both expressions are true. If both compared Boolean expressions return TRUE, the AND expression also returns TRUE. Otherwise, a value of FALSE is returned.	5 > 7 AND 6 < 15
ANY	Compares a single scalar value with a column of values that are returned from a subquery. This operator returns TRUE if any value in the returned column is true. If no values are true, FALSE is returned to the calling query. The ANY operator is the same as the SOME operator.	5 > ANY (SELECT qty FROM sales)
BETWEEN	Checks to see whether a value lies within a specified range. If the value is contained in the range, the operator returns TRUE; otherwise, a value of FALSE is returned to the calling query.	5 BETWEEN (3 AND 10)
EXISTS	Checks to see if any results are returned from the execution of a query. If results are returned, the operator returns a TRUE value; otherwise, it returns FALSE.	EXISTS (SELECT * FROM test)

continues

10

PROGRAMMING
STRUCTURES
IN SQL

TABLE 10.3   Continued

Operator	Meaning	Example
IN	Checks to see whether a value exists in a specified range of values. If the value being checked is in the range, the operator returns TRUE; otherwise, the operator returns FALSE.	`5 IN (SELECT qty FROM sales)`
LIKE	Checks to see if the specified value matches the search value that can include wildcards. The valid wildcards for this operator can be found in Chapter 5, "Creating and Altering Stored Procedures."	`SELECT name WHERE name LIKE 'S%'`
NOT	Negates a Boolean operator and uses the reverse of that value. With NOT *expression*, if the expression is true, NOT returns FALSE, and vice versa.	`NOT 5 > 2`
OR	Checks to see whether either of two Boolean operations is true. If either operator returns TRUE, OR also returns TRUE. If neither operation returns TRUE, OR returns FALSE.	`5 > 2 OR 10 < 3`
SOME	Compares a single scalar value with a column of values that are returned from a subquery. This operator returns TRUE if any value in the returned column is true. If no values are true, FALSE is returned to the user. The SOME operator works in the same way as the ANY operator.	`5 > SOME (SELECT * FROM sales)`

String Concatenation Operator

String concatenation is the process of combining two separate strings into one new one. You can concatenate data of char, varchar, nchar, nvarchar, text, and ntext. The string concatenation operator in SQL Server is the plus sign (+). An example of string concatenation is as follows:

```
SELECT 'This ' + 'is a test.'
```

Bitwise Operators

Bitwise operators are used to perform bit-level manipulations with integer data types. Table 10.4 outlines the supported bitwise operators.

TABLE 10.4   Bitwise Operators

Operator	Meaning	Example
&	Bitwise AND; takes two expressions of integer type and performs a logical bitwise AND operation. To perform this operation, SQL Server converts the data that was passed in into binary equivalents and resolves them. With each bit in the number, the new number will have a bit value of 1 only if the corresponding bit in both original numbers was a 1. Otherwise, the bit will be set to 0.	7 & 51 = 3
|	Bitwise OR; takes two expressions of integer type and performs a bitwise OR operation. To perform this operation, SQL Server converts the data that was passed in into binary equivalents and then resolves them. With each bit in the number, the new number will have a bit value of 1 if the corresponding bit in either number was a 1. If both bits were 0, that bit will be set to 0.	7 | 51 = 55
^	Bitwise exclusive OR; takes two expressions of integer type and performs a logical bitwise exclusive OR operation against them. To perform this operation, SQL Server converts	7 ^ 51 = 52

continues

10

TABLE 10.4   Continued

Operator	Meaning	Example
	the data that was passed in into its binary equivalents and then resolves them. With each bit in the existing numbers, a new number is generated in the following manner. If either corresponding bit is 1 or 0, the new bit is set to 1. If both bits are 1 or both bits are 0, the new bit is set to 0.	
~	Bitwise NOT; takes a single integer value and performs a logical NOT operation against it. During this operation, SQL Server converts the input data into its binary equivalent and processes it one bit at a time. If the current bit is 0, the corresponding bit in the new number is set to 1. Likewise, if it's 1, the corresponding bit will be set to 0.	~7 = -8

Unary Operators

The unary operators are simply the way of telling SQL Server if the value that's being passed in is positive or negative. These operators only work with numeric data. Table 10.5 outlines the accepted unary operators.

TABLE 10.5   Unary Operators

Operator	Meaning
+	Positive; indicates that the number is a positive value
-	Negative; indicates that the number is a negative value

An example of the unary operators is as follows:

```
SELECT -4 + (+6)
```

Looping Structures

Many times within an application, you will need to loop. Looping is the process of repeating a certain section of code until a specific criteria is met. SQL Server can loop. There are only two real looping structures within SQL Server and they are extremely similar. One is a loop using a WHILE statement and the other is a loop that utilizes a GOTO statement. Of course, as anyone who has ever taken a programming class can tell you WHILE is the preferred method; you should try to avoid using GOTO because it can create code that's extremely difficult to read.

WHILE Loop

The WHILE loop is a loop in which you check the criteria before the statement executes. All you have to do is specify the WHILE keyword, the criteria you are checking for, and a BEGIN...END loop containing the code that you want repeated. The syntax for creating a WHILE loop is as follows:

```
WHILE Boolean_expression
    {sql_statement | statement_block}
    [BREAK]
    {sql_statement | statement_block}
    [CONTINUE]
```

Table 10.6 lists the options for the WHILE loop.

TABLE 10.6   WHILE Syntax Options

Option	Description
WHILE	Use this keyword to tell SQL Server that you are going to start a loop.
Boolean_expression	This is the criterion that you will check for during the loop's execution. When the expression stops being evaluated as true, SQL Server stops the loop's execution.
sql_statement | statement_block	This is the SQL statement or block of SQL statements that you want repeated. If you have more than one SQL statement that will be repeated, you must delimit the entire statement with the BEGIN and END keywords.
BREAK	This keyword tells SQL Server to stop executing the current loop. Any statements after the BREAK statement and before the END keyword are ignored.

continues

TABLE 10.6   Continued

Option	Description
CONTINUE	This keyword restarts the current loop at the beginning. All statements after the CONTINUE statement and before the END keyword are ignored.

Listing 10.1 shows an example of a simple WHILE loop.

LISTING 10.1   A Simple WHILE Loop

```
CREATE TABLE WhileLoopTest
(
    LoopID        INT,
    LoopValue     VARCHAR(32)
)
GO

SET NOCOUNT ON

DECLARE    @intCounter      INT
DECLARE @vchLoopValue       VARCHAR(32)

SELECT @intCounter = 1

WHILE (@intCounter <= 1000)
BEGIN
    SELECT @vchLoopValue = 'Loop Interation #' +
           CONVERT(VARCHAR(4), @intCounter)
    INSERT INTO WhileLoopTest(LoopID, LoopValue)
           VALUES (@intCounter, @vchLoopValue)
    SELECT @intCounter = @intCounter + 1
END
```

GOTO Loop

The other type of loop available to you is GOTO. Like the WHILE loop, GOTO enables you to repeat a series of statements until a certain criteria is met.

> **NOTE**
>
> The GOTO statement doesn't necessarily have to be used for looping. You can also use it to exit other loops.

To use the GOTO statement, you must do two things. First, you need to define a label. The *label* is a statement that specifies where the GOTO statement will jump. The label itself doesn't actually perform the jump and, without the presence of a GOTO statement, doesn't change the execution of the SQL statement. To create a label, use the following syntax:

LABEL :

where *LABEL* is how you want to reference the label in your code. This, in and of itself, doesn't affect the code in any way. When you want to jump to that label during code execution, use the GOTO statement. The syntax for this is as follows:

GOTO *LABEL*

where *LABEL* is the name of a label that you defined previously in your code. By using the GOTO statement, you can jump forward or backward in code. Listing 10.2 outlines a piece of code similar to the one in Listing 10.1, only this code uses the GOTO statement instead of a WHILE loop.

LISTING 10.2 A Simple GOTO Loop

```
CREATE TABLE GotoLoopTest
(
    GotoID        INT,
    GotoValue     VARCHAR(32)
)
GO

SET NOCOUNT ON

DECLARE    @intCounter    INT
DECLARE    @vchLoopValue  VARCHAR(32)

SELECT @intCounter = 0

LOOPSTART:

SELECT @intCounter = @intCounter + 1
SELECT @vchLoopValue = 'Loop Iteration #' + CONVERT(VARCHAR(4), @intCounter)
INSERT INTO GotoLoopTest(GotoID, GotoValue) VALUES (@intCounter, @vchLoopValue)
```

continues

10

PROGRAMMING
STRUCTURES
IN SQL

LISTING 10.2 Continued

```
IF (@intCounter <= 1000)
BEGIN
    GOTO LOOPSTART
END
```

Control-of-Flow Statements

We've actually covered a great deal of the control-of-flow language already. The WHILE and GOTO statements are forms of *control-of-flow statements*, which modify the order in which SQL statements are executed. The last main control-of-flow statements available to you are IF...ELSE and CASE.

IF...ELSE

The IF...ELSE statement block is used to make a decision based on supplied parameters and to perform some action based on that decision. For example, if a variable contains a specific value, SQL Server will perform some action. Otherwise, that action won't be taken. The syntax for the IF...ELSE block is as follows:

```
IF expression
BEGIN
    sql_statements
END
ELSE
BEGIN
    sql_statements
END
```

The options for this statement are quite simple. The IF keyword tells SQL Server to evaluate the expression that follows it. If the statement evaluates as true, the statements in the following block are executed. The block is delimited by the BEGIN and END keywords. The optional ELSE section is executed only if the previous section isn't executed. Listing 10.3 shows an example of an IF...ELSE block.

LISTING 10.3 A Simple IF...ELSE Statement

```
CREATE PROCEDURE uspCheckNumber
    @intNumber    INT
AS
IF @intNumber < 1
```

```
BEGIN
    PRINT 'Number is less that 1.'
    RETURN
END
ELSE IF @intNumber = 1
BEGIN
    PRINT 'One'
    RETURN
END
ELSE IF @intNumber = 2
BEGIN
    PRINT 'Two'
    RETURN
END
ELSE IF @intNumber = 3
BEGIN
    PRINT 'Three'
    RETURN
END
ELSE IF @intNumber = 4
BEGIN
    PRINT 'Four'
    RETURN
END
ELSE IF @intNumber = 5
BEGIN
    PRINT 'Five'
    RETURN
END
ELSE IF @intNumber = 6
BEGIN
    PRINT 'Six'
    RETURN
END
ELSE IF @intNumber = 7
BEGIN
    PRINT 'Seven'
    RETURN
END
ELSE IF @intNumber = 8
BEGIN
    PRINT 'Eight'
    RETURN
END
ELSE IF @intNumber = 9
```

continues

10

PROGRAMMING
STRUCTURES
IN SQL

LISTING 10.3   Continued

```
BEGIN
    PRINT 'Nine'
    RETURN
END
ELSE IF @intNumber = 10
BEGIN
    PRINT 'Ten'
    RETURN
END
ELSE
BEGIN
    PRINT 'Number is greater than 10.'
    RETURN
END
```

CASE

The CASE statement is used to evaluate an expression and returns one of several possible results based on the evaluation's result. There are two different types of CASE statements:

- With the *simple* CASE statement, an expression is compared to a simple set of values to determine a result. Consider the following syntax:

```
CASE case_expression
    WHEN expression THEN result
        [...n]
    [ELSE else_result]
END
```

- A *searched* CASE statement evaluates a set of Boolean expressions to determine the result. Here is its syntax:

```
CASE
    WHEN Boolean_expression THEN result
        [...n]
    [ELSE else_result]
END
```

Table 10.7 lists the CASE syntax options.

TABLE 10.7   Simple and Searched CASE Options

Option	Description
CASE	This keyword tells SQL Server that a CASE statement is about to begin.
case_expression	This placeholder tells SQL Server what expression will be evaluated in a simple CASE statement.
WHEN	This keyword tells SQL Server that you will tell it what expression to look at.
expression	This placeholder is the actual expression to be compared. If the expression is evaluated as true, the result is returned.
THEN	This keyword shows that the result is about to be outlined.
result	This placeholder is what's returned if the expression evaluates as true.
...n	This number indicates that you can use multiple WHEN expression THEN result blocks.
ELSE	This optional keyword is used to define a result that will be returned if no other expression was matched.
else_result	This placeholder is used with the ELSE keyword to show where you would define the result of the ELSE block.
Boolean_expression	This placeholder shows where you would perform a searched CASE.

Listing 10.4 shows an example of a combination searched and simple CASE expression. This stored procedure returns the same results as the one in Listing 10.3.

LISTING 10.4   Combination Searched and Simple CASE

```
CREATE PROCEDURE uspCheckNumberCase
    @chrNumber    CHAR(2)
AS

IF (CONVERT(INT, @chrNumber) < 1) OR (CONVERT(INT, @chrNumber) > 10)
BEGIN
    SELECT CASE
        WHEN CONVERT(INT, @chrNumber) < 1 THEN 'Number is less than 1.'
        WHEN CONVERT(INT, @chrNumber) > 10 THEN 'Number is greater than 10.'
    END
RETURN
END
```

continues

LISTING 10.4   Continued

```
SELECT CASE CONVERT(INT, @chrNumber)
    WHEN 1 THEN 'One'
    WHEN 2 THEN 'Two'
    WHEN 3 THEN 'Three'
    WHEN 4 THEN 'Four'
    WHEN 5 THEN 'Five'
    WHEN 6 THEN 'Six'
    WHEN 7 THEN 'Seven'
    WHEN 8 THEN 'Eight'
    WHEN 9 THEN 'Nine'
    WHEN 10 THEN 'Ten'
END
```

Functions

Functions are used either to format and manipulate data or to return information to the user that would ordinarily not be available to him directly within the SQL language. There are really two classes of functions: system-defined and user-defined. System-defined functions are created by Microsoft and installed when SQL Server is installed. User-defined functions are created by the user by using the CREATE FUNCTION command. (User-defined functions are covered in Chapter 13, "Creating Custom Functions.")

Within the class of system-defined functions are several types of functions:

- *String functions* are used to manipulate strings. These types of functions can be used to pull out certain parts of the string, perform a search against a string for a certain pattern of characters, and determine the length of a string.

- *Date functions* are used to manipulate date information. These functions can be used to add and subtract dates, retrieve certain parts of the date, such as the month or year, from a date, and simply to return the current date on the computer.

- *Mathematical functions* perform mathematical operations such as getting the square root of a number, finding the absolute value of a number, and rounding a number.

- *System functions* are a grouping of all functions that don't fall in any of the other groups. This group of functions enables you to retrieve system data, such as the name of the computer that the user is currently connected from or the name of the user that's currently connected, or to convert data from one data type to another.

String Functions

String functions manipulate how string data is returned to the user or stored in a table. These functions can be used only with character data. The following are some of the most frequently used string functions.

- CHARINDEX() finds the starting position of a specified character string (*string1*) in another string (*string2*). The syntax is

  ```
  CHARINDEX(string1, string2, start_position)
  ```

  As an example,

  ```
  SELECT CHARINDEX('test', 'This is a test', 1)
  ```

  returns 11, which is where the word test starts in the second string.

- LEFT() returns the specified number of characters from the left side of a character string. The syntax is

  ```
  LEFT(string, number_of_characters)
  ```

  As an example,

  ```
  SELECT LEFT('This is a test', 4)
  ```

  returns the word This to the user.

- LEN() determines the length of a character string that's passed into it. The syntax is LEN(*string*). For example,

  ```
  SELECT LEN('Test of LEN')
  ```

  returns 11, which is the total length of the string passed into it.

- LOWER() forces the character string that's passed into it into all lowercase letters. The syntax of the command is LOWER(*string*). As an example,

  ```
  SELECT LOWER('TEST OF LOWER')
  ```

  returns test of lower to the user.

- LTRIM() removes any blank characters from the beginning of a string that's passed into it. The syntax of the command is LTRIM(*string*). As an example,

  ```
  SELECT LTRIM('   This is a test')
  ```

  returns the string This is a test (without any spaces to the left) to the user.

- RIGHT() returns the specified number of characters from the right side of the specified character string. The syntax of the command is

  ```
  RIGHT(string, number_of_characters)
  ```

  As an example,

  ```
  SELECT RIGHT('This is a test', 4)
  ```

  returns the word test to the user.

- RTRIM() removes any blank characters from the end of a string. The syntax of the command is RTRIM(*string*). For example,

  ```
  SELECT RTRIM('This is a test     ')
  ```

  returns the string This is a test (without any trailing spaces) to the user.

- UPPER() forces the character string that's passed into it into all uppercase letters. The syntax is UPPER(*string*). As an example,

  SELECT UPPER('This is a test')

  returns THIS IS A TEST to the user.

> **NOTE**
>
> Be very careful when using functions such as UPPER() on the left side of a comparison operator. This will force SQL Server to perform a table scan to look for the value. To see the difference in this, run the following two queries and look at the execution plans. On my machine, the second query took three times as long to run:
>
> select au_lname from authors where au_lname = 'Green'
>
> select au_lname from authors where upper(au_lname) = 'Green'

Date Functions

Date functions are used to manipulate date information and, of course, can only be used with the datetime data type. Many date functions require that you pass in a special type of information called a *datepart* to make them work.

Before getting too far into the date functions, you need to see what the dateparts are. You use dateparts to tell SQL Server which portion of the date you want to work with. Normally, you work with these as an abbreviation, but you can use the full datepart within a script as well. Table 10.8 shows all the available dateparts.

TABLE 10.8   Available Dateparts for Date Functions

Datepart Abbreviation	Datepart
yy	year
yyyy	year
qq	quarter
q	quarter
mm	month
m	month
dy	dayofyear
y	dayofyear

Datepart Abbreviation	Datepart
dd	day
d	day
wk	week
ww	week
dw	weekday
hh	hour
mi	minute
n	minute
ss	second
s	second
ms	millisecond

Some of the more frequently used date functions are as follows:

- DATEADD() adds an amount of time to a time that's passed in. You type in the portion of the date that you want to add. For example, if you want to add time to the year, type the word year as the datepart. The syntax of the command is

  DATEADD(*datepart*, *amount*, *date*)

  For example,

  SELECT DATEADD(year, 1, GETDATE())

  adds one year to the current date.

- DATEDIFF() determines the difference between two dates by using the datepart, as explained earlier. The syntax is

  DATEDIFF(*datepart*, *date1*, *date2*)

  The function

  SELECT DATEDIFF(hour, '1/1/2000 12:00:00', '1/1/2000 16:00:00')

  returns 4, which is the number of hours difference between the two.

- DATEPART() returns the specified portion of the date as specified by the datepart. The syntax is DATEPART(*datepart*, *date*). As an example,

  SELECT DATEPART(month, '1/1/2000 00:00:00')

  returns 1 to the user.

- DAY() returns the number of the day of the month from a specified date. The syntax of the command is DAY(*date*). An example of this function would be

  SELECT DAY('5/22/1976 00:04:00')

10

PROGRAMMING
STRUCTURES
IN SQL

which returns the number 22 to the user.

- `GETDATE()` returns the current date and time from the system. This function's syntax is, simply, `GETDATE()`. As an example,

```
SELECT GETDATE()
```

returns the current date and time from the system.

- `MONTH()` returns the number of the month of the year from the specified date. The syntax of the function is `MONTH(date)`. For example,

```
SELECT MONTH('12/14/74 08:10:00')
```

returns the number 12 to the user.

- `YEAR()` returns the number of the year from the specified date. The syntax of the function is `YEAR(date)`. As an example of this function,

```
SELECT YEAR('4/12/78 10:00:00')
```

returns the number 1978 to the user, depending on the century cutoff configured on the system.

Mathematical Functions

Mathematical functions perform more complex mathematical operations such as absolute value, square, and square root. The following are some of the more frequently used mathematical functions available to you.

- `ABS()` returns the absolute value of a given number. The syntax of the command is `ABS(number)`. As an example,

```
SELECT ABS(-10)
```

returns the number 10 to the user.

- `CEILING()` returns the smallest integer value that's greater than or equal to the given numeric value. The syntax of the command is `CEILING(number)`. For example,

```
SELECT CEILING(10.50)
```

returns the number 11 to the user.

- `FLOOR()` returns the largest integer value that's less than or equal to the given numeric value. The syntax of the command is `FLOOR(number)`. An example of the function in action would be

```
SELECT FLOOR(10.50)
```

which returns the number 10 to the user.

- `POWER()` returns the result of a number raised to a specific value. The syntax of the command is `POWER(number, power)`. As an example,

```
SELECT POWER(3, 3)
```

returns the number 27 to the user.

- ROUND() returns a numeric expression that has been rounded to the closest precision. The syntax of the command is ROUND(*number*, *precision*). An example would be

  ```
  SELECT ROUND(10.25, 1)
  ```

  which returns the number 10.3 to the user.

- SQUARE() returns the square of the number passed into it. The syntax of the command is SQUARE (*number*). An example of this function in use is

  ```
  SELECT SQUARE(5)
  ```

  which returns the number 25 to the user.

- SQRT() returns the square root of the number passed into it. The syntax of the command is SQRT(*number*). For example,

  ```
  SELECT SQRT(25)
  ```

  returns the number 5 to the user.

System Functions

System functions get system information about objects and settings in SQL Server. The following outlines some of the most frequently used system functions.

- CONVERT() changes an expression of one data type into another data type. The syntax of the command is

  ```
  CONVERT (data type, expression)
  ```

  As an example,

  ```
  SELECT CONVERT(VARCHAR(5), 12345)
  ```

  returns the string "12345" to the user.

TIP

SQL Server will perform many types of data conversions for you without your having to use the convert function. If you have an all-numeric string, such as "12345", and add 5 to it, the result will be the number 12350. The converse of this is also true. For more information on implicit conversions, see the CAST and CONVERT topic in SQL Server Books Online.

- CURRENT_USER returns the name of the current user. The syntax of the command is simply CURRENT_USER. For example,

  ```
  SELECT CURRENT_USER
  ```

  returns the name of the user that you logged in as.

10

PROGRAMMING
STRUCTURES
IN SQL

- `DATALENGTH()` returns the number of bytes used to represent the passed-in expression. The syntax of the command is `DATALENGTH(expression)`. As an example,

  ```
  SELECT DATALENGTH('Test')
  ```

  returns the number 4 to the user.

- `HOST_NAME()` returns the name of the computer from which the current user is logged in to the server. The syntax of the command is simply `HOST_NAME()`. For example,

  ```
  SELECT HOST_NAME()
  ```

  returns the name of the computer that you are logged in from.

- `SYSTEM_USER()` returns the name of the user who is currently logged in. The syntax of the command is simply `SYSTEM_USER`. For example,

  ```
  SELECT SYSTEM_USER
  ```

  returns the name of the user that you are currently logged in as.

- `USER_NAME()` returns the username of the person from a given user ID number. As an example,

  ```
  SELECT name FROM sysobjects WHERE USER_NAME(uid) = 'dbo'
  ```

  returns the names of all objects owned by the dbo in any database.

Conclusion

Transact-SQL is an extension of straight SQL that makes it a true programming language. In this chapter, you saw all the operators available to you when you create SQL scripts and stored procedures. Next, you learned how you can perform looping operations in Transact-SQL by using the WHILE loop and the GOTO statement. Last, you saw some of the more frequently used system-defined functions available to you. All these aspects combined make Transact-SQL a rather powerful programming language.

Writing Utility Stored Procedures

IN THIS CHAPTER

Utility stored procedures are, for me, the type of procedure that is the most fun to write. This type of procedure can help you perform system maintenance, find problems with your server and tables, and make the administrator's job easier by automating some of the tasks that can take up large amounts of his or her time.

In this chapter, I cover the following:

- Defining utility stored procedures
- Utility stored procedures sample code

Defining Utility Stored Procedures

Utility stored procedures give you the ability to maintain your system easily. These stored procedures can be extensions of the Microsoft system stored procedures or can be new ones that, in general, make your life as the administrator easy. When creating utility stored procedures, you interact directly with the system tables in the database by selecting information from them. For the most part, you should never directly change any of the system tables. Microsoft does not recommend, and neither do I, that you directly change any of the data in the system tables. Doing so can damage your SQL Server beyond repair.

Utility stored procedures are procedures that are not tied directly to an application. These stored procedures perform maintenance on your system and, for the most part, can be executed in any database. That means these stored procedures are created in the master database and are prefixed with sp_ so that the query engine can find them.

In this chapter, I give you some analyzed source code to some of my favorite utility stored procedures. Feel free to use them in any way you want. The only thing I ask is that if you change these procedures, send me an email and let me know that you did. With that out of the way, on to the code.

Utility Stored Procedure Code

Over the next few pages, I present you with a great deal of source code. This code has been compiled over the past few years. Some of these procedures are fixes and modifications to Microsoft stored procedures, and others were written to make my life easier. As with any programming language, one good way to learn about utility stored procedures is to look at other people's source code. If you want to use any of these procedures and do not want to type them in, you can download the source code from this book's Web site, at http://www.samspublishing.com.

Writing Utility Stored Procedures

CHAPTER 11

203

11

WRITING UTILITY
STORED
PROCEDURES

Updating Index Statistics

One of the most important things you can do with the indexes on your tables is update the usage statistics on those indexes. This is done by creating a utility stored procedure that issues the UPDATE STATISTICS command with the name of the table on which you want to update the indexes. When you have a large number of tables on which you need to update the indexes, doing so can be extremely tedious. The code in Listing 11.1 creates a stored procedure called sp_update_statistics that updates the statistics on all the tables in the database in which it is run.

LISTING 11.1   sp_update_statistics

```
USE master
GO
CREATE PROCEDURE sp_update_statistics
AS
SET NOCOUNT ON -Turns of row count returns
/* Declare the variables */
DECLARE @dtmTimeStart        DATETIME
DECLARE @dtmTimeEnd          DATETIME
DECLARE @intHours        INT
DECLARE @intMinutes       INT
DECLARE @intSeconds       INT
DECLARE @chrHours        CHAR(2)
DECLARE @chrMinutes        CHAR(2)
DECLARE @chrSeconds        CHAR(2)
DECLARE @chrFinalTime        CHAR(8)
DECLARE @vchRetMessage         VARCHAR(64)
DECLARE @intCurrentUpdateID     INT
DECLARE @intMaxUpdateID      INT
DECLARE @vchTableName        VARCHAR(32)
DECLARE @vchSQLStatement      VARCHAR(255)

/* Get the current time.  This will be used to determine how long the */
/* process runs.  */

SELECT     @dtmTimeStart = GETDATE()

/* Drop the temp table if it exists */

IF EXISTS (SELECT name FROM sysobjects WHERE name = 'IndexUpdate')
BEGIN
    DROP TABLE IndexUpdate
END
```

continues

LISTING 11.1   Continued

```
/*  Create the temp table */

CREATE TABLE IndexUpdate
(
    UpdateID     INT IDENTITY(1, 1),
    TableName    VARCHAR(32),
    Done         BIT,
    CompletedOn    DATETIME NULL
)

/* Get all the user table names */

INSERT INTO IndexUpdate(TableName, Done)
    SELECT      CONVERT(VARCHAR(32), OBJECT_NAME(id)), 0
    FROM        sysindexes
    WHERE       (indid = 0 OR indid = 1) AND
         id > 1000
    ORDER       BY rows

/* Get the id of the last table to be updated */

SELECT    @intMaxUpdateID = MAX(UpdateID)
FROM      IndexUpdate

SELECT    @intCurrentUpdateID = 0

/* Loop through the table and update the statistics */

WHILE     (@intCurrentUpdateID <= @intMaxUpdateID)
BEGIN
    SELECT    @intCurrentUpdateID = MIN(UpdateID)
    FROM      IndexUpdate
    WHERE     Done = 0

    SELECT    @vchTableName = TableName
    FROM      IndexUpdate
    WHERE     UpdateID = @intCurrentUpdateID

    SELECT    @vchSQLStatement = 'UPDATE STATISTICS ' + @vchTableName
    EXEC      ( @vchSQLStatement )

    UPDATE    IndexUpdate
    SET    Done = 1,
        CompletedOn = GETDATE()
    WHERE     UpdateID = @intCurrentUpdateID
END
```

```
/* Get and display the final time figure. */

SELECT @dtmTimeEnd = GETDATE()
SELECT @intSeconds = (DATEDIFF(ss, @dtmTimeStart, @dtmTimeEnd) % 60)
SELECT @intMinutes = (DATEDIFF(ss, @dtmTimeStart, @dtmTimeEnd) / 60)

IF (@intMinutes > 59)
BEGIN
    SELECT @intHours = @intMinutes / 60
    SELECT @intMinutes = @intMinutes % 60
END
ELSE
BEGIN
    SELECT @intHours = 0
END

IF (@intSeconds < 10)
BEGIN
    SELECT @chrSeconds = '0' + CONVERT (CHAR(1), @intSeconds)
END
ELSE
BEGIN
    SELECT @chrSeconds =  CONVERT (CHAR(2), @intSeconds)
END

IF (@intMinutes < 10)
BEGIN
    SELECT @chrMinutes = '0' + CONVERT (CHAR(1), @intMinutes)
END
ELSE
BEGIN
    SELECT @chrMinutes =  CONVERT (CHAR(2), @intMinutes)
END

IF (@intHours < 10)
BEGIN
    SELECT @chrHours = '0' + CONVERT (CHAR(1), @intHours)
END
ELSE
BEGIN
    SELECT @chrHours =  CONVERT (CHAR(2), @intHours)
END

SELECT @chrFinalTime = @chrHours + ':' + @chrMinutes + ':' + @chrSeconds
SELECT @vchRetMessage = 'Time to update statistics: ' + @chrFinalTime
PRINT ''
PRINT @vchRetMessage
```

As you can tell, this stored procedure is relatively complex. It starts by declaring all the variables that will be used in the procedure. After the variables are declared, the stored procedure grabs the time. This will be used at the end to determine how long the procedure ran. For this stored procedure, this information is not as important as it is for longer-running stored procedures. After the time has been collected, the stored procedure builds a table and populates it with the names of all the user tables in the database. After that, the procedure loops through all the rows in the temporary table and runs UPDATE STATISTICS. After all the tables have been looped through, the procedure gets the finish time and then calculates and outputs the total time that the procedure ran.

Reindexing a Database

Another very important activity you can perform on your database is to rebuild the indexes on the tables. Rebuilding the indexes on tables can do several things for you. First, it can speed up access to the data in the tables. Second, this process can reduce the size of your database because, over time, the indexes in your database will develop holes where data has been deleted. Finally, this activity will also update the statistics on the indexes. The code in Listing 11.2 creates a stored procedure called sp_reindex_database that rebuilds the indexes on all user tables in the database.

LISTING 11.2   sp_reindex_database

```
USE master
GO
CREATE PROCEDURE sp_reindex_database
AS
SET NOCOUNT ON

/* Declare the variables */

DECLARE @dtmTimeStart       DATETIME
DECLARE @dtmTimeEnd         DATETIME
DECLARE @intHours        INT
DECLARE @intMinutes        INT
DECLARE @intSeconds        INT
DECLARE @chrHours       CHAR(2)
DECLARE @chrMinutes        CHAR(2)
DECLARE @chrSeconds        CHAR(2)
DECLARE @chrFinalTime         CHAR(8)
DECLARE @vchRetMessage          VARCHAR(64)
DECLARE @intCurrentRebuildID     INT
DECLARE @intMaxRebuildID      INT
DECLARE @vchTableName         VARCHAR(32)
DECLARE @vchSQLStatement      VARCHAR(255)
```

```
/* Get the current time.  This will be used to determine how long the */
/* process runs.  */

SELECT      @dtmTimeStart = GETDATE()

/* Drop the temp table if it exists */

IF EXISTS (SELECT name FROM sysobjects WHERE name = 'IndexRebuild')
BEGIN
    DROP TABLE IndexRebuild
END

/* Build the temp table */

CREATE TABLE IndexRebuild
(
    RebuildID     INT IDENTITY(1, 1),
    TableName     VARCHAR(32),
    Done          BIT,
    CompletedOn   DATETIME NULL
)

/* Gather the names of the tables */

INSERT INTO IndexRebuild(TableName, Done)
    SELECT      CONVERT(VARCHAR(32), OBJECT_NAME(id)), 0
    FROM        sysindexes
    WHERE       (indid = 0 OR indid = 1) AND
          id > 1000
    ORDER       BY rows

/* Get the id of the first table to be rebuilt */

SELECT    @intMaxRebuildID = MAX(RebuildID)
FROM      IndexRebuild

SELECT    @intCurrentRebuildID = 0

/* Loop through the table and rebuild the indexes */

WHILE       ((@intCurrentRebuildID <= @intMaxRebuildID)
BEGIN
    SELECT      @intCurrentRebuildID = MIN(RebuildID)
    FROM        IndexRebuild
    WHERE       Done = 0
```

continues

LISTING 11.2   Continued

```
SELECT    @vchTableName = TableName
FROM      IndexRebuild
WHERE     RebuildID = @intCurrentRebuildID

SELECT     @vchSQLStatement = 'DBCC DBREINDEX(' + @vchTableName +
      ➥ ') WITH NO_INFOMSGS'
EXEC     ( @vchSQLStatement )

SELECT     @vchSQLStatement = 'DBCC UPDATEUSAGE(' + DB_NAME() + ', ' +
      ➥@vchTableName + ')'
EXEC     ( @vchSQLStatement )

update    IndexRebuild
set    Done = 1,
     CompletedOn = GETDATE()
WHERE     RebuildID = @intCurrentRebuildID
END

/* Get the current time and display the total run time */

SELECT @dtmTimeEnd = GETDATE()
SELECT @intSeconds = (datedIFf(ss, @dtmTimeStart, @dtmTimeEnd) % 60)
SELECT @intMinutes = (datedIFf(ss, @dtmTimeStart, @dtmTimeEnd) / 60)

IF (@intMinutes > 59)
BEGIN
    SELECT @intHours = @intMinutes / 60
    SELECT @intMinutes = @intMinutes % 60
END
ELSE
BEGIN
    SELECT @intHours = 0
END

IF (@intSeconds < 10)
BEGIN
    SELECT @chrSeconds = '0' + CONVERT (CHAR(1), @intSeconds)
END
ELSE
BEGIN
    SELECT @chrSeconds =  CONVERT (CHAR(2), @intSeconds)
END
```

```
IF (@intMinutes < 10)
BEGIN
    SELECT @chrMinutes = '0' + CONVERT (CHAR(1), @intMinutes)
END
ELSE
BEGIN
    SELECT @chrMinutes =  CONVERT (CHAR(2), @intMinutes)
END

IF (@intHours < 10)
BEGIN
    SELECT @chrHours = '0' + CONVERT (CHAR(1), @intHours)
END
ELSE
BEGIN
    SELECT @chrHours =  CONVERT (CHAR(2), @intHours)
END

SELECT @chrFinalTime = @chrHours + ':' + @chrMinutes + ':' + @chrSeconds
SELECT @vchRetMessage = 'Time to reindex database: ' + @chrFinalTime
PRINT ''
PRINT @vchRetMessage
```

This procedure is similar in structure to the sp_update_statistics stored procedure.
sp_reindex_database starts by declaring all the variables that will be used in the procedure.
After the variables are declared, the stored procedure gets the system time. This will be used at
the end to determine how long the procedure ran. After the time has been collected, the stored
procedure builds a table and populates it with the names of all the user tables in the database.
After that, the procedure loops through all the rows in the temporary table and runs DBCC
DBREINDEX and DBCC UPDATEUSAGE. DBCC DBREINDEX rebuilds all the indexes on the table that
is specified, and DBCC UPDATEUSAGE verifies the amount of space that each object is using.
After all the tables have been looped through, the procedure gets the finish time and then calculates and outputs the total time that the procedure ran.

Finding Object Permissions

Knowing what permissions are assigned to which users on which objects is extremely important. Depending on what information is stored in your database, having the wrong person see
the wrong piece of information can make or break your organization. Imagine the chaos if a
disgruntled employee gained access to your HR database and sent out the salaries of everyone
who works in your company to the entire company. Using Enterprise Manager or any other
SQL Server stored procedure, there is no way to get a report of all permissions. The code in
Listing 11.3 creates a procedure called sp_get_user_object_permissions that creates a
report of all permissions on all user objects.

LISTING 11.3   sp_get_user_object_permissions

```
CREATE PROCEDURE sp_get_user_object_permissions
AS
SET NOCOUNT ON

/*  Declare the variables */

DECLARE @vchUserName        VARCHAR(32)
DECLARE @vchUserType        VARCHAR(16)
DECLARE @intObjectID        INT
DECLARE @vchObjectType       VARCHAR(32)
DECLARE @vchActionType       VARCHAR(32)
DECLARE @vchObjectName       VARCHAR(32)
DECLARE    @bitActionSelect    BIT
DECLARE    @bitActionInsert    BIT
DECLARE    @bitActionUpdate    BIT
DECLARE    @bitActionDelete    BIT
DECLARE    @bitActionExecute    BIT
DECLARE    @bitActionReferences    BIT
DECLARE @vchRetMessage        VARCHAR(255)
DECLARE @vchSpaces          VARCHAR(64)
DECLARE @vchDashes          VARCHAR(95)

SELECT @vchDashes = REPLICATE('-', 95) -- Used for display

/* Create the table that is used to store object information */

CREATE TABLE #ObjectInfo
(
    ObjectID        INT NOT NULL,
    ObjectName       VARCHAR(64) NULL,
    UserType        VARCHAR(16) NULL,
    UserName        VARCHAR(32) NOT NULL,
    ObjectType       VARCHAR(32) NULL,
    ActionType       VARCHAR(32) NULL,
    ActionSelect      BIT NOT NULL
        DEFAULT 0,
    ActionInsert      BIT NOT NULL
        DEFAULT 0,
    ActionUpdate      BIT NOT NULL
        DEFAULT 0,
    ActionDelete      BIT NOT NULL
        DEFAULT 0,
    ActionExecute      BIT NOT NULL
        DEFAULT 0,
    ActionReferences    BIT NOT NULL
        DEFAULT 0
)
```

11

```
/* Populate the table with the information about objects that have */
/* permissions assigned to them */

INSERT #ObjectInfo (ObjectID, ObjectName, UserName, ActionType)
    SELECT      DISTINCT id AS 'ObjectID', OBJECT_NAME(id) AS 'ObjectName',
                ➥USER_NAME(uid) AS 'UserName',
        CASE protecttype
            WHEN 204 THEN 'GRANT_W_GRANT'
            WHEN 205 THEN 'GRANT'
            WHEN 206 THEN 'REVOKE'
        END AS 'ActionType'
    FROM        sysprotects
    WHERE       id <> 0 AND
        id > 50

/* Add the information about any objects that do not have permissions */
/* assigned to them */

INSERT #ObjectInfo (ObjectID, ObjectName, UserName, ActionType)
    SELECT      DISTINCT id AS 'ObjectID', OBJECT_NAME(id) AS 'ObjectName',
        'No Permissions' AS 'UserName', NULL AS 'ActionType'
    FROM        sysobjects
    WHERE       id NOT IN (SELECT ObjectID FROM #ObjectInfo) AND
        id > 50 AND
        type IN ('P', 'S', 'U', 'V', 'X')

/* Create a cursor that contains information on whether the */
/* entity that has been assigned the permissions is a user  */
/* or a group and then update the table */

DECLARE curCursorUserTypes CURSOR FOR
    SELECT      name,
        CASE issqluser
            WHEN 0 THEN 'GROUP'
            ELSE 'USER'
        END AS 'UserType'
    FROM        sysusers

Open curCursorUserTypes

FETCH NEXT FROM curCursorUserTypes INTO @vchUserName, @vchUserType

WHILE (@@FETCH_STATUS <> -1)
BEGIN
    UPDATE      #ObjectInfo
    SET     UserType = @vchUserType
```

continues

LISTING 11.3   Continued

```
        WHERE      UserName = @vchUserName
        FETCH NEXT FROM curCursorUserTypes INTO @vchUserName, @vchUserType
END

CLOSE curCursorUserTypes
DEALLOCATE curCursorUserTypes

/* Create a cursor that contains information about the object types */
/* and update the table with that information. */

DECLARE curCursorObjectTypes CURSOR FOR
    SELECT      id AS 'ObjectID',
        CASE type
            WHEN 'P' THEN 'Stored Procedure'
            WHEN 'S' THEN 'System Table'
            WHEN 'U' THEN 'User Table'
            WHEN 'V' THEN 'View'
            WHEN 'X' THEN 'Extended Stored Procedure'
        END AS 'ObjectType'
    FROM       sysobjects
    WHERE      type IN ('P', 'S', 'U', 'V', 'X')

OPEN curCursorObjectTypes

FETCH NEXT FROM curCursorObjectTypes INTO @intObjectID, @vchObjectType
WHILE (@@FETCH_STATUS <> -1)
BEGIN
    UPDATE      #ObjectInfo
    SET     ObjectType = @vchObjectType
    WHERE     ObjectID = @intObjectID
    FETCH NEXT FROM curCursorObjectTypes INTO @intObjectID, @vchObjectType
END

CLOSE curCursorObjectTypes
DEALLOCATE curCursorObjectTypes

/*  Create a cursor that contains information about the types of permissions */
/*  on each object that update the table with it */

DECLARE curCursorObjectPermissions CURSOR FOR
    SELECT    id AS 'ObjectID', USER_NAME(uid) AS 'UserName',
        CASE protecttype
            WHEN 204 THEN 'GRANT_W_GRANT'
            WHEN 205 THEN 'GRANT'
            WHEN 206 THEN 'REVOKE'
```

```
            END AS 'ObjectType',
            CASE action
                WHEN 26 THEN 'REFERENCES'
                WHEN 193 THEN 'SELECT'
                WHEN 195 THEN 'INSERT'
                WHEN 196 THEN 'DELETE'
                WHEN 197 THEN 'UPDATE'
                WHEN 224 THEN 'EXECUTE'
            END AS 'ActionType'
    FROM     sysprotects
    WHERE    id <> 0


OPEN curCursorObjectPermissions
FETCH NEXT FROM curCursorObjectPermissions INTO @intObjectID, @vchUserName,
    ➥@vchObjectType, @vchActionType


WHILE (@@FETCH_STATUS <> -1)
BEGIN
    IF @vchActionType = 'REFERENCES'
    BEGIN
        UPDATE      #ObjectInfo
        SET     ActionReferences = 1
        WHERE     ObjectID = @intObjectID AND
            UserName = @vchUserName AND
            ActionType = @vchObjectType

    END

    IF @vchActionType = 'SELECT'
    BEGIN
        UPDATE      #ObjectInfo
        SET     ActionSelect = 1
        WHERE     ObjectID = @intObjectID AND
            UserName = @vchUserName AND
            ActionType = @vchObjectType
    END

    IF @vchActionType = 'INSERT'
    BEGIN
        UPDATE      #ObjectInfo
        SET     ActionInsert = 1
        WHERE     ObjectID = @intObjectID AND
            UserName = @vchUserName AND
            ActionType = @vchObjectType
    END
```

continues

LISTING 11.3   Continued

```
IF @vchActionType = 'DELETE'
BEGIN
    UPDATE      #ObjectInfo
    SET    ActionDelete = 1
    WHERE     ObjectID = @intObjectID AND
        UserName = @vchUserName AND
        ActionType = @vchObjectType
END

IF @vchActionType = 'UPDATE'
BEGIN
    UPDATE      #ObjectInfo
    SET    ActionUpdate = 1
    WHERE     ObjectID = @intObjectID AND
        UserName = @vchUserName AND
        ActionType = @vchObjectType
END

IF @vchActionType = 'EXECUTE'
BEGIN
    UPDATE      #ObjectInfo
    SET    ActionExecute = 1
    WHERE     ObjectID = @intObjectID AND
        UserName = @vchUserName AND
        ActionType = @vchObjectType
END

    FETCH NEXT FROM curCursorObjectPermissions INTO @intObjectID, @vchUserName,
            @vchObjectType, @vchActionType
END

CLOSE curCursorObjectPermissions
DEALLOCATE curCursorObjectPermissions

/*  Create a cursor that contains all of the information in the table */
/*  and loop through it and return the information to the user /*

DECLARE curObjectNames CURSOR FOR
    SELECT DISTINCT ObjectID AS 'ObjectID', ObjectName AS 'ObjectName',
                ➥ObjectType AS 'ObjectType'
    FROM #ObjectInfo
    ORDER BY ObjectName
```

```
OPEN curObjectNames

FETCH NEXT FROM curObjectNames INTO @intObjectID, @vchObjectName,
    ➥@vchObjectType

WHILE(@@FETCH_STATUS <> -1)
BEGIN
    SELECT      @vchRetMessage = 'Object Name: ' + @vchObjectName + ' (' +
                CONVERT(VARCHAR(15), @intObjectID) + ')'
    SELECT      @vchSpaces = SPACE(56 - DATALENGTH(@vchRetMessage))
    SELECT      @vchRetMessage = @vchRetMessage + @vchSpaces
    SELECT      @vchRetMessage = @vchRetMessage + 'Type: ' + @vchObjectType
    PRINT       @vchRetMessage
    PRINT       ''

    DECLARE CursorPermissions CURSOR FOR
        SELECT      UserName, UserType, ActionType, ActionSelect,
        ➥ActionInsert, ActionUpdate, ActionDelete,
            ActionExecute, ActionReferences
        FROM        #ObjectInfo
        WHERE       ObjectID = @intObjectID

    OPEN CursorPermissions
    FETCH NEXT FROM CursorPermissions
        INTO        @vchUserName, @vchUserType, @vchActionType, @bitActionSelect,
        ➥@bitActionInsert, @bitActionUpdate, @bitActionDelete,
        ➥@bitActionExecute, @bitActionReferences
    WHILE (@@FETCH_STATUS <> -1)
    BEGIN
        SELECT      @vchRetMessage = '     ' + ISNULL(@vchUserType, 'WARNING') +
            ': ' + @vchUserName

        IF (DATALENGTH(@vchRetMessage) < 16)
        BEGIN
            SELECT      @vchRetMessage = @vchRetMessage+ '         ' +
                ISNULL(@vchActionType, ' ') + '             '
        END
        ELSE
        BEGIN
            SELECT      @vchRetMessage = @vchRetMessage+ '     ' +
                ISNULL(@vchActionType, ' ') + '             '
        END

        IF @bitActionSelect = 1
```

continues

LISTING 11.3   Continued

```
BEGIN
    SELECT @vchRetMessage = @vchRetMessage + 'SELECT|'
END

IF @bitActionInsert = 1
BEGIN
    SELECT @vchRetMessage = @vchRetMessage + 'INSERT|'
END

IF @bitActionUpdate = 1
BEGIN
    SELECT @vchRetMessage = @vchRetMessage + 'UPDATE|'
END

IF @bitActionDelete = 1
BEGIN
    SELECT @vchRetMessage = @vchRetMessage + 'DELETE|'
END

IF @bitActionExecute = 1
BEGIN
    SELECT @vchRetMessage = @vchRetMessage + 'EXECUTE|'
END

IF @bitActionReferences = 1
BEGIN
    SELECT @vchRetMessage = @vchRetMessage + 'REFERENCES|'
END

SELECT @vchRetMessage = SUBSTRING(@vchRetMessage, 1,
➥DATALENGTH(@vchRetMessage) - 1)
PRINT @vchRetMessage

    FETCH NEXT FROM CursorPermissions
    INTO      @vchUserName, @vchUserType, @vchActionType,
    ➥@bitActionSelect, @bitActionInsert, @bitActionUpdate,
    ➥@bitActionDelete,@bitActionExecute,
    ➥@bitActionReferences
END

CLOSE CursorPermissions
DEALLOCATE CursorPermissions
```

```
    PRINT ''
    PRINT @vchDashes
    PRINT ''

FETCH NEXT FROM curObjectNames INTO @intObjectID, @vchObjectName,
    ➥@vchObjectType
END

CLOSE curObjectNames
DEALLOCATE curObjectNames

DROP TABLE #ObjectInfo
```

This procedure, like most of the others in this lesson, starts by declaring all the variables that will be used throughout the rest of the procedure. It then creates and populates a temporary table that is looped through to create the report. After the table has been populated and updated, the procedure opens a cursor that gathers a list of all the object names in the table. For each object name, another cursor is opened that gathers and returns the permissions for that object. When no objects are left to check, the procedure drops the temporary table and exits.

Finding Database-Level Permissions

Like the sp_get_user_object_permissions stored procedure, the following stored procedure gathers permissions information on a database level. These permissions include the creation of tables, stored procedures, views, and defaults and the ability to back up databases and transaction logs. The code in Listing 11.4 creates a stored procedure called sp_get_user_database_permissions that shows database-level permissions.

LISTING 11.4 sp_get_user_database_permissions

```
CREATE PROCEDURE sp_get_user_database_permissions
AS
SET NOCOUNT ON

/* Declare the variables */

DECLARE    @intObjectID             INT
DECLARE @vchActionType          VARCHAR(32)
DECLARE @vchObjectName          VARCHAR(32)
DECLARE @vchObjectType          VARCHAR(32)
DECLARE @vchUserName         VARCHAR(32)
DECLARE    @bitActionCreateTable        BIT
DECLARE    @bitActionCreateDatabase     BIT
```

continues

LISTING 11.4 Continued

```
DECLARE    @bitActionCreateView          BIT
DECLARE    @bitActionCreateProcedure     BIT
DECLARE    @bitActionBackupDatabase      BIT
DECLARE    @bitActionCreateDefault    BIT
DECLARE    @bitActionBackupTLog          BIT
DECLARE    @bitActionCreateRule          BIT
DECLARE @vchRetMessage                VARCHAR(255)

/*  Create the temp table */

CREATE TABLE #DatabaseInfo
(
    ObjectID         INT NOT NULL,
    ObjectName       VARCHAR(32) NULL,
    UserName         VARCHAR(32) NOT NULL,
    ActionType       VARCHAR(32) NULL,
    ActionCreateTable    BIT NOT NULL
        DEFAULT 0,
    ActionCreateDatabase    BIT NOT NULL
        DEFAULT 0,
    ActionCreateView    BIT NOT NULL
        DEFAULT 0,
    ActionCreateProcedure    BIT NOT NULL
        DEFAULT 0,
    ActionBackupDatabase    BIT NOT NULL
        DEFAULT 0,
    ActionCreateDefault    BIT NOT NULL
        DEFAULT 0,
    ActionBackupTLog    BIT NOT NULL
        DEFAULT 0,
    ActionCreateRule    BIT NOT NULL
        DEFAULT 0

)

/*  Insert information about the database permissions into */
/*  the temp table */

INSERT #DatabaseInfo (ObjectID, ObjectName, UserName, ActionType)
    SELECT    DISTINCT id AS 'ObjectID',DB_NAME() AS 'ObjectName',
              ➥USER_NAME(uid) AS 'UserName',
        CASE protecttype
            WHEN 204 THEN 'GRANT_W_GRANT'
            WHEN 205 THEN 'GRANT'
            WHEN 206 THEN 'REVOKE'
        END AS 'ActionType'
```

```
        FROM       sysprotects
        WHERE      id = 0

/*  Create a cursor that contains information about the permissions */
/*  that are held by each user and update the table with it */

DECLARE curDatabasePermissions CURSOR FOR
    SELECT    id AS 'ObjectID', USER_NAME(uid) AS 'UserName',
        CASE protecttype
            WHEN 204 THEN 'GRANT_W_GRANT'
            WHEN 205 THEN 'GRANT'
            WHEN 206 THEN 'REVOKE'
        END AS 'ObjectType',
        CASE action
            WHEN 198 THEN 'CREATE TABLE'
            WHEN 203 THEN 'CREATE DATABASE'
            WHEN 207 THEN 'CREATE VIEW'
            WHEN 222 THEN 'CREATE PROCEDURE'
            WHEN 228 THEN 'BACKUP DATABASE'
            WHEN 233 THEN 'CREATE DEFAULT'
            WHEN 235 THEN 'BACKUP LOG'
            WHEN 236 THEN 'CREATE RULE'
    END AS 'ActionType'
    FROM       sysprotects
    WHERE      id = 0

OPEN curDatabasePermissions
FETCH NEXT FROM curDatabasePermissions INTO @intObjectID, @vchUserName,
    ➥@vchObjectType, @vchActionType


WHILE (@@FETCH_STATUS <> -1)
BEGIN
    IF @vchActionType = 'CREATE TABLE'
    BEGIN
        UPDATE     #DatabaseInfo
        SET    ActionCreateTable = 1
        WHERE    ObjectID = @intObjectID AND
            UserName = @vchUserName AND
            ActionType = @vchObjectType

    END

    IF @vchActionType = 'CREATE DATABASE'
    BEGIN
        UPDATE     #DatabaseInfo
        SET    ActionCreateDatabase = 1
```

continues

LISTING 11.4 Continued

```
        WHERE   ObjectID = @intObjectID AND
            UserName = @vchUserName AND
            ActionType = @vchObjectType
    END

    IF @vchActionType = 'CREATE VIEW'
    BEGIN
        UPDATE      #DatabaseInfo
        SET     ActionCreateView = 1
        WHERE   ObjectID = @intObjectID AND
            UserName = @vchUserName AND
            ActionType = @vchObjectType
    END

    IF @vchActionType = 'CREATE PROCEDURE'
    BEGIN
        UPDATE      #DatabaseInfo
        SET     ActionCreateProcedure = 1
        WHERE   ObjectID = @intObjectID AND
            UserName = @vchUserName AND
            ActionType = @vchObjectType
    END

    IF @vchActionType = 'BACKUP DATABASE'
    BEGIN
        UPDATE      #DatabaseInfo
        SET     ActionBackupDatabase = 1
        WHERE   ObjectID = @intObjectID AND
            UserName = @vchUserName AND
            ActionType = @vchObjectType
    END

    IF @vchActionType = 'CREATE DEFAULT'
    BEGIN
        UPDATE      #DatabaseInfo
        SET     ActionCreateDefault = 1
        WHERE   ObjectID = @intObjectID AND
            UserName = @vchUserName AND
            ActionType = @vchObjectType
    END

    IF @vchActionType = 'BACKUP LOG'
    BEGIN
        UPDATE      #DatabaseInfo
```

```
        SET     ActionBackupTLog = 1
        WHERE   ObjectID = @intObjectID AND
            UserName = @vchUserName AND
            ActionType = @vchObjectType
    END


    IF @vchActionType = 'CREATE RULE'
    BEGIN
        UPDATE      #DatabaseInfo
        SET     ActionCreateRule = 1
        WHERE   ObjectID = @intObjectID AND
            UserName = @vchUserName AND
            ActionType = @vchObjectType
    END


    FETCH NEXT FROM curDatabasePermissions INTO @intObjectID, @vchUserName,
        ➥@vchObjectType, @vchActionType
END


CLOSE curDatabasePermissions
DEALLOCATE curDatabasePermissions


/*  Format and return the information to the user */


SELECT      @vchRetMessage = 'Database Name: ' + DB_NAME()
PRINT       @vchRetMessage
PRINT       ''


DECLARE CursorPermissions CURSOR FOR
    SELECT      UserName, ActionType, ActionCreateTable, ActionCreateDatabase,
                ➥ActionCreateView, ActionCreateProcedure,
                ➥ActionBackupDatabase, ActionCreateDefault, ActionBackupTLog,
        ActionCreateRule
    FROM        #DatabaseInfo


OPEN CursorPermissions
FETCH NEXT FROM CursorPermissions
    INTO        @vchUserName, @vchActionType, @bitActionCreateTable,
                ➥@bitActionCreateDatabase, @bitActionCreateView,
                ➥@bitActionCreateProcedure, @bitActionBackupDatabase,
                ➥@bitActionCreateDefault, @bitActionBackupTLog,
                ➥@bitActionCreateRule


WHILE (@@FETCH_STATUS <> -1)
BEGIN
    SELECT @vchRetMessage = '      ' + @vchUserName
    IF DATALENGTH(@vchRetMessage) < 9
```

continues

LISTING 11.4   Continued

```
BEGIN
    SELECT @vchRetMessage = @vchRetMessage+ '             ' +
        ➥@vchActionType + '            '
END
ELSE
BEGIN
    SELECT @vchRetMessage = @vchRetMessage+ '      ' +
        ➥@vchActionType + '          '
END

IF @bitActionCreateTable = 1
BEGIN
    SELECT @vchRetMessage = @vchRetMessage + 'CREATE TABLE|'
END

IF @bitActionCreateDatabase = 1
BEGIN
    SELECT @vchRetMessage = @vchRetMessage + 'CREATE DATABASE|'
END

IF @bitActionCreateView = 1
BEGIN
    SELECT @vchRetMessage = @vchRetMessage + 'CREATE VIEW|'
END

IF @bitActionCreateProcedure = 1
BEGIN
    SELECT @vchRetMessage = @vchRetMessage + 'CREATE PROCEDURE|'
END

IF @bitActionBackupDatabase = 1
BEGIN
    SELECT @vchRetMessage = @vchRetMessage + 'BACKUP DATABASE|'
END

IF @bitActionCreateDefault = 1
BEGIN
    SELECT @vchRetMessage = @vchRetMessage + 'CREATE DEFAULT|'
END

IF @bitActionBackupTLog = 1
BEGIN
    SELECT @vchRetMessage = @vchRetMessage + 'BACKUP LOG|'
END
```

Writing Utility Stored Procedures

CHAPTER 11

223

11

WRITING UTILITY
STORED
PROCEDURES

```
IF @bitActionCreateRule = 1
BEGIN
    SELECT @vchRetMessage = @vchRetMessage + 'CREATE RULE|'
END

SELECT @vchRetMessage = SUBSTRING(@vchRetMessage, 1,
        ➡DATALENGTH(@vchRetMessage) - 1)
PRINT @vchRetMessage

FETCH NEXT FROM CursorPermissions
INTO      @vchUserName, @vchActionType, @bitActionCreateTable,
          ➡@bitActionCreateDatabase, @bitActionCreateView,
          ➡@bitActionCreateProcedure, @bitActionBackupDatabase,
          ➡@bitActionCreateDefault, @bitActionBackupTLog,
          ➡@bitActionCreateRule
END

CLOSE CursorPermissions
DEALLOCATE CursorPermissions

DROP TABLE #DatabaseInfo
```

This procedure is much like sp_get_user_object_permissions. It creates and populates a temporary table that is looped through to create the report. After the table has been populated and updated, the procedure opens a cursor that gathers a list of all the users that have database-level permissions. For each of the usernames, another cursor is opened that gathers and returns the permissions for that user. When there are no users left to check, the procedure drops the temporary table and exits.

The New sp_who

With the release of SQL Server 7.0, Microsoft finally allows more than 255 characters in a column. This much-heralded modification enables developers to make very powerful applications. This modification creates some rather inconvenient problems, though. One of the major problems, for me, is the difference in the sp_who stored procedure. If you have run this procedure, you know that all the data is returned in a format that is 488 characters wide, making it too wide to fit in a single screen. I know that you can use the grid functionality in SQL Query Analyzer, but it was much more fun to rewrite it. To solve this problem, you can either turn on the grid functionality of Query Analyzer or you can create the procedure shown in Listing 11.5. This procedure is an updated version of sp_who that is only 115 characters wide.

LISTING 11.5 sp_who3

```
CREATE PROCEDURE sp_who3
    @LoginName SYSNAME = NULL
AS

/*  Declare the variables */

DECLARE      @intSpidLow        INT
DECLARE      @intSpidHigh        INT
DECLARE      @intSpid        INT
DECLARE      @bnvSID        VARBINARY(85)

SELECT      @intSpidLow = 0
SELECT      @intSpidHigh = 32767

/* Return only active spids and then exit */

IF(@loginame IS NOT NULL AND UPPER(@loginame) = 'ACTIVE')
BEGIN
    SELECT      spid, status = CONVERT(VARCHAR(16), status),
              ➥loginame = CONVERT(VARCHAR(32), loginame),
              ➥hostname = CONVERT(VARCHAR(16), hostname),
              ➥blk = CONVERT(CHAR(5),blocked),
              dbname = CONVERT(VARCHAR(16), DB_NAME(dbid)), cmd
    FROM      master.dbo.sysprocesses
    WHERE      spid >= @intSpidLow AND
        spid <= @intSpidHigh AND
              UPPER(cmd) <> 'AWAITING COMMAND'

    RETURN (0)
END

/* Returns only a specified spid and then exits */

IF (@LoginName IS NOT NULL AND UPPER(@LoginName) <> 'ACTIVE')
BEGIN
    IF (@LoginName LIKE '[0-9]%')
    BEGIN
        SELECT      @intSpid = CONVERT(INT, @LoginName)
    SELECT      spid, status = CONVERT(VARCHAR(16), status),
              ➥loginame = CONVERT(VARCHAR(32), loginame),
              ➥hostname = CONVERT(VARCHAR(16), hostname),
              ➥blk = CONVERT(CHAR(5),blocked),
                  dbname = CONVERT(VARCHAR(16), DB_NAME(dbid)), cmd
```

Writing Utility Stored Procedures

CHAPTER 11

225

11

WRITING UTILITY
STORED
PROCEDURES

```
        FROM        master.dbo.sysprocesses
        WHERE       spid = @intSpid
    END
    ELSE
    BEGIN
        SELECT @bnvSID = SUSER_ID(@LoginName)
        IF (@bnvSID IS NULL)
        BEGIN
            RAISERROR(15007,-1,-1,@LoginName)
            RETURN (1)
        END
        SELECT      spid, status = CONVERT(VARCHAR(16), status),
                    ➥loginame = CONVERT(VARCHAR(32), loginame),
                    ➥hostname = CONVERT(VARCHAR(16), hostname),
                   ➥blk = CONVERT(CHAR(5),blocked),
                    dbname = CONVERT(VARCHAR(16), DB_NAME(dbid)), cmd
        FROM        master.dbo.sysprocesses
        WHERE       sid = @bnvSID
    END
    RETURN (0)
END

/* If nothing was passed in, return all information and exit */

SELECT      spid, status = CONVERT(VARCHAR(16), status),
            ➥loginame = CONVERT(VARCHAR(32), loginame),
            ➥hostname = CONVERT(VARCHAR(16), hostname),
            ➥blk = CONVERT(CHAR(5),blocked),
            dbname = CONVERT(VARCHAR(16), DB_NAME(dbid)), cmd
FROM        master.dbo.sysprocesses
WHERE       spid >= @intSpidLow AND spid <= @intSpidHigh

RETURN (0)
```

The basic functionality that this stored procedure provides is the same as sp_who. What this procedure does for you, however, is use the CONVERT function to cut down on the number of characters returned for the status, loginame, hostname, and dbname sections.

Checking for Blocks

Blocking is the bane of all SQL Server system administrators and developers. When a block occurs, it can bring down the entire system and can take some investigative work to determine who is the cause of all the problems and what that person is executing. The procedure in Listing 11.6 checks for blocking and helps you find out what is going on if blocking is occurring. For more information on exactly what a block is, see Chapter 16, "Considerations When Using Stored Procedures and Triggers."

LISTING 11.6 sp_check_blocking

```
CREATE PROCEDURE sp_check_blocking
AS
SET NOCOUNT ON

/* Declare the variables */

DECLARE @sinBlockingSPID    SMALLINT
DECLARE @sinRootBlockers    SMALLINT
DECLARE @vchRetMess         VARCHAR(150)

SELECT    @sinRootBlockers = 0

SELECT    @vchRetMess = CONVERT(CHAR(28), GETDATE(), 109)
SELECT    @vchRetMess = @vchRetMess + ': '

/*  Select any blocking spids from the sysprocesses table */

SELECT    @sinBlockingSPID = spid
FROM      sysprocesses
WHERE     blocked = 0 AND
      spid IN (SELECT blocked
          FROM sysprocesses
          WHERE blocked != 0)

SELECT @sinRootBlockers = @@rowcount

/*  If there is blocking occurring, determine what they are doing */
/*  and return that information to the user */

IF (@sinRootBlockers > 0)
BEGIN
    DECLARE @sinBlockedSPIDS    SMALLINT
    DECLARE @vchBlockingSPID    VARCHAR(10)
    DECLARE @vchSQLString       VARCHAR(100)

    SELECT    @sinBlockedSPIDS = COUNT(*)
    FROM      sysprocesses
    WHERE     blocked != 0

    SELECT    @vchBlockingSPID = CONVERT(VARCHAR, @sinBlockingSPID)
```

```
    SELECT      @vchRetMess = @vchRetMess + CONVERT(VARCHAR, @sinBlockedSPIDS)
    SELECT      @vchRetMess = @vchRetMess + ' blocked processes from '
    SELECT      @vchRetMess = @vchRetMess + CONVERT(VARCHAR, @sinRootBlockers)
    SELECT      @vchRetMess = @vchRetMess + ' root blocker(s)'
    PRINT       @vchRetMess
    SELECT      spid, 'blk' = blocked, waittype, dbid, status, cmd, cpu,
        physical_io, memusage, suid, hostname, program_name
    FROM        sysprocesses
    WHERE       (spid >= 10 and blocked <> 0) or
        spid = @sinBlockingSPID
    PRINT       ''
    SELECT      @vchRetMess = 'Blocking spid ' + @vchBlockingSPID
    PRINT       @vchRetMess
    SELECT      @vchSQLString = 'DBCC INPUTBUFFER(' + @vchBlockingSPID + ')'
    EXEC        ( @vchSQLString )
END

/*  If no blocking is occurring, return a message that outlines that. */

ELSE
BEGIN
    SELECT @vchRetMess = @vchRetMess + 'No blocking'
    RAISERROR(@vchRetMess, -1, 1) WITH NOWAIT
END
```

The sp_check_blocking stored procedure checks to see whether blocking is present on the system. If there is no blocking situation, the procedure returns the date and time and a message saying that no blocking exists. If a blocking condition does exist, the procedure returns the spid of the root blocker. This is the person who is causing all the problems. Then the stored procedure returns information, in a format similar to sp_who, on all the spids being blocked. After this is complete, the procedure executes DBCC INPUTBUFFER to return information about what the blocking spid is running. To check this stored procedure, go to Chapter 16 and use Listings 16.1 and 16.2.

Checking Table Sizes

As a developer or a database administrator, it is important that you know how your database is growing. This means knowing how large your tables are becoming. As with a number of the other procedures I have shown you, there is no real easy way to get a list of all the tables and how large they are. The code in Listing 11.7 creates a procedure that generates such a list for you.

LISTING 11.7 sp_check_all_object_space

```
CREATE PROCEDURE sp_check_all_object_space
AS

/* Declare the variables */

DECLARE @intID            INT
DECLARE @chrType        CHAR(2)
DECLARE    @intPages        INT
DECLARE @DatabaseName        SYSNAME
DECLARE @decDBSize        DEC(15, 0)
DECLARE @decBytesPerPage    DEC(15, 0)
DECLARE @decPagerPerMB        DEC(15, 0)


/* Create the temporary table */

CREATE TABLE #TableSpaceInfo
(
    id        INT null,
    rows        INT null,
    reserved    dec(15) null,
    data        dec(15) null,
    indexp        dec(15) null,
    unused        dec(15) null
)


SET NOCOUNT ON

/*  Insert information about all user tables into the temporary */
/*  table */

INSERT INTO #TableSpaceInfo (id, reserved)
    SELECT    si.id, sum(si.reserved)
    FROM    sysindexes si, sysobjects so
    WHERE    si.indid IN (0, 1, 255) and
        si.id = so.id and
        so.type = 'U'
    GROUP    BY si.id
    ORDER    BY si.id

/*  Open a cursor that contains information about the tables and */
/*  loop through it updating the system with the space */
/*  information */
```

```
DECLARE     curUsage CURSOR FOR
    SELECT id FROM #TableSpaceInfo


OPEN curUsage
FETCH NEXT FROM curUsage INTO @intID
WHILE (@@FETCH_STATUS <> -1)
BEGIN

    SELECT      @intPages = sum(dpages)
    FROM      sysindexes
    WHERE      indid < 2 AND
        id = @intID

    SELECT      @intPages = @intPages + isnull(sum(used), 0)
    FROM      sysindexes
    WHERE      indid = 255 AND
        id = @intID

    UPDATE      #TableSpaceInfo
    SET     data = @intPages
    WHERE     id = @intID

    UPDATE #TableSpaceInfo
    SET     indexp = (SELECT sum(used)
            FROM      sysindexes
            WHERE  indid IN (0, 1, 255) AND id = @intID) - data
    WHERE     id = @intID


    UPDATE #TableSpaceInfo
    SET     unused = reserved -
        (SELECT sum(used)
        FROM sysindexes
        WHERE indid in (0, 1, 255)
        AND id = @intID)
    WHERE     id = @intID

    UPDATE      #TableSpaceInfo
    SET     rows = i.rows
    FROM     sysindexes i
    WHERE     i.indid < 2 AND
        i.id = @intID AND
        #TableSpaceInfo.id = @intID

    FETCH NEXT FROM curUsage INTO @intID
END
```

continues

LISTING 11.7 Continued

```
CLOSE curUsage
DEALLOCATE curUsage

/*  Return the information to the user */

SELECT   name = SUBSTRING(OBJECT_NAME(id), 1, 32),
     rows = CONVERT(char(11), rows),
     reserved = LTRIM(STR(reserved * d.low / 1024.,15,0) + ' ' + 'KB'),
     data = LTRIM(STR(data * d.low / 1024.,15,0) + ' ' + 'KB'),
     index_size = LTRIM(STR(indexp * d.low / 1024.,15,0) + ' ' + 'KB'),
     unused = LTRIM(STR(unused * d.low / 1024.,15,0) + ' ' + 'KB')
FROM    #TableSpaceInfo, master.dbo.spt_values d
WHERE    d.number = 1 AND
     d.type = 'E'
ORDER    BY name

DROP TABLE #TableSpaceInfo
```

This stored procedure is modeled after the sp_spaceused stored procedure. Unlike that procedure, this procedure gathers information on all tables in the database. It first creates a table of all user tables in the database. Then it opens a cursor that loops through that table and adds information about the amount of space used by those objects. Lastly, it collects all the gathered data from the temporary table and returns it to the user.

Numbering Source Code Lines

When you develop stored procedures, you will find that having a straight listing of the source code you have written can be somewhat difficult to read through. I have found that having line numbers on the code can help somewhat. The procedure in Listing 11.8 creates a stored procedure that numbers the lines of your source code.

LISTING 11.8 sp_helptext_number

```
CREATE PROCEDURE sp_helptext_number
    @nvcObjectName    NVARCHAR(776)
AS

SET NOCOUNT ON

/*  Declare the variables */

declare @DatabaseName       sysname
declare @intBlankSpaceAdded   INT
```

```
declare @intBasePos           INT
declare @intCurrentPos          INT
declare @intTextLength          INT
declare @intLineID        INT
declare @intAddOnLen          INT
declare @intLFCR          INT
declare @intDefinedLength      INT
declare @nvcSysCommentsText      NVARCHAR(4000)
declare @nvcLine            NVARCHAR(255)

SELECT @intDefinedLength = 255
SELECT @intBlankSpaceAdded = 0

/*  Create the temporary table */

CREATE TABLE #CommentText
(
    LineID    INT,
    Text      NVARCHAR(255)
)

/*  Verify the location of the objects and if it exists in the */
/*  current database */

SELECT @DatabaseName = PARSENAME(@nvcObjectName ,3)

IF @DatabaseName IS NOT NULL AND @DatabaseName <> db_name()
        BEGIN
                RAISERROR(15250,-1,-1)
                RETURN (1)
        END

IF (OBJECT_ID(@nvcObjectName) IS NULL)
        BEGIN
        SELECT @DatabaseName = db_name()
        RAISERROR(15009,-1,-1,@nvcObjectName,@DatabaseName)
                RETURN (1)
        END

IF (SELECT COUNT(*) FROM syscomments c, sysobjects o
    ➥WHERE o.xtype NOT IN ('S', 'U') AND
    o.id = c.id AND o.id = OBJECT_ID(@nvcObjectName)) = 0
        BEGIN
                RAISERROR(15197,-1,-1,@nvcObjectName)
                RETURN (1)
        END
```

continues

LISTING 11.8 Continued

```
IF (SELECT COUNT(*) FROM syscomments
    ➥WHERE id = OBJECT_ID(@nvcObjectName) AND encrypted = 0) = 0
        BEGIN
                RAISERROR(15471,-1,-1)
                RETURN (0)
        END

SELECT @intLFCR = 2
SELECT @intLineID = 1

/*  Declare a cursor that contains the comment text and loop through */
/*  it adding that text to the temp table */

DECLARE SysComCursor CURSOR FOR
    SELECT      text
    FROM        syscomments
    WHERE       id = OBJECT_ID(@nvcObjectName) AND
        encrypted = 0 ORDER BY number, colid
FOR READ ONLY

OPEN SysComCursor

FETCH NEXT FROM SysComCursor INTO @nvcSysCommentsText

WHILE @@fetch_status >= 0
BEGIN

    SELECT  @intBasePos     = 1
    SELECT  @intCurrentPos   = 1
    SELECT   @intTextLength = LEN(@nvcSysCommentsText)

    WHILE @intCurrentPos  != 0
    BEGIN
        SELECT @intCurrentPos =   CHARINDEX(CHAR(13)+CHAR(10),
            @nvcSysCommentsText, @intBasePos)
        IF @intCurrentPos != 0
        BEGIN
            WHILE    (ISNULL(LEN(@nvcLine),0) + @intBlankSpaceAdded +
                @intCurrentPos-@intBasePos + @intLFCR) > @intDefinedLength
            BEGIN
                SELECT      @intAddOnLen = @intDefinedLength -
        ➥(ISNULL(LEN(@nvcLine),0) + @intBlankSpaceAdded)
```

```
            INSERT      #CommentText
            VALUES      ( @intLineID, ISNULL(@nvcLine, N'') +
                        ➥ISNULL(SUBSTRING(@nvcSysCommentsText,
                        @intBasePos, @intAddOnLen), N''))
            SELECT      @nvcLine = NULL, @intLineID = @intLineID + 1,
                        ➥@intBasePos = @intBasePos + @intAddOnLen,
                        ➥@intBlankSpaceAdded = 0
        END
        SELECT      @nvcLine = ISNULL(@nvcLine, N'') +
                    ➥ISNULL(SUBSTRING(@nvcSysCommentsText,
                    @intBasePos, @intCurrentPos-@intBasePos +
                    @intLFCR), N'')
        SELECT      @intBasePos = @intCurrentPos+2
        INSERT      #CommentText VALUES( @intLineID, @nvcLine )
        SELECT      @intLineID = @intLineID + 1
        SELECT      @nvcLine = NULL
    END
    ELSE
    BEGIN
        IF @intBasePos <= @intTextLength
        BEGIN
            WHILE      (ISNULL(LEN(@nvcLine),0) + @intBlankSpaceAdded +
                    @intTextLength-@intBasePos+1 ) > @intDefinedLength
            BEGIN
                SELECT      @intAddOnLen = @intDefinedLength -
                        ➥(ISNULL(LEN(@nvcLine),0) +
                        @intBlankSpaceAdded )
                INSERT      #CommentText
                VALUES      ( @intLineID, ISNULL(@nvcLine, N'') +
                        ➥ISNULL(SUBSTRING(@nvcSysCommentsText,
                        @intBasePos, @intAddOnLen), N''))
                SELECT      @nvcLine = NULL, @intLineID = @intLineID + 1,
                        ➥@intBasePos = @intBasePos + @intAddOnLen,
                        ➥@intBlankSpaceAdded = 0
            END
            SELECT      @nvcLine = ISNULL(@nvcLine, N'') +
                    ISNULL(SUBSTRING(@nvcSysCommentsText, @intBasePos,
                    @intTextLength-@intBasePos+1 ), N'')
            IF CHARINDEX(' ', @nvcSysCommentsText, @intTextLength+1 ) > 0
            BEGIN
                SELECT @nvcLine = @nvcLine + ' ', @intBlankSpaceAdded = 1
            END
            BREAK
        END
    END
END
```

continues

LISTING 11.8   Continued

```
    FETCH NEXT FROM SysComCursor INTO @nvcSysCommentsText
END

IF @nvcLine IS NOT NULL
    INSERT #CommentText VALUES( @intLineID, @nvcLine )

/*  Return the information to the user */

SELECT CASE DATALENGTH(CONVERT(VARCHAR(4), LineID))
        WHEN 1 THEN '000' + CONVERT(VARCHAR(1), LineID) + ':  ' + Text
        WHEN 2 THEN '00' + CONVERT(VARCHAR(2), LineID) + ':  ' + Text
        WHEN 3 THEN '0' + CONVERT(VARCHAR(3), LineID) + ':  ' + Text
        WHEN 4 THEN CONVERT(VARCHAR(4), LineID) + ':  ' + Text
    END
FROM #CommentText order by LineID

CLOSE   SysComCursor
DEALLOCATE      SysComCursor

DROP TABLE      #CommentText

RETURN (0)
```

Listing 11.9 shows an example of what the returned code is.

LISTING 11.9   Output from sp_helptext_number

```
0001:   CREATE PROCEDURE sp_helptext_number
0002:       @nvcObjectName     NVARCHAR(776)
0003:   AS
0004:
0005:   SET NOCOUNT ON
0006:
0007:   declare @DatabaseName          sysname
0008:   declare @intBlankSpaceAdded    INT
0009:   declare @intBasePos            INT
0010:   declare @intCurrentPos         INT
0011:   declare @intTextLength         INT
0012:   declare @intLineID             INT
0013:   declare @intAddOnLen           INT
0014:   declare @intLFCR               INT
0015:   declare @intDefinedLength      INT
0016:   declare @nvcSysCommentsText    NVARCHAR(4000)
0017:   declare @nvcLine               NVARCHAR(255)
0018:
0019:   SELECT @intDefinedLength = 255
```

```
0020:   SELECT @intBlankSpaceAdded = 0
0021:
0022:   CREATE TABLE #CommentText
0023:   (
0024:       LineID      INT,
0025:       Text        NVARCHAR(255) --COLLATE database_default
0026:   )
0027:
0028:   SELECT @DatabaseName = PARSENAME(@nvcObjectName ,3)
0029:
0030:   IF @DatabaseName IS NOT NULL AND @DatabaseName <> db_name()
0031:           BEGIN
0032:                   RAISERROR(15250,-1,-1)
0033:                   RETURN (1)
0034:           END
0035:
0036:   IF (OBJECT_ID(@nvcObjectName) IS NULL)
0037:           BEGIN
0038:           SELECT @DatabaseName = db_name()
0039:           RAISERROR(15009,-1,-1,@nvcObjectName,@DatabaseName)
0040:                   RETURN (1)
0041:           END
0042:
0043:   IF (SELECT COUNT(*) FROM syscomments c, sysobjects o WHERE o.xtype
    ➡NOT IN ('S', 'U') AND
0044:       o.id = c.id AND o.id = OBJECT_ID(@nvcObjectName)) = 0
0045:           BEGIN
0046:                   RAISERROR(15197,-1,-1,@nvcObjectName)
0047:                   RETURN (1)
0048:           END
0049:
0050:   IF (SELECT COUNT(*) FROM syscomments WHERE id = OBJECT_ID
    ➡(@nvcObjectName) AND encrypted = 0) = 0
0051:           BEGIN
0052:                   RAISERROR(15471,-1,-1)
0053:                   RETURN (0)
0054:           END
0055:
0056:   SELECT @intLFCR = 2
0057:   SELECT @intLineID = 1
0058:
0059:   DECLARE SysComCursor CURSOR FOR
0060:       SELECT      text
0061:       FROM        syscomments
0062:       WHERE       id = OBJECT_ID(@nvcObjectName) AND
0063:           encrypted = 0 ORDER BY number, colid
0064:   FOR READ ONLY
```

continues

LISTING 11.9   Continued

```
0065:
0066:    OPEN SysComCursor
0067:
0068:    FETCH NEXT FROM SysComCursor INTO @nvcSysCommentsText
0069:
0070:    WHILE @@fetch_status >= 0
0071:    BEGIN
0072:
0073:        SELECT  @intBasePos     = 1
0074:        SELECT  @intCurrentPos    = 1
0075:        SELECT    @intTextLength = LEN(@nvcSysCommentsText)
0076:
0077:        WHILE @intCurrentPos  != 0
0078:        BEGIN
0079:            SELECT @intCurrentPos =   CHARINDEX(CHAR(13)+CHAR(10),
            ➥@nvcSysCommentsText, @intBasePos)
0080:            IF @intCurrentPos != 0
0081:            BEGIN
0082:                WHILE    (ISNULL(LEN(@nvcLine),0) + @intBlankSpaceAdded +
0083:                    @intCurrentPos-@intBasePos + @intLFCR) >
                    ➥@intDefinedLength
0084:                BEGIN
0085:                    SELECT    @intAddOnLen = @intDefinedLength -
            ➥(ISNULL(LEN(@nvcLine),0) + @intBlankSpaceAdded)
0086:                    INSERT     #CommentText
0087:                    VALUES    ( @intLineID, ISNULL(@nvcLine, N'') +
                            ➥ ISNULL(SUBSTRING(@nvcSysCommentsText,
0088:                        @intBasePos, @intAddOnLen), N''))
0089:                    SELECT    @nvcLine = NULL, @intLineID = @intLineID + 1,
0090:                        @intBasePos = @intBasePos + @intAddOnLen,
                        ➥@intBlankSpaceAdded = 0
0091:                END
0092:                SELECT    @nvcLine    = ISNULL(@nvcLine, N'') +
            ➥ISNULL(SUBSTRING
            ➥(@nvcSysCommentsText,
0093:                @intBasePos, @intCurrentPos-@intBasePos + @intLFCR), N'')
0094:                SELECT    @intBasePos = @intCurrentPos+2
0095:                INSERT    #CommentText VALUES( @intLineID, @nvcLine )
0096:                SELECT    @intLineID = @intLineID + 1
0097:                SELECT    @nvcLine = NULL
0098:            END
0099:            ELSE
0100:            BEGIN
```

```
0101:                    IF @intBasePos <= @intTextLength
0102:                    BEGIN
0103:                        WHILE   (ISNULL(LEN(@nvcLine),0) + @intBlankSpaceAdded +
0104:                            @intTextLength-@intBasePos+1 ) > @intDefinedLength
0105:                        BEGIN
0106:                            SELECT      @intAddOnLen = @intDefinedLength -
                            ➥(ISNULL(LEN(@nvcLine),0) +
0107:                                @intBlankSpaceAdded )
0108:                            INSERT      #CommentText
0109:                            VALUES    ( @intLineID, ISNULL(@nvcLine, N'') +
                                        ➥ISNULL(SUBSTRING(@nvcSysCommentsText,
0110:                                @intBasePos, @intAddOnLen), N''))
0111:                            SELECT    @nvcLine = NULL,
                                    ➥@intLineID = @intLineID + 1,
0112:                                @intBasePos = @intBasePos + @intAddOnLen,
                                ➥@intBlankSpaceAdded = 0
0113:                        END
0114:                        SELECT    @nvcLine = ISNULL(@nvcLine, N'') +
0115:                            ISNULL(SUBSTRING(@nvcSysCommentsText, @intBasePos,
0116:                            @intTextLength-@intBasePos+1 ), N'')
0117:                        IF CHARINDEX(' ', @nvcSysCommentsText,
                        ➥@intTextLength+1 ) > 0
0118:                        BEGIN
0119:                            SELECT @nvcLine = @nvcLine + ' ',
                            ➥@intBlankSpaceAdded = 1
0120:                        END
0121:                        BREAK
0122:                    END
0123:                END
0124:        END
0125:
0126:    FETCH NEXT FROM SysComCursor INTO @nvcSysCommentsText
0127: END
0128:
0129: IF @nvcLine IS NOT NULL
0130:     INSERT #CommentText VALUES( @intLineID, @nvcLine )
0131:
0132: SELECT CASE DATALENGTH(CONVERT(VARCHAR(4), LineID))
0133:         WHEN 1 THEN '000' + CONVERT(VARCHAR(1), LineID) + ':  ' + Text
0134:         WHEN 2 THEN '00' + CONVERT(VARCHAR(2), LineID) + ':  ' + Text
0135:         WHEN 3 THEN '0' + CONVERT(VARCHAR(3), LineID) + ':  ' + Text
0136:         WHEN 4 THEN CONVERT(VARCHAR(4), LineID) + ':  ' + Text
0137:     END
0138: FROM #CommentText order by LineID
0139:
0140: CLOSE  SysComCursor
```

continues

LISTING 11.9 Continued

```
0141:   DEALLOCATE      SysComCursor
0142:
0143:   DROP TABLE      #CommentText
0144:
0145:   RETURN (0)
```

Retrieving Index Members

The final stored procedure can help you find information about the indexes created on your user tables. This stored procedure, shown in Listing 11.10, looks at all the tables and returns to you the names of the indexes, the types of indexes, and the member keys in those indexes. This information can be very useful to you if you have recently taken over a database on which you don't have much information. This information allows you to get a general sense of the indexing scheme on the database and if there are any modifications that you can make to them. I have used this stored procedure to find redundant indexes that were taking up more than 2GB of space.

LISTING 11.10 sp_get_index_members

```
CREATE PROCEDURE sp_get_index_members
AS
SET NOCOUNT ON

/*  Declare the variables */

DECLARE @vchObjectName     VARCHAR(64)
DECLARE @intIntObjectID    INT
DECLARE @sinIndexID        SMALLINT
DECLARE @sinGroupID        SMALLINT
DECLARE @intIndexName      SYSNAME
DECLARE @GroupName         SYSNAME
DECLARE @intIntStatus      INT
DECLARE @nvcKeys           NVARCHAR(2048)
DECLARE @DatabaseName      SYSNAME
DECLARE @vchRetMessage     VARCHAR(255)
DECLARE @empty             VARCHAR(1)
DECLARE @des1              VARCHAR(35)
DECLARE @des2              VARCHAR(35)
DECLARE @des4              VARCHAR(35)
DECLARE @des32             VARCHAR(35)
DECLARE @des64             VARCHAR(35)
DECLARE @des2048           VARCHAR(35)
```

```
DECLARE @des4096          VARCHAR(35)
DECLARE @des8388608          VARCHAR(35)
DECLARE @des16777216          VARCHAR(35)
DECLARE     @intI             INT
DECLARE @ThisKey          SYSNAME

/* Create a cursor that contains information about every */
/* user table in the database loop through it and gather */
/* information from the sysindexes table about the keys  */
/* in the indexes */

DECLARE curTables INSENSITIVE CURSOR FOR
    SELECT id FROM sysobjects WHERE type = 'U'
OPEN curTables

FETCH NEXT FROM curTables INTO @intIntObjectID
WHILE (@@FETCH_STATUS <> -1)
BEGIN
    SELECT @vchObjectName = object_name(@intIntObjectID)
    DECLARE curIndexes INSENSITIVE CURSOR FOR
        SELECT indid, groupid, name, status FROM sysindexes
        WHERE  id = @intIntObjectID AND indid > 0 AND indid < 255
        ➡ORDER BY indid
    OPEN curIndexes
    FETCH curIndexes INTO @sinIndexID, @sinGroupID, @intIndexName,
        ➡@intIntStatus

    CREATE TABLE #IndexInfo
    (
        index_name    VARCHAR(24) NOT NULL,
        stats         INT,
        groupname     VARCHAR(32) NOT NULL,
        index_keys    VARCHAR(2048) NULL
    )

    WHILE (@@FETCH_STATUS <> -1)
    BEGIN
        SELECT    @nvcKeys = INDEX_COL(@vchObjectName, @sinIndexID, 1),
            @intI = 2, @ThisKey = INDEX_COL(@vchObjectName, @sinIndexID, 2)
        WHILE     (@ThisKey is NOT NULL )
        BEGIN
            SELECT @nvcKeys = @nvcKeys + ', ' + @ThisKey, @intI = @intI + 1
            SELECT @ThisKey = INDEX_COL(@vchObjectName, @sinIndexID, @intI)
        END

        SELECT     @GroupName = groupname
```

continues

LISTING 11.10   Continued

```
            FROM      sysfilegroups
            WHERE       groupid = @sinGroupID

            IF @intIndexName NOT LIKE '_WA%'
            BEGIN
                INSERT INTO #IndexInfo
                VALUES (CONVERT(CHAR(24), @intIndexName), @intIntStatus,
                       ➥ CONVERT(CHAR(32), @GroupName), @nvcKeys)
            END
            FETCH curIndexes INTO @sinIndexID, @sinGroupID, @intIndexName,
                ➥@intIntStatus
        END
        DEALLOCATE curIndexes

/*  Get information from the spt_values table about the system */
/*  definitions */

        SELECT    @empty = ''

        SELECT    @des1 = name
        FROM      master.dbo.spt_VALUES
        WHERE     type = 'I' AND
            number = 1

        SELECT    @des2 = name
        FROM      master.dbo.spt_VALUES
        WHERE     type = 'I' AND number = 2

        SELECT    @des4 = name
        FROM      master.dbo.spt_VALUES
        WHERE     type = 'I' AND number = 4

        SELECT    @des32 = name
        FROM      master.dbo.spt_VALUES
        WHERE     type = 'I' AND
            number = 32

        SELECT    @des64 = name
        FROM      master.dbo.spt_VALUES
        WHERE     type = 'I' AND
            number = 64

        SELECT    @des2048 = name
```

```
FROM        master.dbo.spt_VALUES
WHERE       type = 'I' AND
      number = 2048

SELECT      @des4096 = name
FROM        master.dbo.spt_VALUES
WHERE       type = 'I' AND
      number = 4096

SELECT      @des8388608 = name
FROM        master.dbo.spt_VALUES
WHERE       type = 'I' AND
      number = 8388608

SELECT      @des16777216 = name
FROM        master.dbo.spt_VALUES
WHERE       type = 'I' AND
      number = 16777216

/*  Return the information to the user */

SELECT      @vchRetMessage = 'Indexes for table: ' +
            ➥object_name(@intIntObjectID)
PRINT       @vchRetMessage

/*  Format the type of index */

SELECT    'Index Name' = index_name,
      'Index Description' = CONVERT(VARCHAR(56),
         CASE
            WHEN (stats & 16) <> 0 THEN 'clustered'
            ELSE 'nonclustered'
         END + CASE
            WHEN (stats & 1) <> 0 THEN ', ' + @des1
            ELSE @empty
         END + CASE
            WHEN (stats & 2) <> 0 THEN ', ' + @des2
            ELSE @empty
         END + CASE
            WHEN (stats & 4) <> 0 THEN ', ' + @des4
            ELSE @empty
         END + CASE
            WHEN (stats & 64) <> 0 THEN ', ' + @des64
            ELSE CASE
               WHEN (stats & 32) <> 0 THEN ', ' + @des32
               ELSE @empty
```

continues

LISTING **11.10**   Continued

```
                    END
            END + CASE
                WHEN (stats & 2048) <> 0 THEN ', ' + @des2048
                ELSE @empty
            END + CASE
                WHEN (stats & 4096) <> 0 THEN ', ' + @des4096
                ELSE @empty
            END + CASE
                WHEN (stats & 8388608) <> 0 THEN ', ' + @des8388608
                ELSE @empty
            END + CASE
                WHEN (stats & 16777216) <> 0 THEN ', ' + @des16777216
            ELSE @empty
            END + ' located on ' + groupname),
        'Index Keys' = CONVERT(VARCHAR(64), index_keys)
    FROM #IndexInfo

    PRINT ''

    DROP TABLE #IndexInfo
    FETCH NEXT FROM curTables INTO @intIntObjectID
END
CLOSE curTables
DEALLOCATE curTables
```

This stored procedure first opens a cursor that gathers the names of all the indexes in the data-base. It places this information into a temporary table, one index at a time. It then formats the data and returns it to the user one row at a time.

Conclusion

Utility stored procedures are the type of procedures that is the most fun to write. You get to use your imagination and create something that can save you quite a bit of time. You should always work on utility stored procedures on a nonproduction SQL Server because you are using sys-tem tables directly. The stored procedures that I have shown you here are ones that I have cre-ated over the past several years and updated with each new release of SQL Server. Some of these procedures, such as the ones that update index statistics and rebuild indexes, can and should be run on a scheduled basis. It would be best to run these during off-peak hours. The others are primarily information-gathering procedures that you can use to find information about your system.

Extended Stored Procedures

IN THIS CHAPTER

Extended stored procedures are a special type of procedure that you can use to add extremely powerful functionality to your SQL Server applications. Unlike normal stored procedures, extended stored procedures aren't written using the SQL language—instead, they are written using C or C++.

In this chapter, the following topics are covered:

- How extended stored procedures work
- Writing the required C code
- Registering extended stored procedures
- Useful system extended stored procedures

How Extended Stored Procedures Work

Extended stored procedures enable you to add extremely powerful functionality to your SQL Server. These types of procedures are written by using C or C++ and then compiled into dynamic link libraries (DLLs). A DLL is a type of executable that can be called on and used by another application. The DLL that makes up the functionality of the extended stored procedure is registered with the SQL Server and then can be called on, as with any normal SQL Server stored procedure. Users can pass parameters into extended stored procedures and receive data back from them as with any other stored procedures.

SQL Server dynamically loads and executes the code in extended stored procedures when they are called. This code runs in the same process and memory space in which the SQL Server engine runs. This can cause problems if the stored procedure isn't well written. Calling an improperly written DLL can cause SQL Server to fault and kill the server. This is why it's important to do all your development of this type of procedure on a nonproduction development server. When creating extended stored procedures, you utilize the Open Data Services Application Programming Interface (ODS API).

SQL Server executes extended stored procedures by using the following steps:

1. The client requests that an extended stored procedure be executed at the server. That request is prepared using the Tabular Data Stream (TDS) protocol, which formats the data in a specific way that is understood by the database. The formatted request is sent to the SQL Server through the network libraries and ODS.

2. SQL Server checks the extended stored procedure request to see which DLL the extended stored procedure calls. It then searches for the DLL in its memory space. If the DLL doesn't exist in its memory space, SQL Server loads it.

3. After the DLL is found or loaded, it calls the function that is implemented in it.

4. After the DLL is called, the stored procedure passes the resultset and returns parameters back to the calling context by using ODS.

You must keep four important rules in mind when you create and execute an extended stored procedure. These rules have to do with the way the stored procedure executes:

- All extended stored procedures run in the SQL Server security context. That means the extended stored procedure runs under the account that you used to start SQL Server. If your SQL Server instance runs under an account with administrative rights, your stored procedure can do anything an administrator can. If SQL Server is instead running under the LocalSystem account, your extended stored procedure won't be able to do many things, such as access any networked resource, access much of the file system, or perform any task that requires advances rights.

- All extended stored procedures run in SQL Server's process space. Although that means the extended stored procedures can offer performance increases and make SQL Server extremely extensible, it can cause problems if the stored procedure doesn't execute properly. Because the extended stored procedure and SQL Server share the same execution and memory space, problems in the procedure can corrupt the SQL Server stack and cause the server to stop functioning. SQL Server handles any exceptions that occur during the execution of the DLL in the extended stored procedure.

- The thread associated with running the extended stored procedure is the same one used for the client connection that called the extended stored procedure. If any error occurs during the execution of the stored procedure that damages the execution thread's memory space, the thread that handles the client connection also becomes corrupt, thus disconnecting the user.

- After an extended stored procedure executes, the DLL that makes up the stored procedure is held in memory until the SQL Server is restarted or an administrator runs the DBCC `dll_name` (FREE) command. This is important to remember when you are working on debugging an extended stored procedure. You must remember to unload the DLL from memory before you can unregister the stored procedure and then reregister the new one.

Extended stored procedures are executed in the same way as normal SQL Server stored procedures. The syntax for doing this is as follows:

```
EXECUTE @retval = xp_extendedProcName @param1, @param2 OUTPUT
```

Table 12.1 lists the options available.

12

EXTENDED STORED PROCEDURES

TABLE 12.1 EXECUTE Options

Option	Description
EXECUTE	Tells SQL Server that you are going to run a stored procedure.
@retval	Tells SQL Server that the extended stored procedure will pass back a value that indicates the execution status. An output parameter isn't required when you run an extended stored procedure. The use of this type of parameter depends on how the extended stored procedure is written.
xp_extendedProcName	The name of the extended stored procedure you are going to execute.
@param1	Indicates an input parameter. This will be a value that you pass in to the stored procedure that you will use during the processing of the extended stored procedure. You aren't required to use input parameters when you use extended stored procedures; it depends on how the extended stored procedure is written.
@param2 OUTPUT	Indicates an input/output parameter. You pass in a value to the extended stored procedure through this option and it passes a value back to you through it. The use of input/output parameters isn't required when you are using extended stored procedures. The use of input/output parameters depends on how the extended stored procedure is written.

Now that you've seen how extended stored procedures work and how to execute them, the next step is to see how to write the C code required to actually create an extended stored procedure.

Writing the Required C Code

Before you proceed too much further into this chapter, you need to be aware that this isn't a book on the C language. There is some C code presented only as an example. In this chapter, you won't learn how to write C code, and the code won't receive more than a cursory explanation.

Now that we are through that, it's time to jump into the actual creation of extended stored procedures. In C terms, the DLL contained in an extended stored procedure is a function with the following prototype:

```
SRVRETCODE xp_extendedProcName (SRVPROC *);
```

This function is exported by the compiler that you use to create the DLL and then registered with the SQL Server.

> **NOTE**
>
> When you are creating the C code required for your extended stored procedure, remember that the names of the extended stored procedures are case sensitive at all times. It doesn't matter which code page or sort order is installed on the server. You aren't required to use the xp_ prefix for extended stored procedures, but it's recommended.

For all C developers reading this book, the following information is for you:

- All extended stored procedures are implemented as 32-bit dynamic link libraries.

- If you require that an entry point be available in the DLL, write a DLLMain function. SQL Server doesn't require this function and if you don't provide one, the compiler adds one for you. The function that the compiler adds contains no instructions other than to return the value TRUE. The DLLMain function executes immediately when the calling thread attaches to or detaches from the DLL.

- All functions in the DLL called by your extended stored procedures must be exported. This is done in one of two ways:

    - Add the name of the function to the EXPORTS section of the definitions, or .def, file.

    - Add the compiler extension __declspec(dllexport) to the beginning of the name of the function. Note that __declspec() begins with two underscores and is a Microsoft-specific compiler extension. If your compiler doesn't support this function, use the first option for exporting your functions.

When you create a DLL that will be used in an extended stored procedure, you must add two files to the project: Srv.h, which is the Open Data Services header file, and Opends60.lib, which is the import library for Opends60.dll.

To create an extended stored procedure using Microsoft Visual C++, follow these steps:

1. Open Microsoft Visual C++ and create a new project with a type of Win32 Dynamic Link Library.

2. Choose Options from the Tools menu. In the Options dialog box, select the Directories tab. Add the directory C:\Program Files\Microsoft SQL Server\75\Tools\ DevTools\Lib to the Library Files option and C:\Program Files\Microsoft SQL Server\75\Tools\DevTools\Include to the Include Files section.

3. From the Project menu, choose Settings to open the Project Settings dialog box. On the Link tab, click the General Category. Add `opends60.dll` to the Object/Library Modules section.

4. Write the source code for the functions that you want to use in the extended stored procedure. Ensure that you add the following function to the DLL. This function is checked by SQL Server to ensure that the ODS library that you are compiling and linking with is the correct version.

```
__declspec(dllexport) ULONG __GetXpVersion()
{
    return ODS_VERSION;
}
```

5. Compile and link your project.

The code in Listings 12.1 and 12.2 are Microsoft examples of an extended stored procedure. Listing 12.1 shows the actual guts of the extended stored procedure—the C code that makes up the stored procedure. It's a simple extended stored procedure that returns the text Hello, World to the client. Listing 12.2 is the definitions file with the EXPORTS section filled out.

LISTING 12.1   "Hello World" C Code (xp_hello.c)

```
// This is an example of an extended procedure DLL built with Open Data
// Services. The function within the DLL can be invoked by using the
// extended stored procedures support in SQL Server.
//
// For more information on Open Data Services refer to the Microsoft Open
// Data Services Programmer's Reference.
//
// xp_hello stored procedure sets an output parameter and sends a result set.
//
// The Transact-SQL script xp_hello.sql installs and exercises the extended
// stored procedure.

#include <stdlib.h>
#include <stdio.h>
#include <string.h>
#include <ctype.h>
#include <windows.h>
#include <srv.h>
#include <time.h>

// Macros -- return codes
#define XP_NOERROR      0
#define XP_ERROR        1
```

```
#define MAX_SERVER_ERROR 20000
#define XP_HELLO_ERROR MAX_SERVER_ERROR+1

void printUsage (SRV_PROC* pSrvProc);
void printError (SRV_PROC *pSrvProc, CHAR* szErrorMsg);

// It is highly recommended that all Microsoft® SQL Server (7.0
// and greater) extended stored procedure DLLs implement and export
// __GetXpVersion. For more information see SQL Server
// Books Online
ULONG __GetXpVersion()

{
    return ODS_VERSION;
}

SRVRETCODE xp_hello
    (
    SRV_PROC* pSrvProc
    )
    {
    char        szText[15] = "Hello World!";
    BYTE        bType;
    long        cbMaxLen;
    long        cbActualLen;
    BOOL        fNull;

#ifdef _DEBUG
    // In a debug build, look up the data type name for assistance.
    DBCHAR*     pdbcDataType;
    int         cbDataType;
#endif

    // Count up the number of input parameters.  There should only be one.
    if (srv_rpcparams(pSrvProc) != 1)
        {
        // Send error message and return
        //
        printUsage (pSrvProc);
        return (XP_ERROR);
        }

    // Use srv_paraminfo to get data type and length information.
    if (srv_paraminfo(pSrvProc, 1, &bType, &cbMaxLen, &cbActualLen,
        NULL, &fNull) == FAIL)
        {
```

continues

LISTING 12.1   Continued

```
        printError (pSrvProc, "srv_paraminfo failed...");
        return (XP_ERROR);
        }

    // Make sure first parameter is a return (OUTPUT) parameter
    if ((srv_paramstatus(pSrvProc, 1) & SRV_PARAMRETURN) == FAIL)
        {
        printUsage (pSrvProc);
        return (XP_ERROR);
        }

    // Make sure first parameter is of char or varchar datatype
    if (bType != SRVBIGVARCHAR && bType != SRVBIGCHAR)
        {
        printUsage (pSrvProc);
        return (XP_ERROR);
        }

    // Make sure first parameter is large enough to hold data
    if (cbMaxLen < (long)strlen(szText))
        {
        printError (pSrvProc, "output param max. length should be bigger");
        return (XP_ERROR);
        }

    // Describe the results set
//#define METHOD1
#ifdef METHOD1
    srv_describe(pSrvProc, 1, "Column 1", SRV_NULLTERM, bType,
            cbMaxLen, bType, strlen(szText), szText);
#else
    srv_describe(pSrvProc, 1, "Column 1", SRV_NULLTERM, bType,
            cbMaxLen, bType, 0, NULL);

    // Set the column's length
    if (srv_setcollen(pSrvProc, 1, strlen(szText)) == FAIL)
        {
        printError (pSrvProc, "srv_setcollen failed...");
        return (XP_ERROR);
        }

    // Set the column's data
    if (srv_setcoldata(pSrvProc, 1, szText) == FAIL)
        {
```

```
        printError (pSrvProc, "srv_setcoldata failed...");
        return (XP_ERROR);
        }

#endif //METHOD1

#ifdef _DEBUG
    // A debugging aid. Get the name of the data type of the parameter.
    pdbcDataType = srv_symbol(SRV_DATATYPE, (int) bType, &cbDataType);
#endif

    // Send a row to client
    if (srv_sendrow(pSrvProc) == FAIL)
        {
        printError (pSrvProc, "srv_sendrow failed...");
        return (XP_ERROR);
        }

    // Set the output parameter
    if (FAIL == srv_paramsetoutput(pSrvProc, 1, szText, strlen(szText), FALSE))
        {
        printError (pSrvProc, "srv_paramsetoutput failed...");
        return (XP_ERROR);
        }

    srv_senddone(pSrvProc, (SRV_DONE_COUNT | SRV_DONE_MORE), 0, 1);

    return (XP_NOERROR);
}

// send XP usage info to client
void printUsage (SRV_PROC *pSrvProc)
{
    // usage: exec xp_hello <@param1 output>
    // Example:
    // declare @txt varchar(33)
    // exec xp_hello @txt OUTPUT
    // select @txt

    srv_sendmsg(pSrvProc, SRV_MSG_ERROR, XP_HELLO_ERROR, SRV_INFO, 1,
            NULL, 0, (DBUSMALLINT) __LINE__,
            "Usage: exec xp_hello <@param1 output>",
            SRV_NULLTERM);
    srv_senddone(pSrvProc, (SRV_DONE_ERROR | SRV_DONE_MORE), 0, 0);

}
```

12

EXTENDED STORED
PROCEDURES

continues

LISTING 12.1   Continued

```
// send szErrorMsg to client
void printError (SRV_PROC *pSrvProc, CHAR* szErrorMsg)
{
    srv_sendmsg(pSrvProc, SRV_MSG_ERROR, XP_HELLO_ERROR, SRV_INFO, 1,
            NULL, 0, (DBUSMALLINT) __LINE__,
            szErrorMsg,
            SRV_NULLTERM);

    srv_senddone(pSrvProc, (SRV_DONE_ERROR | SRV_DONE_MORE), 0, 0);

}
```

LISTING 12.2   "Hello World" DEF File (xp_hello.def)

```
LIBRARY XP_HELLO

DESCRIPTION    'Sample SQL Server Extended Stored Procedure DLL'

EXPORTS
    xp_hello
    __GetXpVersion
```

After you compile and link your DLL, you need to tell SQL Server that it's an extended stored procedure.

Registering an Extended Stored Procedure

The process of creating an extended stored procedure is known as *registering* the extended stored procedure. This registration allows SQL Server to recognize the functionality that's provided in the DLL. To add the extended stored procedure to SQL Server, someone with system administrator–level privileges must run the sp_addextendedproc system stored procedure, specifying the name of the DLL and the function in the DLL that is the extended stored procedure. The following steps walk you through adding an extended stored procedure to the system:

1. Copy the DLL that contains the extended stored procedure function to the server directory that contains the standard SQL Server DLLs. In a normal installation, this is the \MSSQL7\BINN directory.

2. Log in to the SQL Server using SQL Query Analyzer with an account that has administrative privileges. By default, the only account with these types of privileges is sa.

3. While using the master database, run the `sp_addextendedproc` system stored procedure. The syntax of this stored procedure is as follows:

```
sp_addextendedproc function_name, dll_name
```

where `function_name` is the name of the function in the DLL and `dll_name` is the name of the DLL that contains the function. For example, the following adds the `xp_hello` extended stored procedure that was created in the previous code example:

```
sp_addextendedproc 'xp_hello', 'xp_hello.dll'
```

After you execute the `sp_addextendedproc` system stored procedure, all you have to do is assign permissions to the newly created stored procedure so that all your users can use it. The syntax for using the `xp_hello` extended stored procedure is as follows:

```
DECLARE @vchOutput VARCHAR(32)
EXEC xp_hello @vchOutput OUTPUT
SELECT @vchOutput
GO
```

Useful System Extended Stored Procedures

When you install SQL Server 7.5, Microsoft provides around 190 extended stored procedures. You or any other user on the system will never directly use most of these procedures. These extended stored procedures provide all types of functionality that aren't provided directly in the SQL Server engine. This functionality includes the ability to send, receive, and process email; add, read, and delete Registry keys; and provide direct access to the file system. Table 12.2 lists the most used system extended stored procedures.

TABLE 12.2 Useful System Extended Stored Procedures

Stored Procedure	Description
xp_cmdshell	Executes a command string as an operating system command and returns any output data from the command as rows of text.
xp_deletemail	Deletes a message from SQL Server's email inbox. This stored procedure is used by the `sp_processmail` system stored procedure.
xp_enumerrorlogs	Lists the archive number and date for all the SQL Server error logs on the server.
xp_enumgroups	Returns a list of all local groups on the SQL Server or all global groups defined in the specified domain. This procedure won't run on Windows 9x SQL Servers.

continues

12

EXTENDED STORED
PROCEDURES

TABLE 12.2   Continued

Stored Procedure	Description
xp_findnextmsg	Accepts a message ID and returns the next message ID. This stored procedure is used by the sp_processmail system stored procedure.
xp_fixeddrives	Returns a listing of all fixed disk drives on the system and the amount of free space on them.
xp_getnetname	Returns the network name of the SQL Server on which the procedure is run.
xp_grantlogin	Grants access to a Windows NT login to the SQL Server. This stored procedure is run by the sp_grantlogin system stored procedure.
xp_logevent	Adds an error to the Windows NT application log and to the SQL Server error log. This stored procedure can be used to log an error without returning any information to the user.
xp_loginconfig	Returns SQL Server's login security configuration. This stored procedure can be run only on Windows NT servers.
xp_logininfo	Returns the account, the type of account, the mapped login to the account, and the path by which the account has access to SQL Server.
xp_readerrorlog	Returns the error log that you select. The procedure accepts either no parameter, which will return the current error log, or the numbers 1–6, which will return the corresponding archived error log.
xp_readmail	Reads a message from SQL Server email inbox. This stored procedure is used by the sp_processmail system stored procedure.
xp_revokelogin	Revokes access from a Windows NT login or group from SQL Server. This procedure is executed by the sp_revokelogin system stored procedure.
xp_sendmail	Sends email from the SQL Server email account. This stored procedure is used by the sp_processmail system stored procedure.
xp_sqlinventory	Gathers all configuration and inventory information from the SQL Server and stores it in the specified table and database.
xp_startmail	Starts the SQL Server email service.
xp_stopmail	Stops the SQL Server email service.

Conclusion

In this chapter, you saw how to use and create extended stored procedures. First, you learned how SQL Server processes extended stored procedures. These procedures are extensions to SQL Server itself. Next, you saw an example of the C code required to create an extended stored procedure. After writing and compiling the code, you learned how to register the extended stored procedure. Last, you saw some of the more useful built-in extended stored procedures.

12

EXTENDED STORED
PROCEDURES

Creating Custom Functions

IN THIS CHAPTER

One of the newest advances in SQL Server 2000 is the ability to create custom functions. In previous versions of SQL Server, all functions were defined by the system developers and couldn't be modified in any way. In SQL Server 2000, developers can create their own functions that return any type of value. These functions can be used in stored procedures or as a column in a table as a computed column.

In this chapter, I cover the following:

- New enhancements to SQL Server functions
- User-defined functions
- Functions that return a table
- Calling user-defined functions
- Function determinism

New Advances in SQL Server Functions

All programming languages, including T-SQL, have functions that can be used to create powerful applications. In most languages, programmers can create their own functions that allow them to expand on what the system can do. In previous versions of SQL Server, you didn't have the ability to create functions. You could create stored procedures but couldn't use them in certain places, such as within the context of a SELECT statement. Now, SQL Server 2000 now enables you to create your own functions.

A *function* is simply a subroutine that encapsulates SQL statements. By creating functions, you can easily reuse the code that you have created to compare and contrast the differences between functions and stored procedures. An example of a built-in function is GETDATE, which returns the current system date. One major difference between this function and a stored procedure is that the function can be called from the context of a SELECT or other DML statement. I go over this in depth later in the chapter.

User-Defined Functions

SQL Server user-defined functions are created using the CREATE FUNCTION command. Any created function can take zero or more input parameters of any type except timestamp, cursor, or table. User-defined functions pass back a single value as defined in the RETURNS section of the CREATE FUNCTION. User-defined functions can return any data type except text, ntext, image, cursor, or timestamp.

All user-defined functions must comply with all naming standards set forth for all objects in the database. Unlike other objects in the database, when you call a user-defined function, you must use the qualified object name, in the format of *owner_name.function_name*, as follows:

```
SELECT * FROM dbo.fncReturnScalarValue
```

As with all rules, there is an exception to the *owner_name.function_name* rule. With built-in functions that return tables, you must preface the name of the function with two colons (::), as follows:

```
SELECT * FROM ::fn_helpcollations()
```

To create user-defined functions, you must have been assigned the CREATE FUNCTION permission. Before other users can use your function, you must assign them EXECUTE permission on the function. Also, if you create a table that references a user-defined function as either a computed column, a CHECK constraint, or a DEFAULT, you must own both the table and the function.

With all objects that you can create, there is also a list of things that you can and can't do. The following are the rules that go along with user-defined functions.

- The function can't perform any actions that have side effects. This basically means that the function can't perform any changes to a resource outside the function itself. You can't create a procedure that modifies data in a table, performs cursor operations on cursors that aren't local to the procedure, sends email, creates database objects, or generates a resultset that is returned to the user.

- You can assign values to local variables.

- The DECLARE statement can be used to create variables and cursors local to the procedure.

- Cursor operations including DECLARE, OPEN, FETCH, CLOSE, and DEALLOCATE can all be performed in the cursor. FETCH statements in the function can't be used to return data to the user. FETCH statements in functions can be used only to assign values to local variables using the INTO keyword.

- All control-of-flow statements are allowed in the context of the procedure.

- SELECT statements that return values to the user aren't allowed. The only allowable SELECT statements assign values to local variables.

- UPDATEs, INSERTs, and DELETEs to objects external to the function aren't permitted. UPDATEs, INSERTs, and DELETEs to table variables local to the function are permitted.

- The last statement in a function must be a RETURN statement.

- User-defined functions can't contain any function that returns different data every time it is run. These functions include the following:

@@CONNECTIONS	@@TIMETICKS
@@CPU_BUSY	@@TOTAL_ERRORS
@@IDLE	@@TOTAL_READ
@@IO_BUSY	@@TOTAL_WRITE
@@MAX_CONNECTIONS	GETDATE
@@PACK_RECEIVED	NEWID

13

CREATING
CUSTOM
FUNCTIONS

@@PACK_SENT	RAND
@@PACKET_ERRORS	TEXTPTR

All these rules are checked when the function is parsed and, if any one of them is broken, the function creation fails and an error is returned. If all the rules are followed and the procedure is syntactically correct, the procedure is created and stored in the sysobjects and syscomments tables. The following is the syntax for the CREATE FUNCTION command:

```
CREATE FUNCTION [owner_name.]function_name
(
[ {@parameter_name scalar_data_type [= default]} [,...n] ]
)
RETURNS scalar_data_type | TABLE(column_definition | table_constraint [,...n])

[WITH ENCRYPTION | SCHEMABINDING [,...n] ]
[AS]
[BEGIN function_body END] | RETURN [(] select_statement [)]
```

The CREATE FUNCTION command syntax is explained in Table 13.1.

TABLE 13.1 CREATE FUNCTION Syntax

Element	Description
CREATE FUNCTION	This statement tells SQL Server that you are going to create a function object in the current database.
owner_name	This is a placeholder for an optional object owner name. You don't have to specify an owner. If you don't, the person who created the object owns it.
function_name	This is a placeholder for the name of the function that you are creating.
@parameter_name	If the function being created will accept input parameters, this is where you declare them. This process is similar to created parameters for stored procedures.
scalar_data_type	This is the data type for the input parameter. A function can take any data type as a parameter except the timestamp, cursor, and table data types.
= default	If you want to provide a default value for the parameter when the user doesn't pass one in, this is where you do so. This is similar to the way you would create a default value in a stored procedure.
,...n	This indicates that you can create multiple parameters that can be passed into the function. Any function that you create can take up to 1,024 parameters.

Element	Description
RETURNS	This section tells SQL Server what data type the function will return. You can either return a single scalar value or a table.
scalar_data_type	If you are going to return a single scalar value, this is where you tell SQL Server the data type, length, and precision of the data type.
TABLE	This data type enables you to return multiple rows of data from a function.
column_definition	This placeholder shows you where the column definitions for the TABLE data type will go. You define columns in the TABLE data type in the same manner that you do when creating a table.
table_constraint	This placeholder shows you that, like a regular table, you can define table constraints on the TABLE data type.
,...*n*	This indicates that you can have multiple column definitions and table constraints in the TABLE data type.
WITH ENCRYPTION	This option indicates that the function's code will be encrypted in the syscomments table.
WITH SCHEMABINDING	This option indicates that the function that is created is bound to all objects that it references.
,...*n*	This indicates that you can use multiple options when you are creating functions. Currently, there are only two options, but there can be many more.
AS	This keyword alerts SQL Server that the code for the function is about to begin.
BEGIN	This keyword, used with the END function, delimits the code for the function.
function_body	This is a placeholder for the code in function.
END	This keyword, used with the BEGIN function, delimits the code for the function.
RETURN	This statement sends a value back to the calling procedure.
select_statement	This placeholder can be used with the RETURN statement to send a value back to the calling procedure.

13

CREATING
CUSTOM
FUNCTIONS

One note on the WITH SCHEMABINDING option: When a function is created with the WITH SCHEMABINDING option, any objects referenced in the function can't be altered or dropped while the function still exists. The binding of the function is removed and the referenced objects can be dropped or altered only if the function is dropped or the function is altered and the WITH SCHEMABINDING option isn't specified. A function can be schema-bound only if all the following conditions are true:

- Any user-defined functions or views referenced by the function to be schema-bound are also schema-bound.

- The objects referenced by the function aren't referenced using a three- or four-part name.

- The function and any objects referenced by the function are all contained in the same database.

- The user creating the object has REFERENCES permissions on all objects referenced in the database.

User-defined functions can either be scalar or tabular. A *scalar* function returns a single value to the user using the RETURN statement. A *tabular* function returns several values in a table.

User-defined scalar functions can be used in a SQL statement where the data type that's returned from the function can be used. Take, for example, the code in Listing 13.1. This function returns a datetime value of three business days from the date that was passed in.

LISTING 13.1   The First Function

```
CREATE FUNCTION fncGetThreeBusinessDays(@dtmDateStart DATETIME)
    RETURNS DATETIME
AS
BEGIN
    IF DATEPART(dw, @dtmDateStart) = 4
    BEGIN
        RETURN(DATEADD(dw, 5, @dtmDateStart))
    END
    ELSE IF DATEPART(dw, @dtmDateStart) = 5
    BEGIN
        RETURN(DATEADD(dw, 5, @dtmDateStart))
    END
    ELSE IF DATEPART(dw, @dtmDateStart) = 6
    BEGIN
        RETURN(DATEADD(dw, 5, @dtmDateStart))
    END
    ELSE IF DATEPART(dw, @dtmDateStart) = 7
    BEGIN
        RETURN(DATEADD(dw, 4, @dtmDateStart))
    END
    RETURN(DATEADD(dw, 3, @dtmDateStart))
END
```

To test this stored procedure, you can run the code in Listing 13.2. This script enables you to enter a date in the `@dtmDate` variable. The script will show you the day that this date represents and then the name of the day after three business days.

LISTING **13.2**   Using the `fncGetThreeBusinessDays` Function

```
DECLARE @dtmDate     DATETIME

SELECT     @dtmDate = '3/12/2000'

SELECT     DATENAME(dw, @dtmDate)
SELECT     DATENAME(dw, dbo.fncGetThreeBusinessDays(@dtmDate))
```

It's possible to use scalar functions in tables. Doing this creates a computed column in the table where the function is used. The code in Listing 13.3 creates a table that uses the `fncGetThreeBusinessDays` function created in Listing 13.1 to determine a product's expected delivery date. The script then populates the table and retrieves the data from the table so you can see the results.

LISTING **13.3**   Using Functions as Computed Columns

```
CREATE TABLE OrderInfo
(
    OrderID         INT NOT NULL,
    ShippingMethod    VARCHAR(16) NOT NULL,
    OrderDate    DATETIME NOT NULL
        DEFAULT GETDATE(),
    ExpectedDate AS
        (
            dbo.fncGetThreeBusinessDays(OrderDate)
        )
)
GO

INSERT OrderInfo VALUES (1, 'UPS GROUND', GETDATE())
INSERT OrderInfo VALUES (2, 'FEDEX STANDARD', DATEADD(dd, 2, GETDATE()))
INSERT OrderInfo VALUES (3, 'PRIORITY MAIL', DATEADD(dd, 4, GETDATE()))
GO

SELECT     OrderID, ShippingMethod, CONVERT(VARCHAR(12), OrderDate, 1) +
    '(' + DATENAME(dw, OrderDate) + ')' AS 'OrderDate',
    CONVERT(VARCHAR(12), ExpectedDate, 1) +    '(' +
    DATENAME(dw, ExpectedDate) + ')' AS 'ExpectedDate'
FROM     OrderInfo
GO
```

13

CREATING
CUSTOM
FUNCTIONS

Functions That Return a Table

There are two types of tabular functions. If the RETURNS statement contains the TABLE data type with all the columns that are contained in the table defined, the function is known as a *multi-statement tabular function*. If the RETURNS section of the function contains the TABLE data type with no columns listed, the function is known as an *in-line function*. In-line functions are table-valued functions that contain a SELECT statement as the body of the function. The returned columns and data types are derived from the SELECT statement.

Multi-Statement Tabular Functions

Multi-statement tabular functions are a powerful alternative to views. Like a view, this type of function can be used in a T-SQL statement in the same place you would use a table or view. Multi-statement tabular functions can be joined on like any other table. The code in Listing 13.4 outlines the creation of a multi-statement tabular function.

LISTING 13.4   Multi-Statement Tabular Function

```
CREATE FUNCTION fncOrdersByOrderNumber(@vchOrderNumber VARCHAR(12))
    RETURNS @tabOrdersByOrderNumber TABLE
    (
        StoreName      VARCHAR(32),
        OrderNumber      VARCHAR(12),
        Quantity     INT,
        Title          VARCHAR(128)
    )
AS
BEGIN
INSERT INTO @tabOrdersByOrderNumber
    SELECT      st.stor_name, sa.ord_num, sa.qty, ti.title
    FROM    sales sa
        JOIN stores st ON (sa.stor_id = st.stor_id)
        JOIN titles ti ON (sa.title_id = ti.title_id)
    WHERE     sa.ord_num = @vchOrderNumber
RETURN
END
GO
```

To test this function, all you need to do is run a SELECT statement against the function with the order number that you want to get data about. The following SELECT statement does just that for order number P2121:

```
SELECT * FROM fncOrdersByOrderNumber ('P2121')
```

In-Line Functions

The functionality provided by in-line functions enables you to achieve parameterized views. In a standard view, you specify either that all the data is to be contained in the view and then filtered during the SELECT or that the view is to contain only a specified amount of data. Take, for example, the two views in Listing 13.5. The first view returns the information about all the authors in the authors table. The second view returns information about all the authors in the authors table who live in California.

LISTING 13.5   In-Line Functions

```
CREATE VIEW vwAllAuthors
AS
SELECT    au_lname + ', ' + au_fname AS 'Name', phone,
    address, city, state, zip
FROM    authors
GO

CREATE VIEW vwAuthorsInCA
AS
SELECT    au_lname + ', ' + au_fname AS 'Name', phone,
    address, city, state, zip
FROM    authors
WHERE    state = 'CA'
```

Some RDBMSs allow you to create views that let you pass in a parameter that filters the returned data. SQL Server doesn't, but in-line functions can provide similar functionality. The function in Listing 13.6 shows the creation of an in-line procedure that acts as a parameterized view.

LISTING 13.6   Returning a Table

```
CREATE FUNCTION fncGetAuthorsByState(@vchState AS CHAR(2))
    RETURNS TABLE
AS
RETURN
(
    SELECT    au_lname + ', ' + au_fname AS 'Name', phone,
        address, city, state, zip
    FROM    authors
    WHERE    state = @vchState
)
```

The major difference between the code in Listings 13.6 and 13.5 is that the RETURNS section doesn't list the columns that will be returned. To test this code, the following SELECT runs against the function while specifying the state that the user is looking for:

```
SELECT     *
FROM       fncGetAuthorsByState('CA')
```

Now that you've seen how to create the different type of functions, you need to be aware of the different ways to call the functions that you've created.

Calling User-Defined Functions

Calling or invoking a user-defined function is quite easy. All you have to do is specify the name of the function you are calling followed by a set of parentheses. Within the parentheses, you must specify any parameters being passed into the function. Of course, all parameters that you pass in must be in the same order as they are defined in the function.

Calling Scalar Functions

As mentioned previously, scalar functions can be used in T-SQL statements in any location that accepts the data type that the function returns. The following is a list of where you can use scalar functions:

- In T-SQL queries, scalar functions are allowed in any of the following locations:
    - In the SELECT clause of a SELECT statement
    - In a WHERE or HAVING clause
    - In a GROUP BY clause
    - In an ORDER BY clause
    - In the SET clause of an UPDATE statement
    - In the VALUES clause of an INSERT statement
- Scalar functions can be used in CHECK constraints if the columns referenced in the function are contained in the table that contains the CHECK constraint.
- DEFAULT constraints can use scalar functions if the parameters passed into the function are constants.
- Computed columns that contain functions can only reference other columns in the table or constants.
- Scalar functions are allowed as right-hand operators in assignment operations (*value1* = *value2*).
- Control-of-flow statements are allowed to use scalar functions in their Boolean expressions.

- Case statements can invoke functions in any part of the statement.

- PRINT statements can use functions that return character strings.

- Other functions can reference functions that return scalar values.

- The RETURN statement can use any scalar function that returns an integer value.

Calling Tabular Functions

Tabular functions are allowed only in the FROM clause of SELECT, UPDATE, INSERT, and DELETE statements. A couple of rules must be followed during the use of tabular functions:

- If a user-defined function is referenced in the FROM clause of a subquery, the arguments of the function can't reference any columns in the outer query.

- If a cursor is being opened based on the results of the execution of a tabular function, the cursor must be declared as a static, read-only function.

Calling Built-in Functions

SQL Server 2000 provides several built-in functions that you can use. Built-in functions that return tables must be prefaced with two colons (::), which distinguish them from any user-defined functions. You also don't use any database or owner name with this type of function. If you are calling a scalar function, you only need to use the one-part name of the function and don't need to use the leading two colons. An example of a built-in table that returns a table is as follows:

```
SELECT * FROM ::fn_helpcollations()
```

Function Determinism

All functions that exist in SQL Server are either deterministic or nondeterministic. The determinism of a function is defined by the data that is returned by the function. The following outlines the determinism of a function:

- A function is considered *deterministic* if it always returns the same result set when it's called with the same set of input values.

- A function is considered *nondeterministic* if it doesn't always return the same result every time it's called with the same set of input values.

This might sound somewhat complicated, but it really isn't. Take, for example, the DATEDIFF and GETDATE functions. DATEDIFF is deterministic because it will always return the same data every time it's run with the same input parameters. GETDATE is nondeterministic because it will never return the same date every time it's run. Look at the code in Listing 13.7. This code repeats the DATEDIFF and GETDATE function 10 times, waiting one second in between each execution.

13

CREATING
CUSTOM
FUNCTIONS

LISTING 13.7   Function Determinism

```
SET NOCOUNT ON

DECLARE    @intCounter    INT
DECLARE    @vchGETDATE    VARCHAR(32)
DECLARE    @intDATEDIFF   INT

SELECT    @intCounter = 0

WHILE (@intCounter <= 10)
BEGIN
    SELECT    @vchGETDATE = CONVERT(VARCHAR(32), GETDATE(), 109)
    SELECT    @intDATEDIFF = DATEDIFF(dd, '1/1/2000', '1/2/2000')
    PRINT    '-------------------------'
    PRINT    @vchGETDATE
    PRINT    @intDATEDIFF
    SELECT    @intCounter = @intCounter + 1
    WAITFOR DELAY '00:00:01'
END
```

Previous versions of SQL Server didn't care about the determinism of the functions that were used. SQL Server 2000 has introduced functionality that depends on the determinism of the functions contained in them. Nondeterministic functions can't be used in two specific types of SQL statements:

- You can't create an index on a computed column if the expression contained in the computed column references a nondeterministic function.

- You can't create a clustered index on a view if the view references any nondeterministic functions.

User-Defined Function Determinism

When you create a user-defined function, SQL Server records the determinism. The determinism of a user-defined function is determined in how you create the function. A user-defined function is considered deterministic if all the following criteria are met:

- The function is schema-bound to all database objects that it references.

- Any functions called by the user-defined function are deterministic. This includes all user-defined and system functions.

- The function doesn't reference any database objects that are outside its scope. That means the function can't reference any outside tables, variables, or cursors.

When you create a function, SQL Server applies all these criteria to the function to determine its determinism. If a function doesn't pass any one of these checks, the function is marked as nondeterministic. Always check to see whether any functions you create are deterministic or nondeterministic, as these checks can sometimes produce functions marked as nondeterministic even when you expect them to be marked as deterministic. To check a function's determinism, you can use the IsDeterministic property of the OBJECTPROPERTY function. If the function returns a 0, it's nondeterministic. If it returns a 1, the function is deterministic. The syntax for OBJECTPROPERTY is as follows:

```
SELELET OBJECTPROPERTY(OBJECT_ID('FunctionName') 'IsDeterministic')
```

Determinism of System Functions

Because you can't modify the functions that are installed with SQL Server, you can't do anything to change the determinism of these functions. You must be aware of the determinism of functions so that you can control the determinism of any functions that you create.

The following system functions are deterministic:

All string functions	ISNULL
All aggregate functions	ISNUMERIC
ABS	LOG
ACOS	LOG10
ASIN	MONTH
ATAN	NULLIF
ATN2	PARSENAME
CEILING	PATINDEX
COALESCE	POWER
COS	RADIANS
COT	ROUND
DATALENGTH	SIGN
DATEADD	SIN
DATEDIFF	SQUARE
DAY	SQRT
DEGREES	TAN
EXP	YEAR
FLOOR	

Several functions can be either nondeterministic or deterministic depending on the data types that they are being used with. You can use these functions in indexes on computed columns and indexed views when they are used in a deterministic way. These functions are as follows:

- CAST is considered deterministic unless it's used with the datetime, smalldatetime, or sql_variant data types.

- CONVERT is considered deterministic unless it's used with the datetime, smalldatetime, or sql_variant data types. The function can be considered deterministic when used with the datetime and smalldatetime data types if you also use a style parameter.

- CHECKSUM is deterministic in all cases except the CHECKSUM(*) operation.

- ISDATE is deterministic if a style parameter is specified and it's not the 0, 100, 9, or 109 style.

- RAND is deterministic if you specify a seed value.

Most system functions are always nondeterministic, no matter how they are used. The following functions are always nondeterministic:

All configuration functions	STATS_DATE
All cursor functions	SYSTEM_USER
All metadata functions	TEXTPTR
All statistical functions	TEXTVALID
All security functions	USER_NAME
@@ERROR	GETANSINULL
@@IDENTITY	GETDATE
@@ROWCOUNT	HOST_ID
@@TRANCOUNT	HOST_NAME
APP_NAME	IDENT_INCR
CURRENT_TIMESTAMP	IDENT_SEED
CURRENT_USER	IDENTITY
DATENAME	NEWID
FORMATMESSAGE	PERMISSIONS
SESSION_USER	

These lists will help you figure out the determinism of system functions so that you can establish the determinism of any functions you are creating.

Conclusion

In this chapter, you have seen how to create user-defined functions. First, you saw the syntax for creating such functions. Next, the differences between scalar and tabular functions were covered. A *scalar* function returns a single value, whereas a *tabular* function returns multiple values using the TABLE data type. Next, the multi-statement and in-line tabular functions were discussed. After the creation and definition of the different types of user-defined functions, you saw how to call these types of functions. Last, the determinism of functions was covered. The addition of user-defined functions to SQL Server should make it easier for you to create powerful applications.

XML and Triggers

IN THIS PART

SQL Server XML Support

IN THIS CHAPTER

XML is designed to work on the Internet. Although this is certainly a primary factor in its design, XML is also intended to work in many other environments outside the WWW. For example, publishing, data interchange, and many commercial applications use XML. For XML to be used successfully in such a wide variety of applications, it had to be very simple, very powerful, and very easy to implement even for inexperienced users.

This chapter does not go into great depth explaining the ins and outs of XML; instead, it concentrates on XML and its use within the SQL Server arena. It is assumed that you already have a basic understanding of the use of the XML functionality, and a basic working knowledge of URL syntax and HTTP methods. Let's now dive into how SQL Server and XML partner up to manipulate data.

What Is XML?

The goal in creating XML (Extensible Markup Language) was to provide a way of creating, processing, and presenting documents as quickly and as easily as possible. The way to achieve this was to create a new customized set of tags, remain faithfully compatible with HTML, and still provide the power of Standard Generalized Markup Language (SGML) without dealing with all the unworldly complexity of the SGML coding itself. Therefore, when the designers of XML began, they created 10 design commandments:

1. Thou shall be straightforwardly usable over the Internet.
2. Thou shall support a wide variety of applications.
3. Thou shall be compatible with SGML.
4. Thou shall easily allow us to write a program that can process XML documents.
5. Thou shall make sure that the number of optional features is kept to the absolute minimum—zero, if possible.
6. Thy documents shall be readable by humans—or at least reasonably clear.
7. Thy XML design shall be prepared quickly.
8. Thy design of XML shall be formal and concise.
9. Thy documents shall be easy to create.
10. There shall not be a 10th commandment.

> **NOTE**
>
> XML is actually a subset of SGML and was never intended to replace HTML, but to complement it. SGML has been used for a long time in publishing applications, but it is highly sophisticated and complex. Despite the fact that HTML was actually an application of SGML, even providing a standard for Web publishing in general, SGML itself never actually reached its full potential. This was primarily because of its complexity and the resulting overhead required to make it work.

XML and HTML

HTML has made the World Wide Web the world's biggest information library—but XML—the new baby by comparison is fast becoming the world's commercial and financial heart on the Web. As this change comes into being, the Web is becoming much more than just a static library. Increasingly, users accessing the Web aren't just flicking through pages like a book. Instead, pages are being generated dynamically as users open the book. This data can come from any information that is made available to the Web server. It can be anything from a database monitoring the actual Web server, providing information about who visits the site and where they go, small internal company information intranets, right up to the company enterprise databases. This information can even be taken from other Web sites.

The clever thing about dynamic information is that it needn't be displayed "as is." The moment it becomes available, it can be analyzed, extracted, styled, and customized to provide the reader with much more information. With a front-end software package linked to a SQL Server, and the SQL Server linked to a Web page, and the Web page linked to the entire Internet, the moment the person at the front end enters any given data, it becomes available to anyone connected via the World Wide Web. For this kind of flexibility, XML is becoming the language of choice.

The following example demonstrates the difference between XML and HTML by comparing them directly.

HTML code looks much like this:

```
<p>Sausages
<br>Local Shop
<br>1.56
```

Whereas, one would see similar information written in XML like this:

```
<FoodProduct>
    <FoodItem>Sausages</FoodIteml>
    <Shop>Local Shop</Shop>
```

```
    <price>1.56</price>
</FoodProduct>
```

Both examples might look the same when viewed in the browser, but the XML data is much more ingenious. HTML describes how the data looks, but XML tells you what it actually means.

For example, examine Listing 14.1.

LISTING 14.1 Demonstrates the Attributes of the Element FoodProduct

```
<FoodProduct>
    <FoodItem>Sausages</FoodIteml>
    <Shop>Local Shop</Shop>
    <price>1.56</price>
    <FoodItem>Bacon</FoodIteml>
    <Shop>Mc Duffs Bacon Co</Shop>
    <price>1.21</price>
</FoodProduct>
```

With XML, your browser knows there is a food product, and it knows what the food item is, it knows where to buy the product, and it knows the price. From a complete set of information like this, with thousands of elements and multiple products, your browser can tell you where you can get the best sausages that money can buy. It can even show you the cheapest and closest dealer without going back and bothering the server. Unlike HTML, in XML you create your own tags, and they describe exactly what you need to know. Because of that capability, it is possible to interrogate data much more effectively, and your programs are much easier to follow.

Microsoft and XML

Microsoft has never really devoted much time to XML in its SQL documentation in the past. Both SQL 6.5 and SQL 7 carry very little information on this topic, and this has only changed since SQL Server 2000 began development. Microsoft has now tightly integrated XML into the forthcoming SQL Server 2000 RDBMS system to help developers create the next generation of Web and e-commerce applications. Because XML allows you to invent your own markup elements, the information content can be easier to use. The hypertext linking capabilities of XML are much better than those of HTML. XML also provides better facilities for browser presentation, and finally, performance is improved. In conjunction with the Internet Information Server and SQL Server, information access is faster, more accessible, and reusable. This is not the case with SQL versions prior to SQL 2000. To get around this problem, Microsoft has released a technology preview that gives XML integration via direct URL access to SQL Server 7.0 and SQL Server 6.5 (SP5). This software allows queries to be sent directly to a SQL Server via a

URL with the results returned as XML-formatted documents. SQL 2000, the next generation of SQL Server, will be fully XML-enabled and will include all the features that are available in the technology preview for SQL Server 7.0.

XML Fundamentals

First, we need to look at a little basic XML. If you are already familiar with the basics of XML, skip this section.

XML groups data much like a Russian doll. If you take the logical top off, you will find another doll happily nested inside, and so on.

```
<DOLL1>
    <DOLL2>
        <DOLL3>
    <DOLL2>
<DOLL1>
```

Unlike a Russian doll, however, the contents can be multiple. You can take the top off an XML Russian doll and discover more than one doll, several, or even hundreds of thousands.

```
<DOLL1>
    <DOLL2>
        <DOLL3/>
    </DOLL2>
    <DOLL2>
        <DOLL3/>
    </DOLL2>
</DOLL1>
```

<DOLL1> is the parent mark up. XML is divided into mark up and content. *Mark up* is information about the contents, and can be described to any level of detail you require.

Correct mark up must follow certain rules, as seen in the following list:

- First, mark up that contains any content must have opening and closing tags. <DOLL1> is the opening tag. </DOLL2> is a closing tag. Opening tags start with < and close with >. Closing tags start with </ and close with >.

- Second, mark up must be nested properly. Mark up tags divide into parents and children. Parent mark up encloses child mark up. A child's opening and closing tags must be contained within its parent's opening and closing tags.

  You can use:
```
<DOLL1>
    <DOLL2>
        <DOLL3/>
```

```
    </DOLL2>
    <DOLL2>
        <DOLL3/>
    </DOLL2>
</DOLL1>
```

This is said to be well-formed XML. For a document to be well formed, all opening and closing tags must be correctly placed and the mark up should be properly nested.

But you cannot use:

```
<DOLL1>
    <DOLL2>
        </DOLL3>
    </DOLL2>
</DOLL2>
        <DOLL2>
    </DOLL3>
</DOLL1>
```

This is said to be badly formed XML. When badly formed, the opening and closing tags within the document are incorrectly placed and it is not properly nested.

- Third, if the mark up contains no content, it must begin with < and end with />. For example, <Nothing here/>.

Thus, by declaring the XML version, setting the start and end opening tags with <DOLLx> and closing tags with </DOLLx>, and ensuring that the child mark up nests completely within parent mark up, the resulting XML is well-formed.

> **NOTE**
>
> Adding <?xml version="1.0"?> to the beginning declares the XML as version 1.0. This is purely to inform programs how to use this version of XML.

The following wellformed.xml syntax is the simplest possible form of XML:

```
<?xml version="1.0"?>
<PARENT>
    <CHILD>
        This is the data content area.
    </CHILD>
<EMPTY/>
</PARENT>
```

A Basic XML Demonstration

In this section, I prepared a code sample demonstrating the use of both XML and XSL files. Don't worry too much about the XSL file at this stage—it will be explained in greater detail later. However, do study the sample and note the nesting.

Enter the code in Listings 14.2 and 14.3 and save the files.

LISTING 14.2   Basic XML Demonstration

Save as FOOD.XML

```
<?xml version="1.0"?>
<?xml-stylesheet type="text/xsl" href="food.xsl"?>
<MeatTdr xmlns:dt="urn:schemas-microsoft-com:datatypes" xml:space="preserve">
  <Sausages Shop="Master Butchers">
    <name>Ye Olde Sausage</name>
    <Product>Best Beef</Product>
    <price dt:dt="number">1.00</price>
  </Sausages>
  <Sausages Shop="Beef R Us">
    <name>Bully Beef Special</name>
    <Product>Pork and Beef</Product>
    <price dt:dt="number">2.25</price>
  </Sausages>
  <Sausages Shop="Beef R Us">
    <name>Prime Porky Worky</name>
    <Product>Buchers Best</Product>
    <price dt:dt="number">13.4</price>
  </Sausages>
  <Sausages Shop="Big Meats Ltd">
    <name>The All American Sausage</name>
    <Product>Whole Cow</Product>
    <price dt:dt="number">2999.99</price>
  </Sausages>
</MeatTdr>
```

14

**SQL SERVER
XML SUPPORT**

LISTING 14.3   Basic XSL Demonstration

Save as FOOD.XSL

```
<?xml version='1.0'?>
<xsl:stylesheet xmlns:xsl="http://www.w3.org/TR/WD-xsl">
  <xsl:template match="/">
    <HTML>
```

continues

LISTING 14.3 Continued

```
      <BODY>
        <TABLE BORDER="2">
          <TR>
            <TD>Product</TD>
            <TD>Name</TD>
            <TD>Price</TD>
          </TR>
          <xsl:for-each select="MeatTdr/Sausages">
            <TR>
              <TD><xsl:value-of select="Product"/></TD>
              <TD><xsl:value-of select="name"/></TD>
              <TD><xsl:value-of select="price"/></TD>
            </TR>
          </xsl:for-each>
        </TABLE>
      </BODY>
    </HTML>
  </xsl:template>
</xsl:stylesheet>
```

Double-click the FOOD.XML file and you are presented with a short table. By creating both of these files, you can now see a simple example of how XML is created. Try adding other items to the content of the XML file.

Using XML with SQL Server and Internet Information Server's Server Extensions

The Microsoft SQL Server XML technology preview demonstrates XML capabilities when combining the power of SQL Server's T-SQL and Internet Information Server (IIS) via the HTTP protocol. It is an IIS ISAPI extension that provides HTTP access to SQL Server using XML's data formatting and updating capabilities.

With the appropriate configuration, it allows URL queries like:

```
HTTP://IISServer/DBVirtualDir?sql=SELECT+*+FROM+Customers+FOR+XML+AUTO
```

It also allows you to store queries (including stored procedure calls) on the IIS server that can be executed from the URL or posted from an HTML form.

The XML SQL technology preview introduces a number of new features to support XML functionality. The combinations of these features are installed as IIS server extensions (see the discussion on server extensions later) and, because of this, they make the earlier versions of

Microsoft SQL Server into XML-enabled database servers. More accurately, it is the IIS server that actually provides the link between the SQL Server and the browser. The XML technology preview can be downloaded from Micrsoft's MSDN public Web site. The URL is provided later in the chapter.

The features included are

- Access to SQL Server through HTTP via URL
- The FOR XML clause in the SELECT statement to support retrieving results in XML
- XML-based update grams to update data in the database
- Access to SQL Server through HTTP

In this release of the technology preview—at the time of writing a newer version was expected soon—it is possible to gain access to the SQL Server using a URL specifying HTTP as the protocol. So, basically, all you do is open up your browser and enter the syntax directly into the address bar. It is also possible to execute SQL queries and stored procedures directly via the URL that has been stored on the IIS. Alternatively, it is also possible to execute a query by simply specifying a template—also from within the URL.

Creating a Test Database

Before delving too deeply into the workings of XML, a small amount of preparation work is required for the examples to work. First, create a simple database and table. Second, enter a little data. Finally, prepare the software extensions on the Internet Information Server. To use the examples, you need access to a nonproduction Windows NT 4 or Windows 2000 server running SQL Server 7 and Internet Information Server 5—although not necessarily on the same server.

I assume that you are familiar with the syntax and execution of T-SQL and have provided a small amount of code for the purpose.

First, create a database—its name can be anything you want—using the SQL Query Analyzer, and then run the script found in Listing 14.4.

14

SQL SERVER XML SUPPORT

LISTING 14.4 Creating the Contacts Database

```
USE DataBase (Replace DataBase with your chosen name)

if exists (select * from sysobjects
where id = object_id(N'[dbo].[Contacts]')
and OBJECTPROPERTY(id, N'IsUserTable') = 1)
drop table [dbo].[Contacts]
```

continues

LISTING 14.4   Continued

```
GO

CREATE TABLE          [dbo].[Contacts] (
    [ID]          [int] IDENTITY (1, 1) NOT NULL ,
    [Name]          [varchar] (40) NULL ,
    [Telephone1]      [varchar] (20) NULL ,
    [Telephone2]      [varchar] (20) NULL ,
    [Mobile]          [varchar] (20) NULL ,
    [Email]           [varchar] (40) NULL ,
    [Comments]        [varchar] (20) NULL
)
GO
```

This creates the Contacts table that will be used for the examples. After this is done, from Enterprise Manager, open the table and add a few rows of data.

Installing the Server Extensions

You need to obtain a copy of the Microsoft SQL Server XML technology preview. If you don't already have a copy, it is available from Microsoft's MSDN public Web site at

`http://msdn.microsoft.com/downloads/webtechnology/xml/msxml.asp`.

This will allow you to install all the functionality described earlier through the server extensions.

> **NOTE**
>
> The installation instructions request that you make special note of the fact that this is a preview with unreleased product code and, therefore, it hasn't been fully tested in high-load and high-stress testing conditions. Additionally, the preview software has only been tested on NT4/IIS4 and Windows 2000/IIS5 and also with SQL Server 7.0 and SQL Server 6.5 (Service Pack 5). Any other combinations are unlikely to work. For example, Windows 98 and Personal Web Server do not work.

The installation is fairly straightforward. After you have downloaded the software, simply run it by double-clicking the file.

> **NOTE**
>
> Internet Information Server must be present on the installation server. The installation will copy the ISAPI dynamic link library (DLL) and create the entry XML Technology Preview for SQL Server in the program group menu.

Using the Registration Tool Snap-in (Regxmlss Utility)

After the software has been installed, the first job is to configure the IIS server using the newly installed regxmlss utility menu—this is called the registration tool in the Program menu.

Before SQL queries can be used at the URL, a virtual directory must be set up using the registration tool. The registration tool is used to set a definition and register a new virtual root on the Internet Information Server. The utility instructs IIS to create the required association between the new virtual root and a specific SQL Server, including a given database—use the one you created earlier. You will also require the necessary connectivity information such as login, password, and access permissions.

To use the graphical interface for regxmlss, select the Registration Tool from the XML technology preview for SQL Server menu.

Setting Virtual Directories

Virtual roots can be both registered and unregistered using the registration tool. The registration tool tells IIS to create an association between the new virtual root, a SQL Server, and a given database, along with the login password and access permissions. Permissions can be set for execute queries using a URL, execute queries from template files, or both. A virtual root created by the registration tool points to an existing directory; if the directory does not exist, the registration tool creates the directory automatically. This directory can then store template files and other Web contents.

As soon as you have connected to an IIS machine using the registration tool, click on the default Web site. If this is an unchanged configuration, you should see nothing in the right-side pane. Assuming that this is a fresh install, right-click in the pane and choose New Virtual Directory from the menu.

Double-click the new entry and the Properties dialog box for the new virtual root will appear. Provide the new virtual root a name and a target directory.

> **NOTE**
>
> If the virtual root already exists as a normal root on the IIS machine, the registration tool will not overwrite it. Instead, the creation of the directory will fail. The virtual directory should be placed in a new physical directory.

SQL XML

With the appropriate configuration, and given that you have now created a database with the table Contacts and added a little dummy data, you will now be able to run URL queries. So, open IE5 and type this directly into the address bar:

```
http://YourServer/Yourvirtualroot?sql=SELECT+*+FROM+contacts+FOR+XML+AUTO
```

It is also possible to store "canned queries" (including stored procedure calls) on the Internet Information Server that can be executed with optional parameters from the URL or POSTed from an HTML form. We now explore how to create a URL query, "can" the query, and pass parameters, and discuss the roles that update grams play in the XML/SQL Server connection.

Creating a URL Query

Create a file using the .xml extension and add the following code. Then save it to the virtual root directory you created earlier with the registration tool. The code in Listing 14.5 will help you generate the desired query.

LISTING 14.5 A Canned Query

```
<ROOT xmlns:sql="urn:schemas-microsoft-com:xml-sql">
<sql:query>
SELECT    name,telephone1,telephone2,mobile,email,comments
FROM      contacts
FOR       XML AUTO
</sql:query>
</ROOT>
```

As you can see, this code is a lot more civilized, much easier to understand, and more familiar to those who have used T-SQL. Once saved to the virtual root directory, this file becomes the template file for that particular data query. With only simple alterations or use of multiple files, many different queries can be made against the same database.

Now, use the template specified directly in a URL using the following syntax:

```
http://YourServer/Yourvirtualroot /FileName.xml
```

If the installation and configuration went well, you should now be able to access the SQL Server from a URL and execute XML directly from the virtual directory. So, to sum up, SQL statements can be entered directly, or alternatively, you can specify a file that contains the template. A template is simply a valid XML document containing one or more SQL statements and is sometimes called a *canned query*. This is the easier option because it avoids having to type long SQL statements at the URL. The resulting output will depend on the information you have entered into the Contacts table, however, it should look very similar to the output shown later in the "FOR XML RAW" section.

Canning a Query

Writing extensive queries (or even basic queries) at the URL can be very unwieldy. The following URL code gives some idea of how much typing is needed for this activity—and it doesn't include the WHERE or ORDER BY statements. Don't be tempted to try this code—it specifies a style file that we haven't created yet. "Canning a query" is a rather quaint expression used by developers to describe the act of placing a T-SQL query into an XML document. An XML document containing this type of query is called a template file and is usually stored in the virtual directory of the Internet Information Server. Later in the chapter, we shall be "canning" a query within a template file.

```
http://Yoursever/virtualdir?sql=SELECT+name,+telephone1,+telephone2+,mobile,
+email,+comments+FROM+contacts+FOR+XML+auto&amp;xsl=phone.xsl&amp;
contenttype=text/html
```

Remember, templates including queries can be stored in a file within the virtual directory of the IIS Server and are much easier to maintain. They also provide a little security in the bargain by hiding all the parameters.

Passing Parameters

It is also possible to pass variables via the URL using a similar method to that of the command-line parameters used in the DOS environment, and, also directly to the SQL Server. Again, the easiest method is via the use of a template file.

To do this, open a text editor, add the syntax in Listing 14.6, and save the file with the .XML extension.

LISTING 14.6   Passing Parameters to the Query from the URL

```
<ROOT xmlns:sql="urn:schemas-microsoft-com:xml-sql">
<sql:query inname = 'John Smith'>
declare @INName as varchar(24)
select @innname = ?
SELECT *
FROM contacts
where name like @inname+'%'
FOR XML AUTO
</sql:query>
</ROOT>
```

Now run the following command directly from the URL:

```
http://indianapolis/xml/test2.xml?inname=John
```

This will return all names that begin with John; for example, John Smith and John Jones. However, this result will depend on the names you added to your test database.

Okay, let's take a closer look at the syntax:

```
<sql:query inname = 'John Smith'>
```

This sets the default value for the query if nothing is typed in.

```
declare @INName as varchar(24)
```

sets up an internal variable.

```
select @innname = ?
```

The ? takes the value after the corresponding ? in the URL and places this value into the variable.

```
SELECT *
FROM contacts
where name like @inname+'%'
```

Finally, the T-SQL selects all fields from the contacts table and filters out any that are not like the @inname variable.

The FOR XML Clause

The FOR XML clause in the SELECT statement has been provided to support retrieving results in XML format. Queries can therefore be created to return a resultset in the form of an XML document instead of a standard row set.

When writing a query, the FOR XML clause in a SELECT statement enables you to specify that the resultset should be returned as an XML document and can be specified in one of three modes:

```
FOR XML RAW
FOR XML AUTO
FOR XML EXPLICIT
```

FOR XML RAW

This mode takes the query result, and transforms each row in the resultset into XML elements with a generic identifier "row" as the element tag. An example of this is seen in the following code:

```
- <root>
      <row name="John" telephone1="777 7777" telephone2="999" mobile="010"
       email="John.smith@JollyHappy.com" />
      <row name="Peter Johnes" telephone1="444 7777" telephone2="777 4444"
       mobile="110110110" email="Pete@NiceMotor.Costapacket.co.uk" />
  </root>
```

Notice how the resultset is nested:

```
<ROOT> <ROW/> <ROW/> </ROOT>
```

RAW mode changes each row in the resultset into an XML element with the generic identifier row. Each column value is mapped to an attribute of the XML element in which the attribute name is the same as the column name from the table. In this code, I used the following simple query on the contacts database to generate the result:

```
http://YourServer/XMLVR?sql=SELECT+*+FROM+contacts+FOR+XML+AUTO
```

FOR XML AUTO

This mode returns the result in a nested XML tree. Each table in the FROM clause—for which at least one column is listed in the SELECT statement—is represented as an XML element. The columns listed in the SELECT clause are mapped to each of the element's attributes.

FOR XML EXPLICIT

Using EXPLICIT mode, you must define the shape of the resulting tree. However, this requires that the query be written using a specific method such that information about nesting is specified explicitly.

An XML document contains all the elements and attributes, whereas a Document Type Definition (DTD) defines the elements and attributes. These items are defined so that, in turn, they can then be used within an XML document, while a stylesheet describes how the data is to be formatted or displayed. The language used within XML documents is Extended Style Language (XSL). XSL is discussed in depth later.

Formatting Data with XSL

XSL is the style sheet language that defines rules for mapping XML data to HTML for presentation. A group of these rules defines a style sheet. With XSL, it is possible to generate a presentation structure that can be very different from the original data structure. XSL enables a given element to be formatted and displayed in multiple locations on a page, rearranged, or removed from display completely. For example, an <ITEM> element described in an XML-based purchase order could be presented in HTML in a list <UL> or in a table <TD>. You can have as many stylesheets for a given data array as you want. Recall the simple XML sample earlier in the chapter. We created both Food.xml and Food.xsl files. Jump back to these files to capture a glimpse of what XSL is doing.

XSL Versus CSS

XSL is compatible with Cascading Style Sheets (CSS). It has been designed to handle the latest capabilities of XML that CSS can't. However, the syntax of XSL is very different from CSS, which can also be used to display XML data. But CSS isn't general enough to handle all the possibilities put forward by XML. For example, CSS cannot add new items or generate text to assign a purchase order number or add a simple footer to the document. XSL has these capabilities.

XML and Style Sheets

Unlike HTML, XML does not contain a predefined display format for any of its elements. Instead, it uses a style sheet. Therefore, XML requires a separate style sheet file to contain the descriptions of how the data will eventually look. This separation of the XML content from the presentation documents allows the content to be easily displayed in multiple formats. Think of XML and XSL as two separate applications, a word processor and a desktop publisher. Usually a writer produces the data via a word processor, but it is the editor who sets up the layout of the text with all the nice pictures and cute typefaces. Also, the editor has the luxury of taking information from several writers, photographers, artists, cartoonists, and the like. Suffice to say that XML provides all the data and XSL displays it and makes it look nice.

Enabling an XML Document for Browsing with Style Sheets

To enable an XML document for browsing, you need to indicate the type and location of a style sheet. You can do this with what is called the style sheet processing instruction, or style sheet PI, for short. The basic form of the style sheet PI follows:

```
<?xml-stylesheet type="text/xsl" href="Anystyleyoulike.xsl"?>
```

When Internet Explorer browses the XML document, the style sheet PI forces it to look for an XSL file on the virtual root and to download the style sheet. Internet Explorer then uses that style sheet to display the XML data.

> **NOTE**
>
> The style sheet PI is used automatically only when displaying the XML directly in the browser without the use of an XSL file.

Every style sheet must have a `type` attribute. The values for that attribute describe the type of style sheet to apply; `"text/css"` indicates a CSS style sheet and `"text/xsl"` indicates an XSL style sheet.

The `href` attribute is a URL to the style sheet. Relative URLs are evaluated relative to the URL of the XML document.

Putting It All Together

As my father-in-law is fond of saying, "Now we're all here, let's have some beer!" I'm sure there's a virtual root beer joke in there somewhere, but I digress. Now that we have all the elements, it's time to put them all together and make it work.

Creating the XML Template File

Earlier, you saw how ungainly the query syntax could be if you were to type in said syntax directly at the URL. Well, here it is again, and once the style sheet has been created, the following will work:

```
http://Yourserver/VirtualDir?sql=SELECT+name,+telephone1,+telephone2+,mobile,
+email,+comments+FROM+contacts+FOR+XML+auto&xsl=phone.xsl&contenttype=text/xml
```

In Listing 14.7—and the previous ungainly version—the code returns all the data relating to all the names within the `contacts` database in the XML format.

LISTING 14.7   Output Result from Contacts Query

```
<?xml version="1.0" encoding="UTF-8" ?>
- <root>
  <contacts name="Fred Smith" telephone1="111 111" />
  <contacts name="Harry Smith" telephone1="222 222" />
  <contacts name="Molly Smith" telephone1="333 333"/>
- <root>
```

> **NOTE**
>
> If you decide to try this out to see the result, you need to remove the XSL file point-
> ers, `<?xml-stylesheet type="text/xsl" href="Phone.xsl"?>` from Listing 14.8 and
> `&xsl=phone.xsl&contenttype=text/xml` from the earlier, ugly example.

Save the code in Listing 14.8 to a file called `phone.xml` in your chosen virtual root directory:

LISTING 14.8   Canned T-SQL Query in a Template File

```
<ROOT xmlns:sql="urn:schemas-microsoft-com:xml-sql">
<?xml-stylesheet type="text/xsl" href="Phone.xsl"?>
<sql:query>
SELECT    name,
          telephone1,
          telephone2,
          mobile,
          email,
          comments
FROM      contacts
FOR       XML AUTO
</sql:query>
</ROOT>
```

Creating the Style Sheet

Save the code in Listing 14.9 to a file called `phone.xsl` in your chosen virtual root directory.

LISTING 14.9   The Contacts Style Sheet

```
<?xml version="1.0"  encoding="ISO-8859-1" ?>
<xsl:stylesheet xmlns:xsl="http://www.w3.org/TR/WD-xsl">
```

```
<xsl:template match = "*">
    <xsl:apply-templates />
</xsl:template>
<xsl:template match = "contacts">
    <TR>
    <TD><xsl:value-of select = "@name" /></TD>
    <TD><B><xsl:value-of select = "@telephone1" /></B></TD>
    <TD><B><xsl:value-of select = "@telephone2" /></B></TD>
<TD><B><xsl:value-of select = "@mobile" /></B></TD>
<TD><B><xsl:value-of select = "@email" /></B></TD>
<TD><B><xsl:value-of select = "@comments" /></B></TD>
    </TR>
</xsl:template>
<xsl:template match = "/">
    <HTML>
    <HEAD>
    <STYLE>th { background-color: #CCCCCC }</STYLE>
    </HEAD>
    <BODY>
    <TABLE border="1" style="width:700;">
    <TR><TH colspan="6">Contacts</TH></TR>
    <TR><TH >Name</TH>
    <TH>Phone</TH>
    <TH>Phone 2</TH>
<TH>Mobile</TH>
<TH>Email</TH>
<TH>Comments 2</TH>
    </TR>
    <xsl:apply-templates select = "root" />
    </TABLE>
    </BODY>
    </HTML>
</xsl:template>
</xsl:stylesheet>
```

After the file is saved, if you double-click the file, it will—if valid—produce a list of information relating to the XSL file. When this is done, double-clicking the XML produces a formatted table in the browser containing all the information you typed into the Contacts table.

Creating the HTML Document

Enter the code in Listing 14.10 or Listing 14.11 directly into a file and save it as Phone.html. This will develop our front end for the URL queries sent to SQL Server.

14

SQL SERVER XML SUPPORT

LISTING 14.10   HTML Front End

```
<html>
<head>
<title>Phone List</title>
</head>
<body>
<p><a
href="http://Yourserver/VirtualDir?sql=SELECT+name,+telephone1,+telephone2,+
mobile,+email,+comments+FROM+contacts+FOR+XML+auto&amp;xsl=phone.xsl&amp;
contenttype=text/html" target="_blank">Show
the XML Contacts Page</a></p>
</body>
</html>
```

I have included two methods—the use of a template file and the full URL syntax—to show the differences in each method. It demonstrates quite nicely how much easier it is to use files when possible.

LISTING 14.11   A Neater Version of the Front End

```
<html>
<head>
<title>Phone List</title>
</head>
<body>
<p><a
href="http://Yourserver/VirtualDir?/phones.xml" target="_blank">Show
the XML Contacts Page</a></p>
</body>
</html>
```

After this is completed, when you click on the HTML file, it opens in your browser and a single hyperlink is displayed. Clicking the hyperlink will—syntax errors permitting—open your fully formatted table.

Update Grams

SQL Server supports XML-based insert, update, and delete operations in much the same way as T-SQL does. Any number of records can be modified, added, or removed using the insert, update, and delete commands.

The Update Gram Standard Format

The standard format of an update gram is

```
<sql:sync xmlns:sql="urn:schemas-microsoft-com:xml-sql">

<sql:Before>
<TableName [sql:id="Value"] Col="Value" Col="Value".../>
</sql:Before>

<sql:After>
<TableName [sql:id="Value"] [sql:at-identity="Value"]
Col="Value" Col="Value".../>
</sql:After>

</sql:sync>
```

Following is a basic breakdown of this syntax.

`Sync`, `Before`, and `After` are keywords that have been defined in the `sql` namespace. The first `<sync>` tag points to the beginning of a procedure to be performed against the database. The entire content falling within the beginning and ending `<sync>` and `<sync>` tags is treated as if it were a single transaction. All the procedures falling within the body of the `<Before>` and `<After>` tags must be successfully executed before the transaction can be completed successfully.

The rows specified in the `<Before>` block refer to existing records in the database. The rows specified in the `<After>` block refer to what the data will be changed to within the database.

`TableName` identifies a database table against which the procedure is to be carried out. As with T-SQL syntax, the table can also be specified as *database.owner.table*; for example, `YourDB.DBO.Contacts`.

The identity column value is assigned by the system, but it is possible to capture the last value added by means using the `at-identity` attribute. The `at-identity` attribute stores the last identity value added by the system. This value can then be used in subsequent procedures.

The `sql:id`—not to be confused with login ID—attribute is used to mark rows. This forces an association between the record specified in the `<Before>` and the record specified in the `<After>` area within the update gram.

Each `TableName` refers to a single table.

Multiple `<TableName.../>` entries are allowed in the same `<Before>` or `<After>` tags, and in both `<Before>` and `<After>` tags—but can never be nested.

Columns of type text, ntext, image, binary, and varbinary are not supported in the <Before> area.

Special attention must be paid to the money data type. Values for this data type must begin with a SQL Server currency character.

Within the <After> area of an update gram—and if only this area is specified—the rows specified in the <After> area are inserted into the table. If both the <Before> and <After> areas are specified, the rows specified in the <After> area for which there are no matching rows in the <Before> area are inserted in the table.

In an update procedure, the rows specified in the <Before> area point directly to specific data that already exists within rows in the database. The corresponding rows in the <After> area contain the information that a given user wants to have within the database. A row update procedure is executed only if there is a row in both areas of the <Before> and <After> tags with a matching set of values for the attributes that uniquely identify a row within the table. The set of rows specified within the <Before> area must be valid within the database for the update gram to successfully update the information stored in the rows of a given table.

When using the delete procedure, only the <Before> area is specified in the update gram; the rows specified within the <Before> area are deleted from the table. If both the <Before> and <After> areas are specified, the rows for which there are no corresponding rows in the <After> area are deleted from the table.

Setting Basic Security

Using the registration tool, select the virtual root, select the Security tab, and enter a valid SQL Server login ID. For ease of testing, use sa as the login with no password. This setting is dependent on the SQL Server configuration and you should not consider doing this on a production SQL Server; use this setting only a test bed server because this procedure makes the server a security risk.

Select a data source, enter the name of a valid SQL Server, and choose the database you created earlier. Incidentally, this is the only time you will see the database name when using XML; the virtual directory name is the one you should take note of.

Under the security settings, you can specify the actions allowed at the virtual root directory. By default, only template files are allowed. For ease, and only if security isn't an issue, select Allow URL Queries as well. Another point to note: The virtual root name chosen—MyXMLDir, for example—can only be used for accessing SQL data. Any other Web files (such as .htm and .asp files) will not be accessible from this virtual root. This area is reserved for template files that contain queries stored in files. These files, or rather the queries contained within them, are also sometimes referred to as *canned queries*.

> **NOTE**
>
> The virtual root allows templates to be stored in a directory structure that is deliberately in a different location from the default `c:\inetpub\wwwroot` home directory. This is done to separate the database functionality from the Web server.

Security Configuration for URL Access

URL access to SQL Server is implemented via the Internet Information Server (IIS). Most commonly, all that is required is the setting of the security settings in regxmlss. However, when needed, more complex configurations are possible by additional configuration of the settings within IIS.

regxmlss provides three security settings during the creation of the virtual root:

- Always log on as—Once set, any user accessing the SQL data will use these credentials to log on. No other access IDs or passwords will be required. This is simplest method, however, depending on the chosen user ID, this method can also be the weakest.

- Use Windows Integrated Authentication—The login ID is taken directly from the Windows NT Workstation or Server using the Logon Account of the current user, the user rights of this account will be dependent on the NT security system configuration.

- Use basic authentication (Clear Text) to the SQL Server account—This setting causes SQL Server to prompt for a login ID and password. This forces the IIS Server extensions to use a clear text password.

Using IIS Directory Security Settings

To further complement security, it is possible to set up the SQL Server and IIS to log in to SQL Server as a Windows NT user using the trusted connection method. If this is decided, make sure the correct access rights to the database are granted to the specified user account.

Alternatively, by changing the default behavior of the IIS Service Manager, and given that the IIS and SQL Server are on the same computer, it is possible to clear the Anonymous user account and allow users to be logged in by means of their Windows NT accounts. This is really only useful for intranet applications. Some NT environments—Site Server, for example—might automatically group users by means of another method. In this instance, their group user IDs will be used.

The use of the SQL Server account, username, and password will set up SQL Server and IIS to log in to the SQL Server with the account name and password specified. This is the simplest security configuration. If configured correctly, this account allows access to only the areas of the database that the users are allowed to access.

During the logon process, it is possible to obtain SQL Server account information directly from the user. This sets up SQL Server and IIS to ask the user for his SQL Server user ID and password, and then to log him in to SQL Server as that user. This is a good idea if you have only a small number of users logging in, and it is a secure connection—an intranet, for example. On its own, this is not a good choice if you have a large number of users. Also, if you are providing access over the general Internet, the administration overhead with a huge number of users becomes very cumbersome.

Conclusion

Extensible Markup Language is flexible—it allows the representation of a wide range of data and it also allows this data to be self-describing. This is so that structured data expressed in XML can be manipulated and displayed by software that does not have a built-in description of that data. XML provides a file format for representing data and schema, and includes a description of its own structure. With its powerful flexibility, XML adds structure to data on the Internet and it has the capability to become the future standard for developing Web technology.

Writing Triggers

IN THIS CHAPTER

You might find it strange that there is a chapter on triggers in a book about stored procedures. When you think about it, though, it's really not that strange. In the most basic of explanations, a *trigger* is a specialized type of stored procedure that's conditionally executed based on certain actions in your database. For example, you can create a trigger that will execute when a row is inserted into a table. Until the release of SQL Server 2000, the only types of triggers available were those that ran in the context of a transaction that added, modified, or deleted data from a table. Microsoft's release of SQL Server 2000 includes a new trigger type. This new trigger type enables you to create triggers on views, so you can modify data in all the base tables of a view in the same statement. Microsoft has also added the ability to have several triggers of the same type on a single table.

This chapter will cover the following:

- How triggers are defined
- How triggers are processed
- Creating triggers
- Nesting triggers
- Problems with triggers

How Triggers Are Defined

As I mentioned in the introduction to this chapter, a trigger is nothing more than a specialized stored procedure that's fired in response to a data modification statement against a table or a view. Triggers can add a powerful dimension to any application that you create, allowing you to react programmatically to the data users are entering into database tables. The only other way to do this would be to code any type of reactionary logic into the application layer. This might not always be the right answer for you.

In the past, the main functionality provided by triggers was enforcing referential integrity—in other words, ensuring that a parent-child relationship was maintained between tables. Today, using primary key and foreign key relationships or Declared Referential Integrity (DRI) usually provides this functionality. You will still find that a number of developers want to maintain relationships between tables using triggers. As you will discover after reading this chapter and seeing the performance hit you can take when using triggers, it's usually better to allow SQL Server to maintain the relationships between tables using DRI and to use triggers in circumstances where relationships aren't the only thing being maintained.

One example of this would be an inventory tracking application. When a product is ordered and the shipment is fulfilled, you will want to decrement the overall number of that particular product on hand by the number ordered and, if the total inventory has fallen below a specified level, send a message to get more of that product ordered. DRI can't handle this type of functionality. Therefore, the only alternative you have to create this functionality within the database is to write a trigger that performs all this for you.

Triggers were also used with DRI to allow for cascading referential integrity. *Cascading referential integrity* means that your users can delete a parent record from one table, and thus also delete that record's children in other tables. In previous versions of SQL Server, triggers were the only way to provide this type of action. SQL Server 2000 has eliminated the need to create cascading referential integrity using triggers because DRI now supports cascading actions. Nevertheless, to remain backward compatible with older versions of SQL Server, when you create an application, you might want to use triggers to create this functionality.

How Triggers Are Processed

From a 40,000-foot view, both triggers and stored procedures are processed similarly. When you take a closer look, you see some major differences. As I mentioned earlier, probably the largest difference is that triggers can't be executed directly. In other words, users can't simply type in an EXECUTE statement and get the trigger to run. Rather, all triggers are fired in response to data modification statements run against either tables or views.

Because there are two basic types of triggers, they are processed differently. The type of trigger that most people are familiar with is known as an AFTER trigger, because that was the type of trigger available in all versions of SQL Server before SQL Server 2000. The other type of trigger is the INSTEAD OF trigger.

AFTER Triggers

When a data modification statement is run against a table that has an AFTER trigger defined on it, several processes occur before the trigger is actually fired. First, the query engine checks to see whether the table has any constraints. If it does, SQL Server performs any data validation defined in the constraints. If the data being added or modified breaks any of the constraints, the query engine ceases the execution of the statement and the trigger isn't fired. If all the constraints check out, SQL Server begins the trigger's execution.

Before any statements contained in the trigger are actually executed, SQL Server creates two special, in-memory tables:

- The INSERTED table contains the values being added to the table.
- The DELETED table contains the values being deleted from the table.

If the trigger is defined as an INSERT trigger, meaning it's fired only when an INSERT is performed against the table, SQL Server creates only the INSERTED table. If the trigger is defined as a DELETE trigger, only the DELETED table is created. Lastly, if the trigger is defined as an UPDATE trigger, SQL Server creates both the INSERTED and DELETED tables. In this case, the INSERTED table will contain an image of the row after the changes are made and the DELETED table will contain the row before the changes are made. At this point, the trigger is recalled from the syscomments table and is processed in the same manner as a stored procedure. I will go over the INSERTED and DELETED tables a little later in this chapter.

INSTEAD OF Triggers

INSTEAD OF triggers are new additions to SQL Server 2000. As the name implies, INSTEAD OF triggers are fired instead of the action used to trigger them. In other words, if a trigger is defined as an INSTEAD OF INSERT trigger, this trigger will fire when an INSERT statement has been executed against the table. When an INSTEAD OF trigger is fired, it's done directly after the data modification statement is sent. Constraints aren't checked before the trigger is fired, although the INSERTED and DELETED tables are still created. After these tables are created, the trigger is processed in the same way that stored procedures are.

INSTEAD OF triggers can be created on either tables or views, but the functionality they provide was really added to overcome a shortcoming in multitable views. As you might recall, previous versions on SQL Server had major restrictions for inserting data into multitable views. The biggest and most difficult restriction to overcome was that you could insert data into only one table at a time through a view. This could, in general, be problematic. The underlying problem still exists in SQL Server 2000, but you can use an INSTEAD OF INSERT trigger on these types of views to solve the problem. On any multitable views that exist in your system, you simply create an INSTEAD OF INSERT trigger on the view that will gather the data being inserted into the view and distribute it across the relevant tables.

Creating Triggers

Like all other objects in SQL Server, triggers are created through a CREATE statement. As you might suspect, this is actually a CREATE TRIGGER statement. The actual syntax for the CREATE TRIGGER statement is as follows:

```
CREATE TRIGGER trigger_name
ON {table | view}
[WITH ENCRYPTION]
{
{{FOR | AFTER | INSTEAD OF} { [DELETE] [,] [INSERT] [,] [UPDATE] }
    [WITH APPEND]
    [NOT FOR REPLICATION]
    AS
    { IF UPDATE (column)
    [{AND | OR} UPDATE (column)]
    [...n]
    | IF (COLUMNS_UPDATED() {bitwise_operator} updated_bitmask)
    { comparison_operator} column_bitmask [...n]
    }
    sql_statement [...n]
}
```

Table 15.1 lists the syntax options available.

TABLE 15.1 Trigger Creation Syntax

Option	Description
CREATE TRIGGER	Tells SQL Server that you're going to create an object in the database that's of the trigger type.
trigger_name	Indicates the name of the trigger you're going to create. This name must conform to the SQL Server naming standards, as outlined in Chapter 4, "Stored Procedures Rules," and usually contains the name of the table that the trigger affects and the actions that activate it. For example, an update trigger on the authors table in the pubs database will be named trAuthorsUpdate.
ON	Specifies that you are about to identify the name of the table or view on which you're going to create the trigger.
{table | view}	Indicates the name of the table or view on which you're creating the trigger.
WITH ENCRYPTION	Specifies that the code for the trigger, which is stored in the syscomments table of the database containing the object, is to be encrypted so that no other user can look at it. This enables you to create source code that's protected from prying eyes.
FOR	Defines the actions that the trigger will be fired in response to and the type of trigger that you are creating.
AFTER	Indicates an AFTER trigger. This option is mutually exclusive of the INSTEAD OF keyword.
INSTEAD OF	Indicates that you are creating an INSTEAD OF trigger. This option is mutually exclusive of the AFTER keyword.
DELETE	Specifies that the trigger you are creating is to be fired in response to a DELETE action against the target table or view. This option can be used by itself or with any other action keyword.
INSERT	Specifies that the trigger you are creating is to be fired in response to an INSERT action against the target table or view. This option can be used by itself or with any other action keyword.
UPDATE	Specifies that the trigger you are creating is to be fired in response to an INSERT action against the target table or view. This option can be used by itself or with any other action keyword.

15

WRITING TRIGGERS

continues

TABLE 15.1 Continued

Option	Description
WITH APPEND	Specifies that you are adding a trigger of the same type. This option is needed only if the database compatibility is set to 65 or less. If compatibility is set higher than 65, the default action is to append a new trigger of the same type.
NOT FOR REPLICATION	Specifies that any replication actions run against the underlying table aren't to fire the trigger.
AS	Indicates that the trigger's code will follow.
sql_statement	Indicates the trigger's actual code. This code might not contain any of the constructs represented in the rest of this table.
IF UPDATE (column)	Used only in the context of an INSERT or UPDATE trigger. This construct is used to test for any modifications to specific columns and then act on them.
AND | OR UPDATE (column)	Used to show that you can string together several UPDATE constructs to check several columns at the same time.
...n	Indicates that you can use the UPDATE construct as often as you need to in the trigger's code.
IF (COLUMNS_UPDATED())	Used only in the context of INSERT and UPDATE triggers. This function will return a bit pattern that indicates which columns were modified during an INSERT or UPDATE statement against the base table.
bitwise_operator	Used to compare the data returned from the COLUMNS_UPDATED function.
updated_bitmask	Used to check which columns were actually updated during an INSERT or UPDATE statement against the base table. An example of this would be a table that contains five columns. To check the first, second, and fourth columns for update, you would specify an integer value of 11, which is equivalent to 1011 in binary. To check only the third column, you would specify a value of 4, which is equivalent to 100 in binary.
comparison_operator	Used to determine whether any of the columns are updated. Use the equal sign to determine whether all the columns represented by the integer bitmask were updated or the greater-than sign (>) to determine whether all or some of the columns have been updated.

Option	Description
column_bitmask	Indicates the bitmask that's returned by the COLUMNS_UPDATED operator.
...n	Indicates that you can use the COLUMNS_UPDATED() function as often as you need to in the trigger's code.

Building an AFTER Trigger

AFTER triggers are the most commonly used triggers in SQL Server and the type with which you are probably the most familiar. As outlined earlier, AFTER triggers are fired in response to a data modification statement that's executed against the table that has the trigger defined on it. Before this type of trigger is fired, all table and column constraints are checked, including primary and foreign key relationships, check constraints, and unique constraints. AFTER triggers are the default type of trigger that SQL Server has always created, even though the AFTER keyword hasn't been supported until SQL Server 2000.

Some circumstances in which you might use AFTER triggers are as follows. This list is just the beginning of what you can do with a trigger:

- Emulating primary and foreign key relationships without defining them as such. For example, you may use a trigger to ensure that a value being inserted into a table is present in another table.

- Performing more complex business rule validation. For example, a trigger could be used to determine the price of certain products on a sliding scale. If user A can buy 5 widgets for $5.00, 10 widgets for $9.50, and 11 or more widgets for $0.90 each, and user B can buy 5 widgets for $4.90, 10 widgets for $9.30, and 11 or more widgets for $0.88 each, a trigger could be implemented to look up all the pricing and quantity information and determine the price.

- Performing data summarization. For example, a trigger could be used to create a running average of certain values in a table.

- Alerting users of the system when specified events occur. For example, a trigger could be implemented to send an email, using the xp_sendmail extended stored procedure, to the person in charge of ordering supplies when the paper clip inventory has reached a level of 10 or fewer boxes.

15

> **NOTE**
>
> Be aware of one interesting pseudo-rule when creating any type of trigger: Avoid returning data to the user during the trigger's execution. Because most applications don't expect any information to return from the system when a row is inserted, updated, or deleted, they could interpret the information being returned as an error that might not be handled. If you must return information out of a trigger, do so with the RAISERROR function. That way, you can be sure that the application will pick up the information as an error that it can handle.

Look at the code in Listing 15.1. This is an example of an AFTER INSERT trigger defined on the table called TriggerTableChild. This trigger is fired when a row is inserted into TriggerTable1 and it checks to see whether there's a corresponding row in TriggerTableParent for the row being inserted. If there isn't a corresponding row, the transaction is rolled back and an error message is returned. If a record is present, the transaction is allowed to proceed as normal. Notice how the INSERTED table is joined against in the trigger to determine the inserted value.

LISTING 15.1   AFTER INSERT Trigger

```
CREATE TABLE TriggerTableParent
(
    TriggerID    INT,
    TriggerText    VARCHAR(32)
)
GO


INSERT INTO TriggerTableParent VALUES (1, 'Trigger Text 1')
INSERT INTO TriggerTableParent VALUES (2, 'Trigger Text 2')
INSERT INTO TriggerTableParent VALUES (3, 'Trigger Text 3')
INSERT INTO TriggerTableParent VALUES (4, 'Trigger Text 4')
INSERT INTO TriggerTableParent VALUES (5, 'Trigger Text 5')
GO


CREATE TABLE TriggerTableChild
(
    TriggerID    INT,
    TriggerSubText    VARCHAR(32)
)
GO
```

```
CREATE TRIGGER trTriggerTableChildInsert
ON TriggerTableChild
FOR INSERT
AS
IF (    SELECT      COUNT(*)
    FROM      TriggerTableParent TTP
        INNER JOIN INSERTED I ON
        (TTP.TriggerID = I.TriggerID)) = 0
BEGIN
    ROLLBACK TRANSACTION
    RAISERROR ('No corresponding record was found in the TriggerTableParent
            table for this insert.', 11, 1)
END
GO

INSERT INTO TriggerTableChild VALUES (1, 'Sub Trigger Text 1')
INSERT INTO TriggerTableChild VALUES (2, 'Sub Trigger Text 2')
INSERT INTO TriggerTableChild VALUES (3, 'Sub Trigger Text 3')
INSERT INTO TriggerTableChild VALUES (6, 'Sub Trigger Text 6')
GO
```

In this example, the first three inserts in the TriggerTableChild table are successful. The fourth insert fails and returns an error that the application can trap. The role of the INSERTED table is to contain the values that are being added to the underlying table so that they can be used to verify other data. To see what the INSERTED and DELETED tables will contain, create the trigger in Listing 15.2 on the TriggerTableParent table. This trigger does exactly what you aren't supposed to do: It returns data directly to the user, but it gives you an idea of what's stored in these tables.

LISTING 15.2   INSERTED and DELETED Tables

```
CREATE TRIGGER trTriggerTableParentUpdate
ON TriggerTableParent
AFTER UPDATE
AS
SET NOCOUNT ON

PRINT     'Contents of the INSERTED Table:'
SELECT    *
FROM      INSERTED

PRINT     'Contents of the DELETED Table:'
SELECT    *
FROM      DELETED
```

15

WRITING
TRIGGERS

continues

LISTING 15.2   Continued

```
PRINT     'Contents of the TriggerTableParent Table:'
SELECT    TTP.*
FROM    TriggerTableParent TTP
    INNER JOIN INSERTED I ON
    (TTP.TriggerID = I.TriggerID)

ROLLBACK TRANSACTION
GO

UPDATE      TriggerTableParent
SET    TriggerText = 'Changed Trigger Text 1'
WHERE     TriggerID = 1
```

When you run the update query at the bottom of the listing, notice that the INSERTED table contains the new values, the DELETED table contains the old values, and the TriggerTableParent table contains the new values. This action will be similar when using delete or insert triggers, except that only one table of the corresponding type will be created.

As outlined earlier, some special functions are available when you create UPDATE triggers. These functions test whether certain columns have been updated. If they have, you can take action based on that. Listing 15.3 outlines the creation of a trigger that checks whether the TriggerID column in the TriggerTableChild table has been updated. If it has, the trigger checks the TriggerTableParent table to see whether the new value exists. If the value does exist, the update is allowed to complete; if the value doesn't exist, the transaction is rolled back and an error is returned.

LISTING 15.3   UPDATE Trigger Using an IF UPDATED Construct

```
CREATE TRIGGER trTriggerTableChildUpdate
ON TriggerTableChild
AFTER UPDATE
AS

IF UPDATE(TriggerID)
BEGIN
    IF (    SELECT     COUNT(*)
        FROM      TriggerTableParent TTP
            INNER JOIN INSERTED I ON
            (TTP.TriggerID = I.TriggerID)) = 0
    BEGIN
        RAISERROR ('No parent record exists for this modification.
                Transaction cancelled.', 11, 1)
        ROLLBACK TRANSACTION
```

```
        RETURN
    END
END
GO

UPDATE      TriggerTableChild
SET     TriggerID = 7
WHERE       TriggerID = 1
GO
```

These are pretty simple examples of AFTER triggers. Most triggers will be more complicated than these and usually depend on your company's business rules.

Building INSTEAD OF Triggers

The INSTEAD OF class of triggers is new to SQL Server 2000. As a result, you probably have very little experience using them. These triggers, like AFTER triggers, are fired in response to a data modification statement being run against the table on which the trigger is defined. Unlike the AFTER triggers, no table or column constraints are checked before the trigger is fired. To create an INSTEAD OF trigger, you must use the INSTEAD OF keyword. If you don't specify a trigger type, an AFTER trigger is created.

You will want to use an INSTEAD OF trigger in several situations:

- The INSTEAD OF trigger was introduced primarily to allow users to modify rows in all tables in a multitable view. This was impossible in previous versions of SQL Server— you had to modify the relevant rows in each table in separate queries.

- You need to insert data into a temporary table, which is then formatted and inserted into another table. In previous versions of SQL Server, you had to declare a trigger that moved that data over, but the data was still inserted into the original table. By using an INSTEAD OF trigger, you can simply insert the data into the second table without having to write the data to the first table.

- For error-trapping purposes, you can declare an INSTEAD OF trigger on a table. I have seen this functionality used for this situation mainly when a company I was consulting for needed to trap for an error in a code incrementing field in a table. Instead of using an identity column, this company was using SELECT MAX(ID) + 1 to retrieve the next entry number into a table. Although this works on an inactive database, as the database became more active, the users began to get errors saying that a duplicate record couldn't be inserted into the table. The company determined a path to take to fix the problem, but wanted to determine how many times the users were getting the error before they fixed it. The company implemented an INSTEAD OF trigger on the table in question and within the code of the trigger checked for a duplicate value. If a duplicate value existed,

15

an error was written out to a table and then the transaction was allowed to complete, returning an error to the user. This allowed the company to find out exactly how frequently this error was occurring.

As with the AFTER triggers, this list barely scratches the surface of the types of situations in which you would use INSTEAD OF triggers. Their use will depend on your company's needs.

As you would expect, because INSTEAD OF triggers are fired before any data is ever modified in the database, the roles of the INSERTED and DELETED tables are modified slightly. Although these tables will still hold the same values that they would when an AFTER trigger is fired, they should be viewed as "about-to-be" INSERTED and "about-to-be" DELETED tables. The data contained in these tables hasn't actually hit the underlying tables yet. An example of this can be seen in Listing 15.4, which is essentially the same as Listing 15.2 except that the trigger is now an INSTEAD OF trigger. Notice the differences in the execution of the two triggers, especially in the base table.

LISTING 15.4 INSTEAD OF Trigger

```
CREATE TABLE TriggerTableParent2
(
    TriggerID      INT,
    TriggerText    VARCHAR(32)
)
GO

INSERT INTO TriggerTableParent2 VALUES (1, 'Trigger Text 1')
INSERT INTO TriggerTableParent2 VALUES (2, 'Trigger Text 2')
INSERT INTO TriggerTableParent2 VALUES (3, 'Trigger Text 3')
INSERT INTO TriggerTableParent2 VALUES (4, 'Trigger Text 4')
INSERT INTO TriggerTableParent2 VALUES (5, 'Trigger Text 5')
GO

CREATE TABLE TriggerTableChild2
(
    TriggerID     INT,
    TriggerSubText    VARCHAR(32)
)
GO

CREATE TRIGGER trTriggerTableParent2InsteadOfUpdate
ON TriggerTableParent2
INSTEAD OF UPDATE
AS
SET NOCOUNT ON
```

```
PRINT      'Contents of the INSERTED Table:'
SELECT     *
FROM       INSERTED

PRINT      'Contents of the DELETED Table:'
SELECT     *
FROM       DELETED

PRINT      'Contents of the TriggerTableParent Table:'
SELECT     TTP.*
FROM    TriggerTableParent2 TTP
    INNER JOIN INSERTED I ON
    (TTP.TriggerID = I.TriggerID)

ROLLBACK TRANSACTION
GO


UPDATE      TriggerTableParent2
SET     TriggerText = 'Changed Trigger Text 1'
WHERE       TriggerID = 1
GO
```

As you can tell from the results, the base table hasn't yet been updated to reflect the changes in the data. Rather, the data is still being held in the INSERTED table for other verification before it's acted on.

The primary reason for the INSTEAD OF triggers was to enable users to perform data modification statements against multitable views. Listing 15.5 outlines the creation of an INSTEAD OF trigger that performs this functionality.

LISTING 15.5   Multitable Views and INSTEAD OF Triggers

```
SET NOCOUNT ON
GO

CREATE TABLE ViewTable1
(
    KeyColumn     INT,
    Table1Column    VARCHAR(32)
)
GO

INSERT INTO ViewTable1 VALUES (1, 'ViewTable1 Value 1')
INSERT INTO ViewTable1 VALUES (2, 'ViewTable1 Value 2')
INSERT INTO ViewTable1 VALUES (3, 'ViewTable1 Value 3')
```

continues

15

WRITING
TRIGGERS

LISTING 15.5   Continued

```
INSERT INTO ViewTable1 VALUES (4, 'ViewTable1 Value 4')
INSERT INTO ViewTable1 VALUES (5, 'ViewTable1 Value 5')
INSERT INTO ViewTable1 VALUES (6, 'ViewTable1 Value 6')
INSERT INTO ViewTable1 VALUES (7, 'ViewTable1 Value 7')
INSERT INTO ViewTable1 VALUES (8, 'ViewTable1 Value 8')
INSERT INTO ViewTable1 VALUES (9, 'ViewTable1 Value 9')
INSERT INTO ViewTable1 VALUES (10, 'ViewTable1 Value 10')
GO

CREATE TABLE ViewTable2
(
    KeyColumn      INT,
    Table2Column    VARCHAR(32)
)
GO

INSERT INTO ViewTable2 VALUES (1, 'ViewTable2 Value 1')
INSERT INTO ViewTable2 VALUES (2, 'ViewTable2 Value 2')
INSERT INTO ViewTable2 VALUES (3, 'ViewTable2 Value 3')
INSERT INTO ViewTable2 VALUES (4, 'ViewTable2 Value 4')
INSERT INTO ViewTable2 VALUES (5, 'ViewTable2 Value 5')
INSERT INTO ViewTable2 VALUES (6, 'ViewTable2 Value 6')
INSERT INTO ViewTable2 VALUES (7, 'ViewTable2 Value 7')
INSERT INTO ViewTable2 VALUES (8, 'ViewTable2 Value 8')
INSERT INTO ViewTable2 VALUES (9, 'ViewTable2 Value 9')
INSERT INTO ViewTable2 VALUES (10, 'ViewTable2 Value 10')
GO

CREATE VIEW TestView1
AS
SELECT      VT1.KeyColumn, VT1.Table1Column, VT2.Table2Column
FROM      ViewTable1 VT1 INNER JOIN
    ViewTable2 VT2 ON
    (VT1.KeyColumn = VT2.KeyColumn)
GO

INSERT INTO TestView1 VALUES (11, 'ViewTable1 Value 11', 'ViewTable2 Value 11')

GO
```

```
CREATE TRIGGER trTestView1InsteadOfInsert
ON TestView1
INSTEAD OF INSERT
AS
DECLARE     @intKeyColumn           INT
DECLARE @vchTable1Column     VARCHAR(32)
DECLARE @vchTable2Column     VARCHAR(32)
DECLARE @intError          INT

SET NOCOUNT ON

SELECT      @intKeyColumn = KeyColumn, @vchTable1Column = Table1Column,
    @vchTable2Column = Table2Column
FROM    INSERTED

BEGIN TRANSACTION
    INSERT INTO ViewTable1 VALUES(@intKeyColumn, @vchTable1Column)
    SELECT @intError = @@ROWCOUNT
    INSERT INTO ViewTable2 VALUES(@intKeyColumn, @vchTable2Column)
    SELECT @intError = @intError + @@ROWCOUNT
    IF ((@intError < 2) OR (@intError % 2) <> 0)
    BEGIN
        RAISERROR('An error occurred during the multitable insert.', 1, 11)
        ROLLBACK TRANSACTION
        RETURN
    END
COMMIT TRANSACTION
GO

INSERT INTO TestView1 VALUES (11, 'ViewTable1 Value 11', 'ViewTable2 Value 11')
GO
```

When you run this script, the first thing that occurs is that two tables are created and a set of 10 dummy rows is inserted into both. These rows share a common value, which is being stored in the KeyColumn column. Then a view is created that returns rows from both tables, tied together using the KeyColumn value. An INSERT is then attempted against the view. This INSERT will fail because there are multiple table names in the FROM clause of the SELECT statement that makes up the view. Next, an INSTEAD OF trigger is created that captures the data being inserted into the view and distributes it across the two tables.

15

> **NOTE**
>
> There's some pretty hefty error checking in this trigger. After each INSERT into the base tables, the @@ROWCOUNT system variable is added to a local variable called @intError. After both inserts are performed, the @intError variable is checked to see whether it's less than 2 or if the modulus of @intError and 2 isn't equal to 0. These checks are performed so that you can know whether fewer than two rows were inserted (one into each table), and whether the overall result was even (each table getting the same number of rows). If either check fails, the trigger rolls back the transactions, returns an error, and exits.

Trigger Restrictions

As with any object that you can create, you must be aware of several restrictions when creating and using triggers in SQL Server. Keep in mind the following points:

- When creating a trigger, the CREATE TRIGGER statement must be the first statement in the batch.
- A trigger is created on the object in the current database only.
- Triggers can access objects that don't reside in the same database as they do.
- When you create a trigger using a fully qualified object name, you must also fully qualify the name of the table on which the trigger is being created.
- DELETE triggers won't be fired when a TRUNCATE TABLE statement is executed. This is because the TRUNCATE TABLE statement is a nonlogged statement.
- Triggers won't fire in response to the WRITETEXT function.
- The following SQL statements are not allowed in the context of a trigger:

ALTER DATABASE	DROP DATABASE
ALTER TRIGGER	DROP PROCEDURE
CREATE DEFAULT	DROP TRIGGER
CREATE RULE	LOAD DATABASE
CREATE TRIGGER	RESTORE LOG
DISK INIT	ALTER PROCEDURE
DROP DEFAULT	ALTER VIEW
DROP RULE	CREATE INDEX
DROP VIEW	CREATE SCHEMA
LOAD LOG	CREATE VIEW
REVOKE	DISK RESIZE
TRUNCATE TABLE	DROP INDEX
ALTER TABLE	DROP TABLE

```
CREATE DATABASE          GRANT
CREATE PROCEDURE         RESTORE DATABASE
CREATE TABLE             RECONFIGURE
DENY                     UPDATE STATISTICS
```

Nested Triggers

Nested triggers aren't a special class of triggers, as the name might imply. Rather, nested triggers are fired in response to an action that's performed during another trigger. The second layer of triggers can then fire other triggers, and those can fire others, up until 32 levels of nesting. If a trigger chain exceeds 32 levels, SQL Server halts execution of the chain and returns an error. Trigger nesting can be turned off at the server level through the use of the nested triggers option, which is turned on by default.

There's another special class of nested triggers, known as *recursive* triggers. By default, when a trigger performs actions against the table on which it's defined, it won't fire off itself. For example, if you define an INSERT trigger and, within the context of that trigger, perform an INSERT into the table on which the trigger is defined, it won't normally fire the trigger a second time. In some cases, you might need the functionality of a trigger that fires in response to itself. To allow this sort of functionality, you need to turn on the recursive triggers database option. There are two different types of recursive triggers:

- With *direct recursion*, the trigger performs an action that would cause it to fire itself again. For example, a table called TriggerTest1 has an update trigger defined on it called trTriggerTest1Update that performs an update to the TriggerTest1 table. When an update is run against TriggerTest1, trTriggerTest1Update is fired. When trTriggerTest1Update updates the TriggerTest1 table, it's fired again.

- With *indirect recursion*, a trigger performs an action against a second table, which fires a trigger that goes back and causes the first trigger to be fired again. For example, a table called TriggerTest1 has an insert trigger defined on it called trTriggerTest1Update that performs an insert into a table called TriggerTest2. This table has a trigger on it called trTriggerTest2Insert that performs an insert into the TriggerTest1 table. When an insert is run against the TriggerTest1 table, its trigger is fired, resulting in an insert into TriggerTest2. That insert fires a trigger resulting in an insert into TriggerTest1, beginning the entire sequence again.

You need to be aware of two things when you are working with nested and recursive triggers:

- If a trigger action results in an infinite loop, when it reaches the 32-trigger nesting limit, it will stop execution and return an error to the user. This keeps the database from going into an infinite cycle of executing the same stored procedure repeatedly.

15

WRITING
TRIGGERS

- All nested triggers, regardless of any explicit transactions declared in them, all reside in a large implicit transaction. If an error occurs at any level of the trigger, all changes made in all triggers are rolled back.

Problems with Triggers

The main two problems that you will encounter when using triggers are performance and concurrency issues. Chapter 16, "Considerations When Using Stored Procedures and Triggers," provides the steps you can take to alleviate these problems.

Although small, fast-executing triggers don't usually result in problems, large and complex triggers can result in performance problems. All triggers, nested or otherwise, execute serially. This action can result in overall transaction length issues that can cause problems in the client layer.

For example, I once worked on a system that had a trigger on the most active table in the database that, when printed, was 27 pages long. Not only that, but the trigger affected other tables in the database that had triggers defined on them as well. The code in this trigger was extremely complex. During no-load testing of the system, the designers told me that an insert into that table would normally take a little over a second. They didn't see this as a problem. When a client of theirs rolled this application out to 450 simultaneous users, the system simply died. Transactions that normally took a little over a second during no-load testing could easily take longer than 30 seconds in production. As most of you probably know, database users aren't very forgiving when it looks like things have locked up. These users weren't any different. They would wait a few seconds before doing a Ctrl+Alt+Delete and ending the task on the client layer, not realizing that doing so only causes more performance issues because the system then has to roll back all the changes that it made.

These types of performance issues can also cause concurrency issues.

Because nested triggers run inside a large transaction, there is the possibility of running into blocking problems. This is because all locks on all objects are held until the trigger completes all operations. Again, for small, fast-executing triggers, this won't normally be a problem. With long-running triggers, where locks are held on a large number of objects for an extended length of time, this can definitely be a problem because other users might need to utilize the locked objects. When this happens, a wait state, called a *block*, occurs, keeping other users from using the objects.

Conclusion

This chapter covered the use and creation of triggers in SQL Server. First, you saw the basics of triggers and when you may want to consider using them. Then, you saw the two types of triggers available in SQL Server: AFTER triggers and the new INSTEAD OF triggers. Next, you saw the implementation of each type of triggers. After the implementation, I covered the rules and restrictions for the creation and use of triggers. Finally, I went over some of the problems that you might encounter when using triggers. In Chapter 16, I will cover some steps that you can take to alleviate these problems.

Considerations When Using Stored Procedures and Triggers

IN THIS CHAPTER

When developing applications that use stored procedures and triggers, you need to be aware of a number of issues. These issues usually revolve around performance issues that can arise with poorly designed stored procedures and triggers. In this chapter, I will cover some of the performance issues that you can run into when using stored procedures and triggers, as well as some concurrency issues.

In this chapter, I will cover the following:

- Problems with stored procedures
- Problems with triggers
- General performance issues

Problems with Stored Procedures

Nearly all programming languages have little problematic things. I can't point out all these things in this chapter—you will have to find and take care of a lot of them on your own. What I can do is point out some of the ones that I have found so that you can avoid them.

Some of the big problems I have found in T-SQL have to do with concurrency. These problems usually come around due to issues introduced by the developer, such as long-running stored procedures, but manifest themselves as problems with the database itself, such as a large amount of blocking. The following sections hit on two of these problems: excessive blocking and sequential numbering in a table.

Blocking

As you know, when data modification is occurring within an object, SQL Server locks that object to keep other users from accessing or modifying the data being modified. This is a required feature of any database management system and it can't be turned off in SQL Server. An example of a lock can be seen using the authors table in the pubs database. If UserA is in the process of updating the record for Ann Dull, who has an author ID of 427-17-2319, at the same time that UserB wants to read the information for the author with ID 427-17-2319, UserB will have to wait until UserA's query completes. This isn't usually a problem because these types of modifications occur very quickly. This activity can manifest itself as a problem when you have long-running data modification statements on frequently accessed tables. When this occurs, the process of locking starts to produce blocks.

A *block* is a lock that keeps another user's statement from completing. When a block lasts longer than a few seconds, users will begin to get frustrated and you will be called on to fix it. Before you can fix a block, you need to know how to find it. Listings 16.1 and 16.2 can be run along with each other to show how a block can affect other server connections and how you can find out who is blocking and information about the block. To perform this exercise, you will need to run each listing in its own query window. With Listing 16.1, you need to make sure that you run the code only up to the point that it tells you to and then run the code in Listing 16.2. This will cause a block to occur. After you investigate the block, you can run the second part of Listing 16.1, which will cancel all the changes you made in the first part. Because you will have created a blocking process on the server, and the process being blocked is Listing 16.2, you won't receive any data back from the server when you execute that listing.

LISTING 16.1   First Part of a Block

```
SET NOCOUNT ON
GO


SELECT CONVERT(VARCHAR(32), GETDATE(), 9)
GO


BEGIN TRANSACTION
GO


UPDATE    authors
SET       au_fname = 'Bill'
GO


-- Stop Execution Here
SELECT CONVERT(VARCHAR(32), GETDATE(), 9)
GO
ROLLBACK TRANSACTION
GO
```

LISTING 16.2   Second Part of a Block

```
SET NOCOUNT ON
GO


SELECT    *
FROM      authors
GO


SELECT CONVERT(VARCHAR(32), GETDATE(), 9)
GO
```

To investigate the block, you will use the sp_who and sp_lock system stored procedures with the DBCC INPUTBUFFER command. After you run Listings 16.1 and 16.2, open a third query window, enter **sp_who**, and execute it. The results from the execution of this stored procedure on my machine while these queries were running are as follows:

```
spid   status               loginame   hostname    blk   dbname    cmd
------ -------------------- ---------- ----------- ----- --------- ---------------
1      background           sa                     0     master    SIGNAL HANDLER
2      background           sa                     0     pubs      LOCK MONITOR
3      background           sa                     0     pubs      LAZY WRITER
4      sleeping             sa                     0     pubs      LOG WRITER
5      background           sa                     0     master    TASK MANAGER
6      sleeping             sa                     0     pubs      CHECKPOINT SLEEP
7      background           sa                     0     master    TASK MANAGER
8      background           sa                     0     master    TASK MANAGER
9      background           sa                     0     master    TASK MANAGER
52     sleeping             sa         TOPHAT      51    pubs      SELECT
53     runnable             sa         TOPHAT      0     pubs      SELECT
```

(11 row(s) affected)

When you suspect that blocking is occurring on the server, and you run the sp_who stored procedure, you will look in the blk column for anything other than a 0. Any number in that column—in the preceding example, in connection 52's row—means that blocking is occurring. The number in that column is the *spid* that's blocking and the row that contains the number is the spid being blocked.

At this point, you have confirmed your suspicion that blocking is occurring, but you don't know anything about the block or the query being executed. The first step is to run the sp_lock system stored procedure. This will return information about all the locks on the server. The results from this query run on my machine are as follows:

```
spid   dbid    ObjId          IndId   Type Resource          Mode      Status
------ ------- -------------- ------- ---- ----------------- --------- ------
1      1       0              0       DB                     S         GRANT
5      1       0              0       DB                     S         GRANT
7      1       0              0       DB                     S         GRANT
8      1       0              0       DB                     S         GRANT
9      1       0              0       DB                     S         GRANT
51     5       0              0       DB                     S         GRANT
51     5       117575457      1       KEY  (2d0250cc7b55)    X         GRANT
51     5       117575457      2       KEY  (b50a011fa684)    X         GRANT
51     5       117575457      2       KEY  (8c06b208fa36)    X         GRANT
51     5       117575457      2       KEY  (420545c60c78)    X         GRANT
51     5       117575457      2       KEY  (2206101c00e2)    X         GRANT
51     5       117575457      2       KEY  (83078580c41d)    X         GRANT
51     5       117575457      2       KEY  (36068064e703)    X         GRANT
51     5       117575457      1       KEY  (3d0206142720)    X         GRANT
51     5       117575457      2       KEY  (0607f38e08d1)    X         GRANT
51     5       117575457      2       KEY  (fd065e73080b)    X         GRANT
51     5       117575457      2       KEY  (060761536c5c)    X         GRANT
```

51	5	117575457	2	KEY	(2806844516dd)	X		GRANT
51	5	117575457	2	KEY	(21067353456b)	X		GRANT
51	5	117575457	1	KEY	(3f02eded9d6f)	X		GRANT
51	5	117575457	2	KEY	(e5078f93b573)	X		GRANT
51	5	117575457	2	KEY	(120900e18c18)	X		GRANT
51	5	117575457	0	TAB		IX		GRANT
51	5	117575457	2	KEY	(f3069264605b)	X		GRANT
51	5	117575457	1	KEY	(42022ac245ed)	X		GRANT
51	5	117575457	2	KEY	(260699a5b826)	X		GRANT
51	5	117575457	1	KEY	(2802064deb43)	X		GRANT
51	5	117575457	1	KEY	(3102300cfd8e)	X		GRANT
51	5	117575457	2	KEY	(0307953819b3)	X		GRANT
51	5	117575457	2	KEY	(0d07e4198bc9)	X		GRANT
51	5	117575457	2	KEY	(2a07be19a3f3)	X		GRANT
51	5	117575457	2	KEY	(0c07a65da6fa)	X		GRANT
51	5	117575457	2	KEY	(090645dabbcb)	X		GRANT
51	5	117575457	1	KEY	(30025a207880)	X		GRANT
51	5	117575457	1	KEY	(380210bc705e)	X		GRANT
51	5	117575457	1	PAG	1:104	IX		GRANT
51	5	117575457	2	KEY	(770797236d53)	X		GRANT
51	5	117575457	1	KEY	(3d0218e12779)	X		GRANT
51	5	117575457	1	KEY	(3002a3ef0af5)	X		GRANT
51	5	117575457	1	KEY	(2e0295bf5d26)	X		GRANT
51	5	117575457	1	KEY	(360232ad0cb8)	X		GRANT
51	5	117575457	1	KEY	(3302bb52f6b7)	X		GRANT
51	5	117575457	1	PAG	1:135	IX		GRANT
51	5	117575457	2	KEY	(e90639640ee4)	X		GRANT
51	5	117575457	1	KEY	(3802c561c7bc)	X		GRANT
51	5	117575457	1	KEY	(330237055e31)	X		GRANT
51	5	117575457	2	KEY	(5b076ad36def)	X		GRANT
51	5	117575457	2	KEY	(2c06ffbf82b3)	X		GRANT
51	5	117575457	2	KEY	(f20704a430d8)	X		GRANT
51	5	117575457	2	KEY	(a806853a1861)	X		GRANT
51	5	117575457	2	KEY	(e5077dd3e42f)	X		GRANT
51	5	117575457	1	KEY	(320246df7cc6)	X		GRANT
51	5	117575457	2	KEY	(a50519d3d29d)	X		GRANT
51	5	117575457	1	KEY	(35020772d288)	X		GRANT
51	5	117575457	2	KEY	(c008af9950df)	X		GRANT
51	5	117575457	2	KEY	(8807e2066586)	X		GRANT
51	5	117575457	2	KEY	(390761e049a9)	X		GRANT
51	5	117575457	2	KEY	(a706419e22e9)	X		GRANT
51	5	117575457	2	KEY	(1a06717b0b94)	X		GRANT
51	5	117575457	2	KEY	(fe06acdf78f8)	X		GRANT
51	5	117575457	2	KEY	(1006eb2f7ae3)	X		GRANT
51	5	117575457	2	KEY	(170788cffe3f)	X		GRANT
51	5	117575457	1	KEY	(3102424acb8a)	X		GRANT

51	5	117575457	2	KEY	(dc042ddc7418)	X	GRANT
51	5	117575457	2	KEY	(5607dfa116fa)	X	GRANT
51	5	117575457	2	KEY	(b005357b9b75)	X	GRANT
51	5	117575457	1	KEY	(35020115ac1f)	X	GRANT
51	5	117575457	2	KEY	(46085c0dcceb)	X	GRANT
51	5	117575457	2	KEY	(cb07544f5627)	X	GRANT
51	5	117575457	2	KEY	(e508cdc552aa)	X	GRANT
51	5	117575457	1	KEY	(33026fa70fa3)	X	GRANT
51	5	117575457	2	KEY	(a5080c4f08b0)	X	GRANT
51	5	117575457	1	KEY	(39021758dc10)	X	GRANT
51	5	117575457	1	KEY	(350257b46837)	X	GRANT
51	5	117575457	2	KEY	(1a09faf15399)	X	GRANT
52	5	0	0	DB		S	GRANT
52	5	117575457	0	TAB		IS	GRANT
52	5	117575457	1	PAG	1:104	IS	GRANT
52	5	117575457	1	KEY	(3102424acb8a)	S	WAIT
53	1	0	0	DB		S	GRANT
53	2	0	0	DB		S	GRANT
53	5	0	0	DB		S	GRANT
53	1	1968726066	0	TAB		IS	GRANT

As you can tell, many locks are being held by spid 51. To interpret what's going on, you need to look at the Type column, which tells you the type of object that the lock is being held on. Table 16.1 outlines the different types of locks that can be held.

TABLE 16.1   Lockable Objects

Object	Description
RID (RID)	A row identifier locks individual rows within a table. This allows for rows to be updated, inserted, and deleted without locking entire pages.
Key (KEY)	A key lock is a row lock in an index. These locks are acquired only while SQL Server is updating an index.
Page (PG)	A page lock locks an entire 8KB page in a table or index, including all rows on that page. This is done while one user is updating more than one row on a page; it's more efficient to lock the entire page than to lock all the individual rows.
Extent (EXT)	An extent lock locks a contiguous group of eight pages. As with a page lock, it locks all rows contained on all pages within the extent. These types of locks are acquired when the data being modified spans several pages and it's more efficient to lock the entire extent than to lock each individual page.
Table (TAB)	A table lock locks an entire table, including all data and indexes in the table. This type of lock is acquired when a data modification affects a great deal of data in a table and SQL Server decides that it's much easier to lock the entire table than to lock any of the smaller objects.

Object	Description
File (FIL)	This lock type allows SQL Server to lock an entire database file during operations such as a database load.
Index (IDX)	This lock type locks an entire index on a table during index value modifications.
DB (DB)	A database lock locks an entire database and all tables in the database. These locks are acquired only during operations that affect the entire database, such as database restores.

As you can tell, SQL Server can lock quite a few different types of objects. When looking at the output from the sp_lock stored procedure, you will find the information about the object lock type in the Type column. SQL Server also has different ways of locking objects, as listed in Table 16.2.

TABLE 16.2   Lock Modes

Lock Mode	Description
Shared (S)	Shared locks are used for operations that don't modify data, such as SELECT statements. Shared locks are released as soon as the data is read. Multiple users can acquire shared locks on the same objects.
Update (U)	Update locks are used when an UPDATE operation takes place. They prevent a type of deadlock that can occur when two users try to modify the same record at the same time. An update operation first reads a record and then modifies the record. If the update lock wasn't used, two users could acquire shared locks on the same record, and then both of them would attempt to upgrade those locks to exclusive locks. This would cause both connections to eventually deadlock. Because only one user at a time can acquire an update lock on a particular object, this keeps this type of activity from occurring.
Exclusive (X)	Exclusive locks are used during data modification operations such as INSERTs, UPDATEs, and DELETEs. This lock type ensures that no other users can access the locked object.
Schema Stability (Sch-S)	Schema stability locks are taken every time a user initiates any type of statement against a table within a database. These locks keep other users or processes from changing the definition of the table that the user is executing against.

continues

TABLE 16.2 Continued

Lock Mode	Description
Schema Modification (Sch-M)	Schema modification locks are taken when a user initiates a schema change. This type of lock keeps users from accessing the object being modified while another user is changing the schema.
Bulk Update (BU)	A bulk update lock is taken when a user is bulk copying data, either through BCP or the BULK INSERT command, and the TABLOCK hint was specified.
Intent Shared (IS)	Intent shared locks indicate that the transaction intends to place shared locks on some but not all resources lower down the hierarchy. For example, a transaction might place an intent shared lock on a table if it appears that most of the rows in a table will be read.
Intent Exclusive (IX)	Intent exclusive locks indicate that a transaction intends to modify some but not all resources lower down the hierarchy.
Shared with Exclusive Intent (SIX)	Shared with exclusive intent locks indicate that a transaction will read all the resources further down the hierarchy and modify some of them by placing intent exclusive locks on them.

When looking at the sp_lock information, the lock mode can be found in the Mode column. Going back to the sp_lock information, you can see that the UPDATE statement is holding an exclusive lock on the table and many locks on key pages. It's locking the keys to update individual key values in the index and the table to update the actual values in the table. During normal operation, you won't usually know the object where the blocking is occurring. To determine this, you would run the following code:

```
SELECT OBJECT_NAME(object_id)
```

where object_id is the ID of the object where the locks are being held. In the preceding case, this is object ID 117575457. Lastly, you will want to determine what SQL statement is actually causing the block. To do this, you would use the DBCC INPUTBUFFER. This statement checks the input stream for the specified connection and returns its contents. If the statement has already completed and returned some results to the user, as is the case with Listing 16.1, it will tell you that there is NULL information in the input buffer. The syntax of DBCC INPUTBFFER is as follows:

```
DBCC INPUTBUFFER(user_spid)
```

where user_spid is the spid of the user that you want to return information on.

Now, back to creating smarter stored procedures. You can do very little from an operational standpoint to eliminate blocking. What you can do, on the other hand, is write smarter code. Some things you should keep in mind when writing your code to help limit the number of blocking situations are as follows:

- Write code that gets in and out of the database as quickly as possible. Don't perform any operation in the database layer that can easily be performed within the application. A good example of this that I have seen was a stored procedure that converted pounds to kilograms. This heavily hit procedure caused a huge bottleneck on this system. It would have made much more sense to perform this conversion at the application layer. You need to avoid performing any type of operation in the database that can be performed at the application layer mainly because any locks acquired by the process are held until all calculations are complete.

- Don't hold transactions open for long periods of time. As you saw in the examples earlier in this chapter, leaving transactions open for long periods of time can cause havoc in your database. An example of this that I have seen was an application that tracked help desk tickets. When a user called in, the help desk operator clicked a button that created a new trouble ticket. At this point, a transaction was opened on the SQL Server. As you know, help desk calls can sometimes take a long time to work through. This left the transaction open, with the potential to cause blocks, until the ticket was closed.

  If you have this type of functionality in your applications, you also might face problems with your transaction log filling up. When a transaction log backup is taken, it can truncate the transaction log only up until the last open transaction. After that, all data must remain in the transaction log. Although this might not sound like a big deal, it has been known to cause problems. I have seen users who would open a transaction on a Friday afternoon and then go home, or even on vacation, and the transaction log would rapidly fill up.

- Use dirty reads when applicable. A *dirty read* is a read of uncommitted data. This allows users to read through locks that have been placed on a resource. Don't use this type of functionality on data where it's imperative that it's always correct, but on frequently read, frequently updated nonsensitive data, this is sometimes a good approach. It's very important that you know all the implications of using dirty reads in your applications, though, because in some cases this type of functionality can produce extremely unexpected and incorrect results. You can accomplish dirty reads in two ways, as discussed in Chapter 5:

  - With a `SELECT` statement, you can use the `NOLOCK` option.
  - Use read-only or scrolling cursors.

- Use smart indexing schemes. When you design the indexes on the tables and views in your database, always know exactly how the data in the tables will be accessed. This way, you can create smart indexes that your applications can take advantage of. Creating good and well-used indexes on your tables can reduce locking by helping your applications find the data they're looking for more quickly. For example, if you are updating a single row in a table that doesn't have an index, SQL Server has to perform a table scan on the entire table, locking the entire table as it does. For more information on indexing, see the Table Indexes topic in SQL Server Books Online.

Sequential Numbering

Sequential numbering is one area that I have seen several companies run into problems with. Many times, you will have applications that rely heavily on sequential numbering and knowing ahead of time what the sequential number will be. In these cases, I have seen two different approaches. Although both of these approaches work well, they tend to fail as the databases grow larger and more active.

The first method is to have a table in the database that contains either the most recently used sequential value, or the next available value. This approach looks something like that shown in Listing 16.3.

LISTING 16.3   Table Method of Sequential Numbering

```
CREATE TABLE SequentialNumbers
(
    NextID          INT
)
GO

INSERT INTO SequentialNumbers VALUES (1)
GO

CREATE PROCEDURE uspGetNextNumber
@intNextNumber    INT OUTPUT

AS

SELECT    @intNextNumber = NextID
FROM      SequentialNumbers

UPDATE    SequentialNumbers
SET       NextID = @intNextNumber + 1
GO
```

```
DECLARE @intNextID    INT

EXEC uspGetNextNumber @intNextID OUTPUT
PRINT @intNextID
GO
```

Again, this option will work in smaller, less utilized databases, but this method comes with a couple of major drawbacks:

- This method can create a *hot spot* in the database. This means that one area in the database is heavily accessed and utilized by nearly all processes in the database. If several users access this hot spot at the same time, you can run into a blocking problem with several users lining up to access the next number and waiting for the user in front of them to get the next number and update the value so they can get it.

- You can run into problems with two users getting the same number. It will be rare, but if two users run this stored procedure at exactly the same time, they could get the same value.

The other approach that you can use is the SELECT MAX method. Of the two approaches I am presenting here, this is the most problematic. In this method, the stored procedure goes to the table where the data is being stored and selects the maximum number in it, adds one, and then uses that number. The code for this approach looks something like that in Listing 16.4.

LISTING 16.4   The SELECT MAX Approach

```
CREATE TABLE OrderTest
(
    OrderID        INT
)
GO

INSERT INTO OrderTest VALUES (1)
GO

CREATE PROCEDURE uspSelectNextOrderID

AS

SET NOCOUNT ON

DECLARE   @intOrderID    INT

SELECT    @intOrderID = OrderID + 1
FROM      OrderTest
```

continues

LISTING 16.4   Continued

```
INSERT INTO OrderTest VALUES (@intOrderID)
GO
```

To test the problems with this sort of approach, type the code in Listing 16.5 into two separate query windows, execute it at the same time, and then run a count and a count distinct against the tables. Note the large differences in the numbers.

LISTING 16.5   Finding the Problems with the SELECT MAX Method

```
DECLARE @intCounter     INT

SELECT      @intCounter = 1

WHILE (@intCounter <= 10000)
BEGIN
    EXEC uspSelectNextOrderID
    SELECT @intCounter = @intCounter + 1
END

SELECT COUNT(OrderID) FROM OrderTest
SELECT COUNT(DISTINCT(OrderID)) FROM OrderTest
```

On my machine, the table had 20,001 records, of which there were only 19,963 unique records. In most systems, this isn't acceptable.

When I run into this type of situation, I implement a method that guarantees that no two records will receive the same number. This method looks similar to the update table method, but with one major difference—you don't perform any updates. Rather, you will perform an insert into a table that has an identity value on it. This way, you know what the sequential number will be before you actually insert data into the orders table. This code looks something like that in Listing 16.6.

LISTING 16.6   The Identity Method of Sequential Numbering

```
CREATE TABLE NextIdentityValue
(
    NextValue     INT
        IDENTITY (1, 1),
    DummyValue     BIT
)
GO
```

```
CREATE PROCEDURE uspGetNextIdentityValue
@intNextValue    INT OUTPUT

AS

SET NOCOUNT ON

INSERT INTO NextIdentityValue(DummyValue) VALUES (0)
SELECT @intNextValue = @@IDENTITY
GO

DECLARE @intNextValue     INT

EXEC uspGetNextIdentityValue @intNextValue OUTPUT
PRINT @intNextValue
GO
```

With this option, you will never run into a problem with overlapping values in the table because you will never have multiple identity values in the dummy table. The only problem that I have ever run into with this sort of approach is when I had a user decide that the dummy table had too many values in it and that it needed to be shrunk. To do this, he truncated the table. When you truncate a table with an identity column on it, SQL Server resets the identity value to its original value. If you ever decide to shrink the table, you should delete all the rows in the table, not truncate it.

Problems with Triggers

Triggers, a type of stored procedure (as discussed in Chapter 15, "Writing Triggers,"), can run into the same problems we have already discussed. Triggers are very complex and can be used to add a great deal of functionality to any application that you write. This functionality can come with some performance issues as well. The main piece of advice I can give you is that you need to make your triggers as lean as possible so that they execute quickly. Don't try to pack too much functionality into the trigger. If you can, move some of the functionality out of the trigger and into the application that performs the data modification that executes the trigger. You need to keep in mind the following things when writing triggers:

- Trigger execution occurs within the context of the calling transaction. The transaction will remain open until all the code in the trigger has completed.

- All locks acquired on all objects during the execution of the trigger are held until the trigger completes execution. That means if you explicitly open a transaction and perform a data modification against a table that fires a trigger that modifies 15 other tables, all the locks on those 15 other tables are held until the transaction is explicitly committed or rolled back.

- It's possible to have more than one trigger of the same type on a single table. These triggers aren't executed in parallel; they are executed serially. Multiple triggers are executed in the same context of the calling transaction.

- Triggers are executed asynchronously. When a trigger executes, it executes each line in the trigger and waits for each line to complete executing until it moves to the next line. If you are performing long-running tasks such as sending an email, copying or moving a file from one location to another, or other activities outside the system, it's important to realize that the calling application—and, hence, the user—will be waiting for the results to come back from the server. If this takes too long, your application could time out or the user could exit the application thinking that something has gone wrong.

- Try to minimize the number of nested triggers that you have. The more nested triggers you have, the slower your data modification statements will run.

General Performance Issues

You need to be aware of a number of general performance issues when writing any type of SQL statement, whether the statement is a simple script, a stored procedure, or a trigger. The following outlines some of the things that you need to keep in mind:

- When applicable, use fully qualified object names. This approach allows the SQL Server query engine to match existing query plans with the statement being executed, thus speeding up overall execution time.

- If you know that you will have several applications that will all retrieve the same data from the database using the same parameters, use a stored procedure as opposed to a straight SQL statement. This will allow SQL Server to more easily match the query plans.

- Close open transactions as quickly as possible, as outlined earlier in this chapter.

- When connecting to the server with an outside application, be sure to process or close result sets as quickly as possible. This is because open result sets are usually maintained on the server and take resources to do so.

- When writing queries that return results to the user, make sure that you limit the number of rows returned to the front end by using a WHERE or HAVING clause in the SELECT statement. This is extremely important. I have seen a single user take down a high-end server by executing a poorly written query against a large table. This particular table had well more than 1 million rows in it and this user didn't know the application he was using. He built the query and then specified that the application would filter the data. All data in the table was pulled down to his computer, where it filtered it out for the 15 rows that he was looking for.

- Limit the number of ad-hoc queries that you execute against your server. Ad-hoc queries can cause problems because you haven't planned them in your indexing schemes.

- Try not to use the not-equal operators when you query the database. The not-equal operators are extremely inefficient because SQL Server must scan all the rows in the table to find those that don't match the given criteria.

- When sending several statements to the SQL Server, try to group as many of them as possible into batches.

- As with all database management systems, try to limit the number of server-side cursors that you use. Server-side cursors are resource intensive and require a lot of network traffic between the server and the client. Every row in the cursor must be requested by the application and returned by the server one at a time. It's more efficient to use client-side cursors because all the data is returned at one shot and then looped through there.

- Apply some of the logic required for your application at the database layer. This enables you to return a smaller result set to the application than if you returned all the data and then applied the logic in the application.

- When working with temporary tables, ensure that all modifications to the structure of the temporary table occur together. Every time you perform any type of modification to a temporary table, the stored procedures and batches that reference that temporary table must be recompiled.

- In general, try to reduce the number of temporary tables that you use. Temporary tables can be very resource intensive to create and destroy every time they are used.

- Using temporary tables inside stored procedures or triggers can cause them to be recompiled every time they are executed. By reducing the number of temporary tables you use, you can reduce the number of stored procedures that are recompiled at each execution.

- Looking back on the Y2K scare, you should always remember to use four-digit years in your stored procedures and triggers, for two reasons: It makes your code easier to read and interpret, and it eliminates confusion as to the windowing date that is configurable on SQL Server. The *windowing date* is a cutoff date in which SQL Server will assume that the date is in one century or another. The default for the windowing date, also known as the two-year cutoff date, is 2049. If 49 is entered as a two-digit century, SQL Server will interpret it as 2049. If 50 is entered, SQL Server will interpret it as 1950.

Conclusion

In this chapter, you saw some of the pitfalls of writing stored procedures and triggers. First, we looked at locking and blocking issues with stored procedures. Then you saw some of the issues that you can run into when using a sequential numbering system within stored procedures. Next, I outlined some of the things that you need to keep in mind when you write triggers.

Last, I pointed out some general rules that you should remember when you write any SQL code. To write good code, you should always keep these rules in mind and document any new ones that you find so that you will remember what to do.

INDEX

SYMBOLS

The IT site
you asked for...

InformIT is a complete online library delivering
information, technology, reference, training, news,
and opinion to IT professionals, students,
and corporate users.

Find IT Solutions Here!

www.informit.com

Other Related Titles

Sams Teach Yourself Microsoft SQL Server 7.0 in 21 Days

Richard Waymire, Rick Sawtell
ISBN: 0-672-31290-5
$39.99 U.S./$57.95 CAN

Sams Teach Yourself SQL in 10 Minutes
Ben Forta
ISBN: 0-672-31664-1
$12.99 U.S./$19.95 CAN

Sams Teach Yourself Data Structures and Algorithms in 24 Hours
Robert LaFore
ISBN: 0-672-31633-1
$24.99 U.S./$37.95 CAN

XML Unleashed
Michael Morrison
ISBN: 0-672-31514-9
$49.99 U.S./$74.95 CAN

Sams Teach Yourself Microsoft SQL Server 7 in 24 Hours
Matthew Shepker
ISBN: 0-672-31715-X
$19.99 U.S./$37.95 CAN

Sams Teach Yourself Microsoft SQL Server 7 in 10 Minutes
William Robison
ISBN: 0-672-31663-3
$12.99 U.S./$19.95 CAN

Microsoft SQL Server 7.0 Unleashed
Simon Gallagher, Sharon Bjeletich, Greg Mable, Vipul Minocha, et al.
ISBN: 0-672-31227-1
$49.99 U.S./$74.95 CAN

Sams Teach Yourself XML in 21 Days
Simon North
ISBN: 1-57521-396-6
$29.99 U.S./$44.95 CAN

F. Scott Barker's Microsoft Access 2000 Power Programming
F. Scott Barker
ISBN: 0-672-31506-8
$49.99 U.S./$74.95 CAN

Microsoft OLAP Unleashed
Timothy Peterson, Jim Pinkelman
ISBN: 0-672-31671-4
$49.99 U.S./$74.95 CAN

Microsoft SQL Server 7.0 Programming Unleashed

John Papa, Matthew Shepker
ISBN: 0-672-31293-X
$49.99 U.S./$74.95 CAN

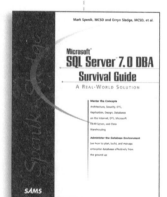

Microsoft SQL Server 7 DBA Survival Guide

Mark Spenik, Orryn Sledge
ISBN: 0-672-31226-3
$49.99 U.S./$74.95 CAN

SAMS

www.samspublishing.com

All prices are subject to change.